THE ROLE OF HELPING IN A BROKEN WORLD

A Faith Perspective

Samson Chama

Quantum
Discovery
A LITERARY AGENCY

ISBN
978-1-963254-03-7 (Paperback)
978-1-963254-04-4 (eBook)

TABLE OF CONTENTS

CHAPTER 1

A Broken World

A Broken world

The world today is very different from the world that existed 100 years ago. Much has happened over the years and some of what has occurred involves developments that have taken shape in a positive trajectory. Unfortunately, there have been a lot of negative developments as well. Unlike in the past, millions of people today living in different parts of the world are struggling with poverty, and with some surviving on as little as a dollar per day (Del Ponte, & DeScioli, 2019)

To this end the developing countries have been impacted the most with most people in these regions living below the poverty line. Men, women, seniors, and children alike are all affected in ways that, though different from people living in developed countries, have similar consequences that include hopelessness, despondency, and marginalization. The developed world has not been spared by the scourge of poverty and some problems being faced in most developed countries require the same kind of attention as those in developing countries. Although the scope and gravity of these problems differ in many ways, the impact they exert on local populations is similar. For example, many vulnerable population groups in developed countries are struggling with daily living efforts and survival, and as they strive and daily spend countless hours on eking out a living, their conditions of living are getting worse and worse by the day. Paradoxically, the richer and the affluent in these countries are getting richer and richer by the day thereby creating a growing rich-poor gap. The widening gap between the rich and poor in developed countries is a phenomenon that cannot be ignored. It needs urgent attention because as more people in these countries get pushed into the poverty cycle, unforeseen and unanticipated social and economic problems and tensions are bound to increase. There is a plethora of problems in the world today and in this chapter, I focus on the most evident, obvious, and crucial problems. These problems particularly revolve around health, water, racism, politics, war, religious persecution, environment, economics, and international refugees. The next sections discuss these problems in detail.

Health

Health is an important topic because it affects everyone. Health is an imperative that affects many areas of our lives, and it also affects societies and communities at many levels. Bellantine and Roberts (2014) define health as "a state of physical, mental, and social well-being, or the absence of disease" (p. 514). Health is a human right, and every person should have access to resources that ensure and promote optimal health. Having and enjoying optimal health is critical because when people are in good health, they can live out their lives in an operative and efficient way. Further, with good health they may be able to perform their daily activities in an efficient and beneficial way. When health is compromised, families and communities suffer and get disrupted in many ways. For example, if two parents with six children are dying from AIDS, their illness will not only disrupt the way their family functions, but it will have an adverse effect on their community as well. In such a case this family would need health care support to delay or prevent early death. In many societies the onus or responsibility of providing health care to its citizens falls on the communities themselves. However, this is not easy as many of the communities are "limping" and crippled with other challenges that make it difficult for them to move forward with providing good health care.

Today, we are witnessing the devastation and negative impact brought about by health related diseases and outbreaks such as AIDS, SARS, bird flu, swine flu (H1N1) and a host of other illnesses (Ching, 2018). COVID-19 is another pandemic that shook the world with millions of people having died because of this virus. It has become common to witness the outbreak of diseases and consequential illnesses that sometimes are fatal. Poor food or lack of it and environmental challenges are other factors that exacerbate the situation (Naeem, Cao, Fatima, Najmuddin, & Acharya, 2018). These lead to more new diseases such as an uncommon type of meningitis that emerged in several U.S. cities in 2012 (Kim, et al., 2019).

Health affects individuals, families, communities, and societies at three levels namely, micro, mezzo, and macro. At the micro level it affects individuals with illnesses and other related challenges. For example, a school that experiences a serious and uncontrollable outbreak of influenza may be forced to close and send student's home. It is possible that some of the students sent home may have already contracted the disease and consequently this could eventually place a heavy burden on their parents. Once a family member comes down with a serious illness or disease, this scenario will disrupt the normal functioning of that family. Dealing with health at the micro level calls for good hygiene and maintenance of acceptable health standards such as health-enhancing lifestyles. At the mezzo level health affects communities especially, those communities hit hardest by outbreaks. For example, hundreds of people were affected by bilharzia, a water borne disease that impacted many people living in some parts of urban and rural Zambia (Shehata, Chama, & Funjika, 2018). This disease affected the well-being of several affected families and although the families did everything possible to prevent the disease including providing care for sick individuals, their overall capacity was limited. Addressing healthcare challenges at the mezzo level requires deliberate and tailor-made interventions by state programs and other stakeholders such as non-profit and faith-based organizations. In addition, this calls for a strong response that is based on solid and a well-established social and economic system (Terziev, Banabakova, & Georgiev, 2018).

Combating health care barriers at a national level requires national and global cooperation and this may involve different countries coming together to roll out tests and trying international strategies. This was the case with smallpox, polio and river blindness which were completely eradicated through inter-country cooperation involving national governments and international organizations such as the World Health Organization (WHO) (Roche, Broutin, & Simard, 2018). Despite the threats of possible pandemics, some of which could come from bioterrorism, there is hope for the future. However, to prevent a resurgence of some of the outbreaks like measles, sustained and well-coordinated efforts are needed.

Discussion Questions

1. In what ways is health care a human right?
2. What are the results of a lack of health care and how might these be addressed?
3. What can poor communities do to combat poverty?
4. In ways might organizations collaborate to promote healthcare delivery?

Water

Water is an essential element of life, and without it there can be no life. Water is a resource as well as a gift we have been given and it should be well managed, processed, purified, and made available to everyone. However, the scenario is different as not every person has access to good and safe water. Every person wants to drink good and safe water, and, in a way, water is a human right. Water is a powerful resource from God and on it depends on our lives. Human bodies are made up of 90 percent water, and as such our bodies should always be nourished with drinkable water (Falkenmark & Lindh, 2019). However, the demand for water is so high in many places that sometimes people go without good drinkable water. Even in some places where water is available in abundance, it is not safe to drink, and people are encouraged to take precautionary measures to purify the water.

There are many ways of purifying water which include tools that are out there for water purification. Not everyone can afford many of these tools as they are beyond their reach. In developing countries, the situation is different as clean water is hardly available and even when it is available its flow is interrupted with constant and often unbearable water shortages. For example, in Zambia where I grew up, it was common to see women walking long distances in search of water. These women would spend almost half of their days just looking for water. When they found it they would fill their containers with it and, they would then walk back carrying these containers on their heads. Water is not safe as it used to be many, many years ago and even in the affluent communities it is strongly advisable to not drink tap because it is not "safe." Drinking unclean water could have a ripple effect that might lead to challenges that include diseases and a host of other health issues. Every person has a right to good and safe water and, where this is not possible every effort should be made at both the micro, mezzo, and macro levels to ensure that people have access to good and drinkable water (Fu, Li, Liu, & Wang, 2018).

Discussion Questions

1. What are ways in which water is useful for life?
2. What are ways safe water might be made available to all?
3. Why is water an important and essential element of life?

Racism and Prejudice

The world is made up of people from different ethnicities and racial backgrounds. People in these ethnic and different racial backgrounds are socialized within their cultures. They learn norms and values that anchor them in society and that act as compasses for positive functioning in society. It is also important to note that ever person is important because each person has been made in the image of the Creator God and has been endowed with inalienable rights. These rights include being respectable and demonstrating respect toward others, and vice versa. Respect should transcend human differences, whether these differences are manifested in skin color or in visible cultural practice differences. Respect should be the norm for every society, civilized or uncivilized. The scenario today, unfortunately, is not like what one would want to see. Some groups of people have given themselves mandates to become superior and above other people resulting in racism. Racism is the treatment of people because they do not measure up to the standards set by another self-proclaimed superior group. Racism and prejudice in most cases co-occur with the latter being an unjustified or incorrect attitude, which is usually negative, toward an individual based solely on the individual's membership in a social group. For example, a person may hold prejudiced views towards a certain race or gender. Racism has had a history that can be traced to many years aback. Its history is tinted with spilled innocent blood and often undeserved death. Many have lost their innocent lives due to the uncalled-for ravages of racism. People have been uprooted from their ancestry homes and pushed into new culture contexts in which their lives have been subjected to the miseries of racism (Hughey, 2018).

Many are broken down by the effects of racism and, they are thought to be less human with their precious lives being equaled to objects that can be traded and kicked left, right and center. Racism is an evil that is very alive today and, in some circles, it has been carefully masked and embedded within the infrastructural fabric thereby making it difficult for the "less than human" to function and lead lives with absolute normalcy. Racism has caused many a tension between different population groups and these tensions have resulted in mistrust and in all kinds of melodramas. It has infuriated the different systematic elements that keep and maintain the economic machinery of many societies (Loewen, 2018). It has led to the creation of social programs that in more cases than not perpetuate oppression, prejudice, socio-economic challenges, and bigotry (Gorski, 2019). It has fueled uncalled for gun rampages and hate crimes which have become an ongoing phenomenon in many cities of the United States. What can be done to confront racism in a manner that is constructive and that helps broken people to regain their dignity and respect? This is a question that requires constructing answers.

Politics

Politics is an important game that has a direct bearing on lives and welfare of citizens and other members of a given society. Politics can unite or divide people, and it can create a positive environment or sometimes an environment tented with division, tension, bitterness, and hatred. Our societies today in these United States are framed within ideologically driven politics (Mallett, &

Monteith, 2019). People of different persuasions and ideological perspectives choose political parties they share their beliefs and values with. The extent to which they support political parties of their choice depends on the commitment demonstrated by the same parties of their choice to address their needs. Unfortunately, today we have a political arena populated with some individuals who enter the game of politics to fulfill their selfish and ego centered ambitions. Others are genuine politicians driven by a commitment and desire to deliver well on their promises. These are individuals whose lives are driven by principle. However, many are dubious politicians who often campaign on camouflaged slogans and make empty promises they hardly fulfill. They are crafty, egocentric and use very carefully calculated tactics to usurp the system for their own good. They feed on people's fears to make their upward mobility, and their insatiable desire to control the upper echelons of society through deceit, is unfathomable. Their main concern is self-aggradation and popularity, which they use as nets to catch poor unsuspecting individuals.

We live in a world where in many cases politics is used as a tool of oppression by a few who control or desire to control and take advantage of the system (Ram, 2018). Many people living under untruthful political systems, particularly the powerless, suffer in many ways and consequently they are broken in many ways. They are broken because the political system deliberately keeps them on the margins and prevents them from becoming active participants in the system. They are broken because they don't understand the political system including how it functions and oppresses. They are broken because they are targets of bigotry, prejudice, racism and discrimination and, they are broken because in some quarters of the society they are thought of as being less human. Politicians do not care that there are masses out there who are marginalized and oppressed by the very system they control (Cox & Devine, 2019). Some of them mask their selfish and self-propelling desires and intentions. They often demonstrate pretentious postures and portray gestures of goodwill that do not align with the broken. They are not ashamed of their manipulations and if it were possible, they would rather remain in their loft positions and continue to exploit the poor and broken folks for as long as they can. Their overall goal is simple, to use the system to break as many people as possible, to continue to feed on people's fears and to create a type of populism that turns them into demigods. It is a dangerous thing to be broken down by a political system that is biased, untrustworthy, and suspect. Further, it is a dangerous thing for anyone person to be powerless, hopeless and be exploited by a system that pretends to care for him or her. People broken down by a political system need not remain broken. They can overcome and can take full command and control of their lives and future (McClain, 2018). They can garner all needed energy and will to steer their future in the right direction. The following suggestions might help broken people not to lose hope and faith when living under an unfavorable political system that has betrayed them:

1. People should take every step necessary to understand the political system. This can be achieved through education.

2. Education is key and should be included on every agenda and goal of a broken individual. Education provides the ladder by which people can climb the social strata of society.

3. Broken people should demonstrate unity and cohesiveness in the midst of a harsh and uncaring political system. This unity should act as a buffer against all assaults from selfish political leaders.

4. Broken people should not give up but should foster a spirit of hope and positive anticipation. They should cultivate a positive mindset and should look into the future as if has already happened.

Discussion Questions

1. War is bad because in many ways it has negative outcomes. What are ways by which you might raise awareness around the dangers of war?

2. What wars are you familiar with and what damage did these wars do to people and societies?

3. Why do countries spend billions of dollars in developing war or military technology?

4. Why is there so much competition among developed and semi-developed nations today to be the most militarily powerful in the world?

References

Ching, F. (2018). Bird Flu, SARS and Beyond. In 130 Years of Medicine in Hong Kong (pp. 381-434). Springer, Singapore.

Cox, W. T., & Devine, P. G. (2019). The prejudice habit-breaking intervention: An empowerment-based confrontation approach. In Confronting Prejudice and Discrimination (pp. 249-274). Academic Press.

Del Ponte, A., & DeScioli, P. (2019). Spending too little in hard times. *Cognition, 183*, 139-151.

Gorski, P. C. (2019). Fighting racism, battling burnout: causes of activist burnout in US racial justice activists. Ethnic and Racial Studies, 42 (5), 667-687.

Falkenmark, M., & Lindh, G. (2019). *Water for a starving world*. Routledge

Fu, H., Li, Z., Liu, Z., & Wang, Z. (2018). Research on big data digging of hot topics about recycled water use on microblog based on particle swarm optimization. Sustainability, 10 (7), 2488.

Hughey, M. W. (2018, September). Of Riots and Racism: Fifty Years Since the Best Laid Schemes of the Kerner Commission (1968–2018). In Sociological Forum (Vol. 33, No. 3, pp. 619-642).

Kim, S. H., Chung, D. R., Song, J. H., Baek, J. Y., Thamlikitkul, V., Wang, H.,... & Lye, D. (2019). Changes in serotype distribution and antimicrobial resistance of Streptococcus pneumoniae isolates from adult patients in Asia: Emergence of drug-resistant non-vaccine serotypes. *Vaccine*.

Loewen, J. W. (2018). Sundown towns: A hidden dimension of American racism. The New Press.

Mallett, R. K., & Monteith, M. J. (2019). Confronting prejudice and discrimination: Historical influences and contemporary approaches. Confronting Prejudice and Discrimination: The Science of Changing Minds and Behaviors.

Mallett, R. K., & Monteith, M. J. (2019). Confronting prejudice and discrimination: Historical influences and contemporary approaches. Confronting Prejudice and Discrimination: The Science of Changing Minds and Behaviors.

McClain, L. C. (2018). The Rhetoric of Bigotry and Conscience in Battles Over'Religious Liberty v. LGBT Rights'. Religious Freedom, LGBT Rights, and the Prospects for Common Ground (William S. Eskridge, Jr. & Robin Fretwell Wilson, eds., Cambridge University Press, Forthcoming), 18-05.

Naeem, S., Cao, C., Fatima, K., Najmuddin, O., & Acharya, B. (2018). Landscape greening policies-based land use/land cover simulation for Beijing and Islamabad—An implication of sustainable urban ecosystems. Sustainability, 10 (4), 1049.

Ram, U. (2018). Postcolonials: Confronting Neocolonialism (1993–2018). In Israeli Sociology (pp. 125-145). Palgrave Macmillan, Cham.

Roche, B., Broutin, H., & Simard, F. (2018). Optimizing public health strategies in low-income countries: the challegens to apply the scientific knowledge for disease control and for which diseases. Ecology and Evolution of Infectious Diseases: Pathogen Control and Public Health Management in Low-income Countries, 309.

Shehata, M. A., Chama, M. F., & Funjika, E. (2018). Prevalence and intensity of Schistosoma haematobium infection among schoolchildren in central Zambia before and after mass treatment with a single dose of praziquantel. Tropical parasitology, 8 (1), 12.

Terziev, V., Banabakova, V., & Georgiev, M. (2018). Social activity of human resource as a basis of effective social policy. Available at SSRN 3138140.

CHAPTER 2

War and Brokenness

War has always had consequences which disrupt normal functioning and the wellbeing of those impacted by it. Today there is war between Israel and Hamas in which both Israelites and Palestinians have been affected. For example, many Palestinians have been misplaced and killed in thousands. War displaces people and forces them into unfamiliar territories. It breaks, disrupts, and distorts families to the extent that families get torn apart. It creates untold suffering on all and creates a new generation of refugees and displaced populations (Okazaki, Guler, Haarlammert & Liu, 2019. Almost every part of the world has known and experienced war in one way or the other. In all cases war is fueled and started by different reasons that range from tribal differences, ethnic conflicts and tensions, quest for regional control, political and economic differences, geographical tensions, and technological competition. There are many other reasons for war and, whatever it might be, war causes nations, particularly the rich countries, to spend billions of dollars on building military arsenals as well as developing advanced military weaponry and technology.

The United States has been involved in four major wars namely the War of 1812, Mexican American War, Civil War, and the Spanish-American war. The first War of 1812 was about regional control and lasted from 1012 through 1815 (Stone, 2019) when the United States declared war on Great Britain. Great Britain wanted to maintain its sovereignty and control of the United States and fraudulently engaged in a malicious strategy of stopping American ships (Jones, 2019). The British were also secretly arming American Indians thereby creating internal resistance against the Americans (McNeill, 2019). This war had serious consequences that included disruptions of trade and the eventual burning of the U.S. capitol. Despite the big push from the British, the Americans won this war in which for the first time they fought a foreign country in order to protect their independence (Marks, 2019). The Mexican American war was a geographical between Mexico and America. It began in 1846 when the then President James Polk ordered General Zachary Taylor and his forces to occupy land claimed by both countries, the United States and Mexico. The President of the United States had strong belief in the United States to expand further west for it to grow. Mexico was the aggressor and attacked first thereby forcing the United States into war. The war ended in February of 1848 and the two countries signed the Treaty of Guadalupe Hidalgo (de Bichara, 2019). This treaty surrendered Texas to the United States and further expanded America's border westward.

The Civil War involved internal tensions and conflict in which the Americans fought one another. Those in the north vehemently supported federal government, also referred to as the Union, whereas those American in the south wanted a separate region known as the Confederacy. The war lasted four years from 1861 to 1865 when finally, the Confederacy army surrendered to the Union army. One of the consequences of this war was the more than 600,000 many lives that were broken down through death and another more than 3 million Americans whose lives were broken because of fighting in the war (Janney, 2019).

The United States fought Spain in the war of 1898 in which it wanted to help Cuba become independent from Spain (Lambe, 2019). The United States had big economic interests in Cuba and wanted to pursue these interests without Spain being an obstacle. The war was ignited by a battleship that was sunk near Cuba and the United States did not doubt that Spain had engineered this attack (Meyer, 2019). The United States won the war at end of 1898 and Cuba got its independence. The United States also fought five wars during the 1900s and these were World War I, World War II, the Korean War, the Vietnam War, and the Persian War. World War I was a bloody war that lasted for a long time and in which many lives were broken. The United States was forced into this war after German submarines attacked British and United States ships, and when the Germans asked Mexico to start a war against the United States (Olmsted, 2019). World War I officially ended in 1919 when The Treaty of Versailles was signed (Olmsted, 2019). During WW II the United States joined forces with France, Great Britain, and the Soviet Union to fend off the German juggernaut. This ended in the eventual liberation of Europe from the German onslaught. During this war many lives were broken as they suffered the vestiges of WW II. The Korean War was equally damaging, and many lives were broken because of this war which resulted in the establishment of North and South Korea. In the Vietnam War many Americans lost their lives with almost 600,000 men and women dying or were missing because of the war. There have been wars in other parts of the world including Africa, Latin America, Asia and Europe where millions of lives were broken through war that resulted in many uncalled-for deaths (Renzi & Roehrs, 2019). Consequently, many families of those broken by war were severely affected. Today, rumors of war and the eminency of war loom all over our world with fears and possibilities of inter-country rivalry escalating at a faster pace.

War within and between nations can be avoided. However, for that to happen there has to be total trust and willingness on the part of those involved to resolve any disagreements amicably. The following suggestions might help in easing tensions that often lead to war within and between nations and that result in brokenness:

1. Countries with existing disputes with other nations should be willing to iron out their differences amicably.

2. International awareness and campaign efforts should be mounted about the dangers of war and its implication on individuals, families, and communities.

3. International organizations such as the United Nations should take an enhanced active, pragmatic, and leading role in mediating and arbitrating in incidents of war.

4. Other platforms and avenues such as schools and institutions of higher learning should be actively engaged in creating more awareness regarding the dangers of war and of how billions of dollars spent on war machinery and technology could be channeled into social and cultural development.

Discussion Questions

1. In what ways is war a danger to humanity?

2. How might you prevent war from occurring between and within nations?

3. War often results from an insatiable quest for control and domination or ideological differences. Explain what each of these concepts might mean in the context of war?

References

Stone, J. P. (2019). American Spheres, British Zones, and the "Special Relationship". In *British and American News Maps in the Early Cold War Period, 1945–1955* (pp. 97-150). Palgrave Macmillan, Cham.

McNeill, W. H. (2019). *The great frontier: Freedom and hierarchy in modern times* (Vol. 5456). Princeton University Press.

Marks, R. B. (2019). *The origins of the modern world: A global and environmental narrative from the fifteenth to the twenty-first century*. Rowman & Littlefield.

de Bichara, D. M. K. (2019). Late 19th-Century Periodical Print Culture in the US-Mexico Border Region. In *Oxford Research Encyclopedia of Literature*.

Janney, C. E. (2019). Free to Go Where We Liked: The Army of Northern Virginia after Appomattox. *The Journal of the Civil War Era, 9* (1), 4-28.

Jones, N. (2019). Global Strategies: The United Kingdom as a Case Study. *Cyber Security: Threats and Responses for Government and Business*, 213.

Lambe, A. M. (2019). *No Barrier Can Contain it: Cuban Antifascism and the Spanish Civil War*. UNC Press Books

Meyer, C. A. (2019). Farming in the Spanish Caribbean: Rural Identity, Culture, and Food Production in the Dominican Republic, Haiti, and Cuba.

Olmsted, K. S. (2019). *Real enemies: Conspiracy theories and American democracy, World War I to 9/11*. Oxford University Press.

Olmsted, K. S. (2019). *Real enemies: Conspiracy theories and American democracy, World War I to 9/11*. Oxford University Press.

Okazaki, S., Guler, J., Haarlammert, M., & Liu, S. R. (2019). Translating psychological research on immigrants and refugees.

Renzi, W. A., & Roehrs, M. D. (2019). Never Look Back: History of World War II in the Pacific: History of World War II in the Pacific.

CHAPTER 3

Physical and Social Environment

Humanity has graciously been endowed by our Creator the responsibility of taking good care of the environment. We are stewards of our environment, and the environment is a crucial part of human existence because it provides important elements for survival. For example, the environment provides natural habitats for animals and all types of living organisms. As human beings we get our food from the environment. Even the air we breathe is made possible by the environment through a natural purification process (Yurtsever, 2019). Trees, plants, and bushes are all part of the environment, and they have different functions such as providing food medicines and even acting as shelter and blocker to winds and other disasters. Unfortunately, not everyone realizes the significant role our environment plays in enhancing human wellbeing and ensuring human existence.

The environment needs to be protected and sadly not everyone has responded positively to ensure environmental protection. Some nations have designed policies that are environmentally friendly, and these policies are developed with a view to fully protecting the environment. Other nations have not paid attention to the environment and consequently are suffering vestiges of their negligence and lack of concern. The environment is also affected by bad farming practices. For instance, in some countries certain farming practices are agriculturally detrimental and do unprecedented damage to the environment. For example, in Zambia the Chitemene system practiced in the Northern Province, accelerated desertification (Tembo, & Phiri, 2019). Desertification has adversely affected some regions of Africa such as Somalia where thousands of families including children face huge hunger problems because of drought (Tembo, & Phiri, 2019). There are consequences that have implications for brokenness that come with paying lip service to the environment. These consequences include drought which often leads to other problems such as hunger and death, and global warming. Global warming has had many implications that have included a rise in unprecedented melting of glaciers and thereby increasing earth water levels (Varela et al., 2019). Global warming has also impacted global weather patterns. This situation has often resulted in changing weather patterns evidenced in such phenomena as soaring heat temperatures, heavy rainfall, and floods in some parts of the world. Several environmental international treaties have been signed with a view to be protecting the environment. The performance of these treaties depends on how countries that have ratified them commit to their success.

People get broken by the environment in several ways. First, when there is no commitment to preserving the environment, people suffer the repercussions of this negligence and these repercussions may include hunger, diseases and consequently poverty and death. Millions of families have been broken by environmental negligence in such countries as Somalia, Ethiopia, and India including other parts of the world. Today, India is struggling with pollution problems and many people are impacted by this situation (Kar, 2019). Second, where there are not carefully and meticulously designed policies to protect the environment, people and animals alike suffer. Thousands of animals die from drought and crop harvests are affected negatively leading to food shortages which in turn lead to diseases such as malnutrition and kwashiorkor in children (Namusalisi, 2019). Third, even in places with robust and promising environmental policies such as the United States, people are broken by the brunt of environmental degradation such as destruction caused by floods and bad weather patterns like cyclones and hurricanes (Namusalisi, 2019). Natural disasters resulting from environmental degradation lead to loss of lives in some parts of the United States.

Unfortunately, environmentalism in the United States is driven by ideology with some people believing in global warming and others saying that it is a fallacy. Depending on which side of the environmental ideological isle one finds him or herself, the debate on global warming continues to impact society in unexpected ways. Meanwhile, while those engaged in this debate push, argue and justify their positions, people on the ground are being affected and dying from environmentally related natural disasters driven by bad policies and environmental neglect.

Pollution, highlighted previously, is another environmental factor that impacts and destroys many people. Pollutants from pollution are dangerous to the environment and unless controlled and regulated they not only lead to untold suffering but to a plethora of other health and emotional challenges. Countries like China and India suffer from heavy pollutants and gas emissions and a lack of strong regulation and targeted environmental policies in these countries creates many public health challenges. The United States too is a big contributor to emission of gases into the atmosphere and policy response to this situation is very weak because of the ideological division between those who believe that gas emission is a factor in global warming and those who do not believe that it is a factor (Grubb, Koch, Thomson, Sullivan &

Munson, 2019). As alluded to earlier, the environment is central because it impacts the well-being of almost everyone living on this planet. Increased environmental awareness is needed now more than ever and, the following suggestions might help create and increase environmental awareness:

1. Environmental groups should be organized at different levels of society with a view to creating more awareness around the environment. Groups could focus on promoting areas such as water preservation and encouraging recycling.

2. In societies where good environmental policies do not exist, deliberate and concerted efforts should be made to design policies that would protect the environment.

3. Townhall meetings and special platforms should be organized where those who have less environmental knowledge and awareness can come and learn from those with knowledge on promising models and best environmental practices.

4. Enhanced local and international collaboration and networking needs to be promoted involving environmental groups and this should include how they might respond to natural disasters such as floods occurring in local or international contexts.

Discussion Questions

1. What comes to your mind when you think of the term environmental justice?

2. Identify ways in which you may help protect the environment?

3. What environmental organizations exist in your area? What do these organizations do? Who funds their work and what other agencies do they work with?

4. In some societies people engage in negative practices that hurt the environment. If you lived in such a society, what steps might you take to address this issue?

References

Bandyopadyay, M., & MacPherson, S. (2019). *Women and health: Tradition and culture in rural India.* Routledge.

Grubb, M., Koch, M., Thomson, K., Sullivan, F., & Munson, A. (2019). *The Earth Summit Agreements: A Guide and Assessment: An Analysis of the Rio'92 UN Conference on Environment and Development* (Vol. 9). Routledge.

Namusalisi, J. (2019). *Evaluation of Hermetic Technologies in the Control of Insect Infestation, Mold Proliferation and Mycotoxin Contamination of Stored Maize in Kenya* (Doctoral dissertation, UoN).

Kar, P. S. (2019). *Air pollution in Delhi and six blind men.* SAGE Publications: SAGE Business Cases Originals.

Tembo, M. N., & Phiri, E. C. (2019). The impact of modern changes in the Chitemene farming system in the northern province of Zambia. In *Gender Issues in Farming Systems Research and Extension* (pp. 361-372). CRC Press.

Varela, M. R., Patrício, A. R., Anderson, K., Broderick, A. C., DeBell, L., Hawkes, L. A.,... & Godley, B. J. (2019). Assessing climate change associated sea-level rise impacts on sea turtle nesting beaches using drones, photogrammetry and a novel GPS system. *Global change biology, 25* (2), 753-762.

Yurtsever, M. (2019). Glitters as a Source of Primary Microplastics: An Approach to Environmental Responsibility and Ethics. *Journal of Agricultural and Environmental Ethics, 32* (3), 459-478.

CHAPTER 4

Immigration and International Refugee Crisis

Immigration is the international movement of people to a destination country of which they are not natives or where they do not possess citizenship in order to settle as permanent residents or naturalized citizens. Related to immigration is the refugee crisis. This century has seen a proliferation of refugee crises that is perhaps the most severe in recent times. The refugee crisis has involved millions of people running away from their countries of origin in pursuit of a better and decent life in other affluent societies (David, 2019). However, being a refugee is not easy and people who experience this life get broken at different levels (Gough & Gough, 2019). For example, they leave their immediate and extended families and friends and associates. Some leave their employment or investments that they might have made in their own countries. They leave their cultures behind and often find themselves in new cultures in which they face unanticipated challenges as they try to acculturate (Myers & Roberts, 2019). Life in their new homelands gets complicated and takes years before many of them begin to culturally adjust to the new social and economic levels (Akhter, 2019).

Generally, refugees and people running away from their home countries do so for various reasons and these include the following: economic reasons for which they leave because they hope to work and attain decent lives in new countries; some others leave because of political reasons because their lives are placed in life threatening dangers and their only safety is fleeing to other countries (Hamber, 2019). Others leave because they want to pursue further education (Peet, 2019. Whatever the reasons may account for fleeing one's own countries, refugees do not often have knowledge and a good sense of what their new lives would turn out to be in their newfound lands (Horst, 2019).

It is not easy to be a refugee and although reasons for becoming a refugee which involves fleeing one's country may be valid and justifiable, those who flee their countries go through arduous and dangerous contours before they reach their desired destinies (Bayraktar, 2019). Some are forced to cross hot and sandy deserts on foot. Others risk their precious lives by venturing to cross seas in unsuitable and very vulnerable unsafe boats. Thousands who have taken this route have perished on seas and only the fortunate ones have managed to reach shores on the other side (Khalifa & Stephens, 2019). Innocent babies and young children have been lost in these seas thereby depriving them of the dignity and decency of a normal burial. As stated previously, those who make it in new lands begin a new life filled with fears, anxieties, and other unexpected challenges. They go through culture shocks as they try to settle down in new societies (Akhter, 2019). They struggle to find employment that is compatible with their earned skills and, some end up doing jobs that are sub-par and incommensurate with their credentials (Jack, Chase & Warwick, 2019). They face challenges of language and of how to fit in cultures that are radically different from their own (Tesser, 2019). Balancing acculturation becomes an insurmountable task particularly for those refugees with young families who they want to bring up within parameters of their own cultural values and norms.

Given a choice, people would rather live, work, retire and die in their own countries. It is not good to be a refugee as this life has many social, culture and economic complications. It is a life in which individuals and families are broken into different uncalled for ways. What can be done to address the refugee problem? There are several suggestions that might help, and these include the following:

1. Countries where refugees are running away should provide appropriate social and economic opportunities for all its citizens.

2. Local institutions should be established to assist in the resolution of political differences, tensions and disagreements involving those individuals running away for political reasons.

3. There needs to be intentional and targeted international collaboration in the management of refugees particularly international cross border refugee movements.

4. Countries receiving refugees should work closely with refugee countries of origin to promote cultural understanding including making it easy for people to experience acculturation.

Discussion Questions

1. What are ways in which you might play a role in assisting refugees?

2. What are the major needs of refugees and what are the reasons for these needs?

3. What services exist in your area to help any refugee resettlement? How do these services' function? In other words, is there any collaboration between agencies providing services to refugees? To what extent are these services and what is their impact on the well-being of refugees?

4. From what countries do refugees in your country come? Which of the countries are top four on your list? What are the reasons why there are so many refugees from these countries?

References

Myers, K., & Roberts, S. (2019). Expulsion, emotion and refugee children: forced European migration and refugee pedagogy (1912-1947). *Educació i Història: revista d'història de l'educació,* (34), 43-63.

Peet, C. (2019). World in Crisis. In *Practicing Transcendence* (pp. 33-61). Palgrave Macmillan, Cham.

Bayraktar, N. (2019). Beyond the spectacle of 'refugee crisis': Multi-directional memories of migration in contemporary essay film. *Journal of European Studies,* 0047244119859155.

Akhter, M. (2019). The proliferation of peripheries: Militarized drones and the reconfiguration of global space. *Progress in human geography, 43* (1), 64-80.

Tesser, L. M. (2019). Identity, Contingency, and Interaction: Historical Research and Social Science Analysis of Nation-State Proliferation. *Nationalities Papers, 47* (3), 412-428.

David, L. G. (2019). Implication of Small Arms and Light Weapons Proliferation for Regional Security. *International Scholar Journal of Arts and Social Science Research, 1* (2), 6-6.

Gough, H. A., & Gough, K. V. (2019). Disrupted becomings: The role of smartphones in Syrian refugees' physical and existential journeys. *Geoforum.*

Hamber, B. (2019). Changing Context and Changing Lenses: A Contextual Approach to Understanding the Impact of Violence on Refugees. In *An Uncertain Safety* (pp. 3-22). Springer, Cham.

Horst, C. (2019). Refugees, peacebuilding, and the anthropology of the good. *Refugees' Roles in Resolving Displacement and Building Peace: Beyond Beneficiaries,* 39.

Khalifa Al Nahyan, S. S. B. S. B., & Stephens, M. (2019).

Perspective—Reforming Policies on Refuge for Refugees. In *Future Governments* (pp. 119-134). Emerald Publishing Limited.

Jack, O., Chase, E., & Warwick, I. (2019). Higher education as a space for promoting the psychosocial well-being of refugee students. *Health Education Journal, 78* (1), 51-66.

CHAPTER 5

Being Broken

Meaning of broken

We all get broken in one way or the other and no one individual is protected from brokenness. What does it mean to be broken? To be broken means to experience an unexpected or expected life challenge in which one's capacity to live or survive is disturbed and stretched to the limit. In brokenness one's strength to survive or to endure a challenge is pushed to the limit. The brokenness limit is in many cases unbearable, and comes with a plethora of implications for employment, health, children, and family. When one is broken or is being broken, the experience of being broken itself is very weakening and causes liturgy and pain for those affected. Brokenness causes hope to be dashed and those affected experience a diminished vision for the future.

It is worth noting that being broken impacts life at different levels. What does it mean to be broken through loss of a job? Being employed accords one security, status, and a sense of pride. Being employed ensures that one can provide the necessary ingredients he or she needs for survival and for his or her wellbeing. It does not matter how one loses a job as the impact on self or on the family is the same. For example, if a breadwinner with a family loses employment, then his or her family may suffer because they are not able to get livelihood support from the breadwinner in absence of employment. I have friends who once enjoyed good lucrative jobs in the corporate world. However, when they lost their employment, the repercussion this loss had on them, and their families was unfathomable and consequently some of them ended up developing mental health problems.

People get broken through poor health, and as alluded to earlier, having and maintaining good health is critical to leading a normal, positive functioning life. Poor health affects many facets of life such as the ability to perform on a job, family, and relationships. We live in a society where people get broken through poor health, and poor health leads to diseases and illnesses. Those who are broken and do not have health insurance cannot afford to access or receive medical services they need for recovery (O'Brien, Jordan, Honeycutt, Wilsnack & Davison, 2019). Consequently, their condition worsens and unless they receive medical support and needed health care their brokenness worsens. Many people in this country struggle to maintain their health because they do not have health care. One of the most essential areas of one's well-being is the physical and mental aspects of life. Poor health is detrimental to wellbeing and can be a precursor to individual economic degradation (Lugo, 2019). It limits economic participation in society and makes it difficult for the young and old alike to engage in education and employment (Munford & Sanders, 2019). In 2013 approximately 42 million people lacked health insurance and of these 5.4 million were children under 18 years (Sniekers, & Brink, 2019). The figures are not any different today as more people are threatened with being broken through poor health and lack of health care.

Brokenness comes through the loss of a child or family member. The pain that results from losing a loved one is unbearable and to be broken in this way is not something one would wish on anybody. Loss of a loved one can come through illness, sudden death such as drowning or heart attack or it can come through a fatal motor vehicle accident (Ritter & Solt, 2019. Over the years I have known people who have experienced loss in its various forms and fashion. I have also seen the devastation this loss brings to families and others affected by brokenness. The following vignettes provide real life cases of individuals who have experienced challenges and brokenness in one form or another. The vignettes describe how they have addressed brokenness and the various challenges. In addition, the vignettes provide lessons for social work practice arising out of the challenges. Names used in the following vignettes are pseudonyms:

Vignette 1

I Donna Anderson, born in Decatur, AL, have faced many challenges in my life both as a child raised by a single mother, and a headstrong and independent female. In life, having to learn lessons of perseverance and independence, as well as understanding abandonment at a young age helped to mold me into the person I am today. I learned at a young age that the only person you can really depend on is yourself, (or in my case, myself, and my mother) and that having a supportive and strong mother helped me to realize my calling as a social worker in my adult life. The struggle my mother faced having to play two roles led me to desire to help people, as my mother helped and continues to help me.

Being a single mother brings challenges of providing and supporting a child alone, and having to play two roles is hard when you are trying to raise a child correctly and support them mentally and physically. The love and support I was given while growing up and am still given today helps me to strive to be as great of a person as my mom was and is. The feeling of abandonment at a young age can sometimes cripple a person, but discovering ways to rise above the ashes allows one to strive to be better than the stereotypes that you are labeled with.

Lessons for Practice

1. ### Understanding Abandonment and Facing Trials and Tribulations is Critical

    As a social worker, understanding abandonment and facing trials and tribulations throughout your life does not have to hurt you in your profession, it can give you the skills to be better than you ever thought you could. Understanding what your calling is, and what you desire to do in life can be indicative of past experiences. In all aspects, deciding whether to be handicapped by your challenges or choosing to use these challenges to better yourself in your career makes all the difference.

2. ### Understanding the Levels of Oppression of Clients

    Social workers need to understand the levels of oppression their clients face and learn to adapt to the familial construct of each specific client. As a social worker, taking past experiences and growing from them can allow you to develop skills to utilize in your profession that you did not think you possessed. Being able to connect to clients on a more personal level, increases the likelihood of success with your clients because you can be seen as "real." Oftentimes we adapt to a robotic way of working with clients, and that leads to severe burnout and lack of motivation to help clients.

3. ### Developing Own Authenticity

    Developing your own personal way of being a social worker allows you to go against the norm and leads you to be the best social worker you can be for your clients. Clients are human, and understanding the unique characteristics of everyone allows us to treat each client with dignity and worth, as well as supporting those clients by giving them the specifically formulated skills they need to help themselves.

Vignette 2

My name is Esther Weber. I was born on August 14, 1992, in Montgomery, AL. I currently reside in Huntsville, AL. I have been living in Huntsville for approximately 10 years. I moved to Huntsville 10 years ago to attend Alabama A &M University. When I graduated from AAMU I felt there were more opportunities for success for me in Huntsville rather than back home in Montgomery. I have experienced some challenges in my life that have changed me significantly. Some of those challenges are the death of my very close cousin and the time when a stranger walked into my grandmother's home with a gun. The aftermath of those two situations impacted me greatly and they currently still do as a 27-year-old adult.

April 28, 2017, I was so ecstatic about graduating college. It took me six and half years to complete my bachelor's degree and I graduated on May 5th. About 11:00 pm I received a phone call from my parents who were in the Dominican Republic for their anniversary. My mom called me to tell me that my very close cousin had passed away. It took me some time to process that information because I had just spoken to her earlier that day as she congratulated me for my accomplishment. After receiving that news, it was hard for me to enjoy my accomplishment of graduating college because I was grieving the death of someone who was extremely close to me and whom I loved very much. It was at that moment I knew that life was not promised, and I learned that it was important to love your loved ones because the time and day of death is unknown.

It was a Monday morning, and I was in the ninth grade. Every morning before school my mother would drop me and my siblings off at my grandmother's house and we would eat breakfast, talk for a while, and then catch the bus to school. This morning my mother decided to take us to school. We had just arrived at my grandmother's house. My baby sister was the last to walk in. I was looking for the door key to lock the door but I could not find it, so I sat down on my grandmother's sofa that she had in her bedroom. My grandmother's bedroom has a back door entrance and that is how everyone enters her house. I had been sitting for about five minutes and I noticed that a man had walked into my grandmother's house. At first, I thought it was someone my grandmother knew because everyone in the neighborhood knew her. I noticed that the man was just standing and looking around and I looked down at his hand and noticed a gun in his hand. My first instinct was to scream "he's got a gun" and run. My mother came in the back where I was to try to open windows and a door so that I could go to a neighbor and call the police, but all the doors were locked, and my grandmother had her windows sealed down. My mother told me to stay back here until the police came and not to come up front no matter what I heard. She said she had to go back for my brother and sister and grandmother. After a few minutes of staying in the back I didn't hear anything and decided to go to the front, and I noticed that the man was gone, and my mother was talking to the police. My mother had informed my father of what had happened because he was at work. He worked from 3 am until 2 pm. My father was very upset and disturbed by the information and he and my uncles went searching for the man but could not find him.

Both challenges impacted me emotionally and mentally. My cousin's death has made me become more loving towards my loved ones. It has also made me more anxious at times. If my wife or parents or siblings call me late at night most times, I am scared to pick up the phone because I fear getting bad news. My cousin died in a car accident, so I am more aware and careful when I am driving. I still cry about my cousin at times. I have never healed from her death, but I have learned to deal with it. The burglar situation has made me become very alert when I am out and when I am at home. When I am out, I am always watching my surroundings. When I am driving, I am always looking in my rearview mirror to make sure no one is following me. If I see that the same car has been behind me for a long time, I will take an alternate route to the police station to see if they still follow me. When I am at home, I always make sure I lock all my doors as soon as I get in. I find myself checking to see if my home doors are locked about five to six times a night. These challenges have made me look at the world differently. My cousin's death has made me look at the world as temporary. Because this place is temporary, I try to make as many memories with my loved ones as possible. The burglar incident made me view the world as evil. I do not know what the burglar's intention was when he walked into my grandmother's home with a gun but after he left my grandmother's home, he tried to kidnap a little girl who stayed around the street. I know there are good people left in the world, but that situation made me feel like this world is wicked and evil with people who want to hurt and inflict pain on others.

Lessons for Practice

1. Live Every Day like it's Your Last

It is very critical to live every day like it's your last. Since we do not know what tomorrow may bring, it's better to live each day doing the best and being good to self and to others.

2. Love Family

Learn to love your family as much as you can and create as many memories with them as possible because when they are gone all you will have are the memories.

3. **Be Alert and Aware of the Surroundings**

   Social workers should encourage their clients to be alert whenever they are out because you never know who is watching you. It is possible to fall into the trap of thinking that everyone in the world is like you. This is not true as everyone has had different upbringings and experiences.

Vignette 3

My name is Mary George, I was born in Kalemie, Democratic Republic of Congo on January 4, 1965. Ever since my young age, I understood that life is a battle and according to my philosophy I believe that people must work hard to get what they deserve. By coming from a polygamous family, I didn't have any choice but to face any situation, because life in a polygamous family is filled with rivalries and other challenges whether you like it or not. Being in that life and that environment taught me to be strong, to fight and to never back down in front of an obstacle. Further, it taught me to always stay hopeful and try to do better even when things were not going our way. That's how I understand and perceive the world. It's always the strongest and those who don't give up become successful. So, the challenge I had and still have been to never give up no matter what. The rivalry in my family had pushed me to never give up to succeed in life.

Lessons for Practice

1. **Dignity of the Individual**

   To value every person with dignity and individual

2. **Encouragement**

   To encourage clients not to give up, and advise them to always do better, and constantly raise their bar for success.

3. **Strength and Self-confidence**

To encourage clients to develop strength and self-confidence in the midst of challenges.

Vignette 4

My name is Victor Hudson and was born in Takoma Park, Maryland. My most significant challenge in my life that changed the way I perceive the world occurred in the summer of 2014. I had returned from visiting my daughter and my wife in Frankfurt, Germany with an uneasy feeling. My plans to move to Europe had changed. My wife had decided she was tired of having a long-distance relationship. She decided it was not necessary for me to move to Germany, and she would not be moving back to the United States. For the last three years we had been separated, and I was desperately trying to reconcile with her. On my way, back from Frankfurt in 2014, I was given the bad news that she had another man in her life. My ego was crushed, and I resorted to drinking to ease the pain. My daughter at age seven could not understand why she couldn't come back to live with her dad. I broke down mentally preparing myself to deal with the generational curse that seemed to plague my family. This was a hard process for me because I did not have a counselor or a therapist to help me adjust to a bad break up. At age three, I went through the same thing when my mother and father split up. I knew what my daughter was feeling, and when I saw the hurt in her eyes, it depressed me. Ever since my parents divorced my dad has been in and out of jail and rehabs my whole life. I couldn't believe that I would suffer the same fate as my dad. Eventually, I would not be able to salvage my marriage and, therefore I honored my ex-wife's wishes and signed the divorce papers in November 2014. After the divorce, I was only able to see my child once every year, or two for the next three years. This was the spark that ignited me to go back to school; I knew that it was time to move on from working meaningless jobs that did not provide me with fulfillment.

Lessons for Practice

My first lesson I learned that I could share with others regarding social work practice is:

1. **Utilize Therapists and Mentors**

   Utilize therapists and mentors who can give you guidance. My mentor Maurice Bond helped me prepare to move to Huntsville, Alabama in 2014. Maurice called me when he heard the bad news and immediately suggested I come to Alabama to enroll in the several HBCU's in the area. At that moment, I had to leave the pity party behind me along with the alcohol and pursue my degree in mental health counseling which had been my passion since I was a teen.

2. **Avoid Self Treatment**

   Using alcohol or drugs as remedies for pain and suffering can only numb the pain for a short time and the only way to change a predicament is to be sober and vigilant. Upon my decision to attend Oakwood University I now had the opportunity to work on the completion of my bachelor's degree, then move on to pursue my graduate degree in Social Work and later get my license.

3. **Don't Blame Anyone Else**

   If I don't try to change my current circumstances, I can't blame anyone else for the outcome of my future. It is my goal to help change the face of America, by bringing awareness to the community about the hazards of drug use in adolescence. My mission is to reach those young people before they choose a lifelong process of jails, institutions, or death.

Vignette 5

My name is Jacklyn Sanders and I was born on July 11th in 1982 in Illinois, Chicago. Due to my mother's addiction, I had no other choice but to get full custody of my seven-year-old sister and my 12-year-old brother at the age of 22. I had just begun to start focusing on myself because I assumed my mother had gotten herself together. Then a few months later I received a call from a social worker stating that they need to remove the children from the home due to neglect. I had already been taking care of them since birth, but to receive that call took me to a totally different emotional level. I felt angry because I felt like I was always being punished for my mother's addiction. I was ready to live my own life but felt like I had to keep putting it on hold because of everyone else. Even though these were difficult times, I would not change it for the world. It made the strong, independent, and educated woman I am today. Don't get me wrong, I had several "Why Me" moments. There were times I felt like giving up, but I knew I had two, soon to be three people depending on me. I perceived the world as a merry-go-round. I knew I had to push myself to be better and work harder to provide for my family, but I felt like I just kept going in circles. No matter how hard I tried, things seemed not to get any better. I felt like it was a repeated cycle to where I was picking myself up just to get knocked back down.

Lessons for Social Work Practice

1. **Keep Family First**

   Family is very important for several reasons. If it was not for me, my siblings would be in foster care, a group home, or even separated. I feel as if Kinship should always be the first choice whenever possible. This is not only to save money but to keep children in a familiar environment. I really do not know what would have happened to my siblings if I did not take them, and I did not want to find out.

2. **Become Selfless and Educate Yourself**

I had to realize that everything was not always about me. They needed me more than ever, we needed each other. It was up to me to show them a better, and different way of life. They felt like our mother had chosen drugs over them, but I had to educate myself and do research to better explain to them that it is a disease and that she does love us. Being objective in such circumstances is crucial.

3. **Don't be Prejudiced**

You should never judge a person by their actions nor their past but allow them to feel comfortable enough to speak openly with you to have a better understanding of their situation. For example, the first thing that was said about my mother was that she stayed out all night getting high and left the children at home by themselves with no food. After she was evaluated, and we started family counseling, I found out that my mother had a troubled childhood, as well as suffered from mental health issues. This evaluation allowed my mother to have access to the proper resources to help her become a better person and mother.

Vignette 6

My name is Veronica Johnson, and I was born February 24th, 1997, in Eutaw, Alabama.

My diagnosis with Systemic Lupus Erythematosus changed me for life. It changed the way I perceived the world. My diagnosis has taught me that life can change at any given moment. For this reason, I choose to live each day like it's my last because I never know the dice, I'm thrown in. Life is just like a game of dice. You move through each day, but you never really know what you're going to feel. You never know what you're going to see. You just never know. All you know is that in whatever battle is set out for you, you must be ready. You must be ready to overcome and persevere through everything. You must be ready to persevere through the people and the things that are ultimately set out to break you. At any given moment, life can cause adjustments and the way I perceive this life and this world matters mostly. This world is not my home eternally, but while I'm here I'll continue bending but I dare not break.

Lessons for Practice

Encourage Others

If a social worker is working with a client who may be facing a similar challenge as prescribed above, they should encourage their clients to:

> *Live life to the fullest without hesitant or regrets*
> *Face every obstacle and master every goal set.*
> *During adversity, during crippled health*
> *Fight until the end with each breath*
> *Conquer fear and remain faithful.*
> *Through what cuts like a knife*
> *"I wanted to live deep and suck out all the marrow of life."*
> —Henry David Thoreau

Vignette 7

I am Rebecca Joseph, and I was born on December 11, 1996, in Birmingham, Alabama. I currently live in Huntsville, Alabama for educational purposes. Life always has its challenges, and it depends on the individual on how they will determine the outcome of their circumstance. Yes, I have experienced a life challenge that changed my life significantly. During the first two days of September in 2018, I was notified that my line sister was missing, and I and other sister decided to go look for her and call local places to look for her. September fourth, 2018, was the day that changed my life significantly. My line sister was pronounced dead from suicide, but the car accident was a cover-up. I was in Talladega, Alabama when I received the news from my other line sister. Because my line sister was not from Alabama and considering the way she died, her funeral arrangements were delayed for about a month. Ignoring the signs of her suicidal attempts or certain conversations I had with her, I felt guilty and wished I could have said something to her to help prevent the suicide. I could also have tried talking her out of it. September 27, 2018, was the first time to visit Detroit, Michigan and, unfortunately this visit was necessitated by a funeral of my line sister who meant a lot to me. When I got to her funeral house I immediately broke down. This challenge made me become more aware of suicidal individuals including how to prevent them from committing suicide. Further, people who are suicidal do not always look sad or dress horribly. Sometimes they hide or mask it with smiles, laughing and continuing their daily life.

Lessons for Practice

1. **Mental Health Awareness**

   I view the world as a place in which we are obliged to create more awareness around mental health and letting our loved ones be able to meet their life challenges without feeling judged.

2. **Spend Time with loved Ones**

   Always spend time with those that matter the most to you. Also, always check on your friends or family members that seem happy all the time because they may be broken and facing life challenges of various scope and gravity.

3. **Connect to Resources**

Upon discovering anyone who may be in danger of committing suicide, it is important to connect them to relevant resources for support. These resources could be sourced from different agents or organizations at the local, state, or national level.

Discussion Questions

1. Choose and carefully read four of the seven vignettes above and identity and discuss the main challenges highlighted in each vignette.

2. Why are these challenges dangerous to the wellbeing of the individuals involved and how might they lead to brokenness?

3. How would you as social worker practitioner assist these individuals? What resources might you refer them to and how would you do that?

Vignette 8

My name is Rushford Stephens born December 31st, 1994, arriving into the world at 10:21 a.m. I was born in a rough city known as Birmingham, Alabama. Birmingham was a rough city. However, it has taught me a lot of life lessons. One significant challenge I recall experiencing in my life that has shaped me is the loss of my mother. My mother was shot and killed when I was only 14 years old and imagine the pain that this situation inflicted on me. As a child losing the woman that knew me best, cared for me unconditionally, and did not judge me in any form was emotionally and physically painful.

Lessons for Practice

There are three things I would recommend assisting a social worker in the field who may have a client facing a similar situation.

1. **Actively Listen to the Client**

   First, I would encourage them to actively listen to their clients. Active listening engages the client and worker so that they can review any events leading up to the situation, or during the situation and after the situation.

2. **Do Not Judge**

   Another suggestion is to not judge how the client comes to the worker because of how vulnerable the client might be. I would recommend building trust between the client and worker. Developing trust or rapport between the worker and client is paramount, this allows the worker to access any information that is vital to the case. Trust must be formed because as an individual who just lost a loved one, they could be experiencing a lack of trust in anyone, feeling lonely, and feeling as if their world has ended too. Furthermore, genuine trust will allow the worker to be an outlet for that client, give the worker an opportunity to empower the client, and remind the client of their strengths.

3. **Allow Clients to Cope and Grieve at Their Own Pace**

   The worker should allow their client to cope and grief at their own pace. The grieving process could be a long- or short-term process, which is contingent upon that person and the relationship that they shared with the deceased. Coping is an essential part of the grieving process that should not be forgotten. Further, coping for a person could be spending time with family/friends, going out to do extracurricular activities that they enjoy, or going to a therapy session. The worker could even suggest coping strategies for a client such as writing in a journal, taking long walks, or exercising for a person who has lost a loved one.

In closing, the loss of my mother has shaped me into becoming a resilient man through adversity. This tragic event has also educated me on how to value people in my life while I have them on this realm. And, remembering that taking a loss doesn't mean you give up on yourself and others who are depending on you.

Vignette 9

My name is Christine Henry, and I was born on March 17, 1982 in Auburn, Alabama. When a child is born, the first attachment is to the mother. Moreover, the father is a very close second, traditionally. However, my life did not begin this way. My mother raised my brother and I as a single parent. Times were hard, but we had all the necessities to thrive. When I was 13, my mother shared with me that she had not been honest, regarding my paternity. I was then introduced to an identity crisis. Who am I? To whom do I belong? In earlier times I had infrequent visits from a "father" figure up until this revelation. Thirteen is a pivotal time for most children; a sense of identity begins, puberty, acne, body changes, and more. Furthermore, a child begins to view the world in abstract ways, as opposed to familial concrete viewpoints. There begins an innate need to "know" from a personal perspective, but through a lack of experience, cannot fully comprehend the extent to which life can alter one's understanding. So, I was introduced to a "new" father, and the process became overwhelming and burdensome. I found myself to be confused and angry, because I had to not only meet this new "father" but a whole new "family, as well." It was a lot. Let us fast-forward five years later, and my mother has a new husband, and my little sister is born, all things new for others; I seemed to have been in a fog. Soon, things became crystal clear to me, however, I was given a court ordered deoxyribonucleic acid test, and the "new" father was found to be indeed, not mine. Queue... another tailspin! So, now I have had a few more life experiences, at eighteen, and just completely done with the paternity issues of my life. It was exhausting. It was painful. It was my life. I have learned a lot from this misadventure.

Lessons for Practice

1. **Mistakes Do Happen**

   Mistakes happen, we're only human. When they do we should face them and learn from them.

2. **Mistakes Lead to Change**

   Sometimes the receptive ones learn from other's mistakes and make drastic changes to their life trajectory. The changes should place them on a path of recovery.

3. **Whatever Doesn't Kill You, Only Makes You Stronger**

   The adage: "whatever doesn't kill you, only makes you stronger," should be placed on a billboard in one's honor. Many families have conducted this play, but the characters are altered. Sadly, some plays are much more tragically performed. Affected individuals should be afforded a great familial support system that values prayer and supplication, along with visions of success through hard work and dedication. Clients should be reminded of the importance of understanding that identity development is an internal journey, as opposed to a search through outside influence. They should constantly strive to forge strong relationships with all their close ties.

My life path with all its hills, mountains, and rough patches led me to pursue a career in social work. As a helping professional, three things I will bring along to strengthen my resolve to succeed are to acknowledge my strengths and weaknesses, first. Second, to become knowledgeable about any cultural differences and/or backgrounds of others that may shape a person's way of life and third to keep an open mind in regard to treatment options, because learned life lessons are a part of any professional's skill set.

Vignette 10

My name is Rebecca Johnson, and I was born in 1995 in Huntsville, Alabama. If someone were asked to describe me in one word five years ago, their answer would be happy. However, five years ago I attempted suicide. I always felt a need to please others and believed that as long as I did for others, I would stay happy- but it didn't. Depression hovered over every aspect of my life from school, to work, to friendships, and to my relationship with Christ. There were days that I did not want to get out of bed or when I wouldn't eat. The challenge for me was not helping others, but positioning myself so that I could help myself. I struggled with being comfortable in knowing that it was okay to open up and let those closest to me know when I was hurting or struggling internally. I had become so overwhelmed with the weight of worldly things that I was suffocating in silence. The first thing that I learned from that day is that I had to anchor myself in Christ to have strength. My faith was shaky and knowing that because I was not standing on God and His promises, my life was bound for destruction at my own hands. I had to learn to live for Him and not solely for myself or others. I was able to understand that it is only in Him that I can be whole.

I now am able to tell others of my story and minister to them in a way that I would have never imagined. I also learned that I wasn't alone. After talking to my family and friends, I was informed that even those closest to me also struggled with depression and were trying to figure out ways to cope with it themselves. I was able to join a support group and they joined with me. I learned in that moment that mental health is as essential to life as a heartbeat. If your mind is not in a healthy place, it is toxic to even the simplest daily tasks. I was grateful that there were people willing to listen to me and understand where I was coming from, not simply because of their textbook knowledge but because they too had overcome depression with the guidance and support of others. It was after this experience that I heard the voice of God and that my calling would be to help adolescents that struggle with depression. I have been able to speak to the youth of my church and not only offer them my struggle but also my saving grace, not only my pain but also my purpose. Although I appeared happy and well put together five years ago— I wasn't. If you were to ask that same individual to describe me in one word today, their answer would be blessed because I not only was given a second chance for myself but to truly care for others in a way that could change lives. As a social worker, I am able to assist those that feel like there is no hope in the situation or circumstance and that I am living testament that anything is possible. I am able to encourage them that second chances are available and even third and fourth, but to never give up. I offer clients a listening ear and try to connect them with a great support system to help and guide them as they recover. As social workers, it is imperative to meet and identify clients' needs even when they don't vocalize them. Whether substance abuse, anxiety, or abandonment, as a social worker I can assist the client with their challenges, linking them to other resources to assist as well if need be. A client overcoming an obstacle or challenge in their life not only brings them joy, but it now brings me genuine joy as well.

Lessons for Practice

1. Listen attentively to those people who may have mental health issues. Let me know that you care and want to help them.

2. Connect clients to the right resources where they will get the needed support.

3. Celebrate with your clients every victory they accomplish as this will give them impetus to keep on striving. This may lead to their ultimate recovery and growth.

Vignette 11

My name is Priscilla London, and I was born in Decatur, GA. A significant challenge in my life that changed me and how I perceive the world is when I lost my grandparents. I was very close to them, especially my dad's parents. When I went off to college, I only had one grandparent left. He lived about 15 minutes away from where I went to school. I was able to spend lots of time with him and he was even able to see me graduate. When he passed, I felt a lot of regret for not keeping in touch with him more after I left. I would talk with him every now and then, but not as often as I did when I was living there. Even towards the end of my college career I was not spending as much time with him as I was when I first got there.

My last conversation with him was the day before he passed. I was in disbelief because I had just talked to him. This changed me because it taught me to not take people for granted. It also showed me that my own parents were getting closer to that age and that they would be the ones coming to the end of the road next. I was able to learn that time is valuable. My perception on the world was one of seeing that people are ungrateful after he passed. I saw how rude we can be and that smiling at someone can change a person's whole mood. I learned to not judge so harshly because people are already having a hard time. My perception of the world definitely changed after he passed.

Lessons for Practice

1. Take the time to get to know the client on a genuine level, not because it is the job requirement. You never know what they are going through or who they might have lost as a support system.

2. Be patient. My grandfather taught me patience and that getting myself worked up over something I cannot change is pointless.

3. Communication. Being able to communicate is key. Had I kept that part of communication up, I would not have felt as much guilt about not calling my grandfather as I had once done.

Vignette Discussion Questions

Choose four vignettes from above and discuss the following:

1. Summarize the main issues in each vignette.

2. Why are these issues important and how do they affect each of the individuals involved?

3. How would you address each of the issues in the vignettes and what policy or programmatic recommendations would you make?

4. What social work core values would come to play as you read these vignettes and why are these relevant?

5. What suggestions would be given to the individuals in each of the vignettes to help them recover fully from their brokenness?

Broken by Poverty

Being poor or living in poverty is another way in which people get broken. Poverty is a social illness that impacts millions around the world including the United States. The United States despite being the wealthiest nation in the world has millions of people who lack basic resources and opportunities (Laurin, Engstrom & Alic, 2019). No one wants to be poor as it strips people of their dignity and worth. Poverty pushes people into a world of difficulties in which life itself becomes a challenge. It demeans and deprives them of purpose and meaning and as they struggle to survive, they lose meaning and direction (Wheeler & Pappas, 2019). They are broken and burdened by the daily challenges of life.

Poverty is relative and those affected by it are impacted relatively. What this means is that someone who is poor in Zimbabwe for example, might not experience poverty in the same way as someone poor in the United States. They are both broken by poverty, but it impacts them differently and at different levels and to different degrees. No one wants to be broken by poverty and given a choice, every person would want to live a decent satisfying life. But because our world is so broken, we always have people living in poverty and we will always have them (Nikolaeva, Adey, Cresswell, Lee, Nóvoa & Temenos, 2019). A society cannot sit idly and watch people get broken by poverty without doing anything about it. It is a moral obligation and responsibility of those with means to help and support the poor. This calls for those with extra resources to share with those who have nothing, and in this way they, who have nothing, will be blessed in ways they cannot imagine.

There are places in this world where people live off one dollar per day. These are people who live on the margins of life and their wellbeing is compromised by their inability to provide for themselves. Some of these individuals are genuinely not able to provide for themselves for various reasons such as a disability or illness (Evans, 2019; Rigles, 2019). There should be caution regarding those individuals who are able to provide for themselves. In such cases individuals who are able bodied should not be enabled by giving those help or support they do not need. Doing this might lead to an ongoing parasitic behavior that is perpetuated through alms and giving from ignorant well-wishers. Instead, deliberate efforts ought to be made to encourage those who are able bodied to care for themselves and their families.

Being broken by poverty leads to many other offshoots such as family dysfunctional. Today, there are many families that are dysfunctional and that have severely been impacted by poverty (Felitti, et al., 2019). These are families that cannot stay together as a unit. They struggle from day to day and their prospects for a good life are so dim that their entire survival occurs on a day-to-day basis. What are some ways in which people broken by poverty might be assisted? The following suggestions might be helpful:

1. Those who are rich or have extra resources should realize and not forget their moral obligation to the poor.

2. Authorities at the state, national, provincial or district levels should design intentional social economic policies targeted at empowering the poor.

3. Non-governmental, for profit and not-for-profit organizations, including churches and other stakeholders should be proactive in creating awareness around poverty and should create service-delivery mechanisms in which food, clothes, shelter, and other types of assistance are made available to the poor.

4. International collaboration involving international groups including philanthropists should be spearheaded by those with international contacts.

5. Efforts should be galvanized around bringing researchers and practitioners together with a view to researching and seeking pragmatic solutions to poverty.

Discussion Questions

1. What are ways you might assist in addressing poverty and those individuals broken by poverty?

2. Identify one social welfare agency in your area and highlight its service delivery system. Who does the agency assist? What are the demographics of those assisted by this agency? Who runs the agency and what is its relationship with the community?

3. If you were asked to work with churches and other faith-based organizations, what steps would you follow to ensure you support the poor?

4. How would you involve and galvanize local politicians and key individuals in your community to become intentional and fully involved in poverty reduction efforts?

Not Broken

To be broken by any challenge or obstacle is a dangerous thing. When one is broken one loses hope and one's aspirations for the future are jeopardized. Those broken have their hearts cut to the core and to them sometimes just living from day to day becomes a nightmare. Their sense of dignity is reduced to crumbs and their hope for the future is drowned in a sea of malaise. Being broken skews one's aspirations and places them on a platform of doubt and a host of other problems. Brokenness is not a welcome phenomenon, and nobody would ever dream of or contemplate asking to be broken. Instead, and as alluded to above, brokenness comes and manifests itself in various ways and sometimes when least expected. However, to be broken is not the end of world, one can be broken and yet not succumb to brokenness. To be broken and not be broken demands an unwavering resolve by any victim of brokenness. It means that one has resolved in his or her heart to stay strong and not focus on brokenness and its offshoots. It means that one who is broken cultivates a positive mindset, a mindset that sees sunrise breaking through the dark clouds of impossibility. Further, it requires that one who is broken sees or envisions a rainbow appearing above and shadowing his or her brokenness. It also means that the broken person makes a conscious choice to not give in to brokenness.

What does it mean to not give in to brokenness? It means that one galvanizes his or her energy and channels that energy into an acceptable path of recovery. Many times, broken people develop negative thoughts that generate negative energy. Negative energy is antithetical to having a positive mind because it supps every ounce of good will and good intentions one may have. So, it is critical that for one not to give in to brokenness, that they hold their head high and realize that despite being broken, they can grow from their brokenness. They can declare victory over their brokenness, and they can decide to stay in the game.

I heard of a man who lost his son to macular degeneration and within a year of his son's passing, his daughter developed a disability. A few years later his wife was diagnosed with cancer and passed shortly after. Yet, despite being severely broken on several fronts, this man made an unshakable resolve to not give in brokenness. After a period of suffering the terrible loses he stayed strong and looked beyond his brokenness. His close friends and family marveled at his sense of hope and the peace that he emanated from him. Although not every person who is broken can demonstrate this type of tenacity and resolve, it can be done by anyone who is broken and chooses and resolves not to stay broken. There was a man who was broken when he lost his job and stayed unemployed for several years. During this time of brokenness, he stayed strong and hopeful. His resolve and positive mindset helped him to weather the brokenness he had experienced during the times of unemployment. Though he may at times feel physically and emotionally weak, he did not entertain self-pity but rather garnered the motivation to stay true to himself.

Considering what has been highlighted above how can people who are broken in various ways stay strong and not feel broken all the time? The following suggestions might be helpful:

1. It is important to realize that the brokenness experienced will pass and will not last forever. It is a season that comes and goes.

2. One who is broken should make an intentional decision to not be broken in the brokenness. This calls for tenacity and absolute resolve to stand strong in the face of any brokenness.

3. If one is pushed to the limits and it seems as if they are about to fall off a mountain cliff, and if they cannot hold on, then they should seek help from family, friends, social services, or the church.

4. Anyone whose life has been negatively impacted by brokenness should not forget that within the brokenness are immense opportunities for growth. Embedded within any negative experience or experiences are seeds of hope, optimism, and purpose.

Discussion Questions

1. What does being broken mean to you?

2. Identify someone you might know who was broken but they decided not to stay broken. What type of brokenness did they face or endure? How did they overcome that brokenness? What made their resolve solid and tenacious?

3. What services are available within your community that might be useful in assisting individuals impacted by brokenness?

4. If you were asked to create a support group for broken people, what type of broken individuals would you recruit for your group and why?

References

Evans, H. D. (2019). 'Trial by fire': forms of impairment disclosure and implications for disability identity. *Disability & Society, 34* (5), 726-746.

Felitti, V. J., Anda, R. F., Nordenberg, D., Williamson, D. F., Spitz, A. M., Edwards, V., & Marks, J. S. (2019). Relationship of childhood abuse and household dysfunction to many of the leading causes of death in adults: The Adverse Childhood Experiences (ACE) Study. *American journal of preventive medicine, 56* (6), 774-786.

Laurin, K., Engstrom, H. R., & Alic, A. (2019). Motivational accounts of the vicious cycle of social status: an integrative framework using the united states as a case study. *Perspectives on Psychological Science, 14* (2), 107-137.

Lugo, A. E. (2019). Recovery and Long-Term Effects. In *Social-Ecological-Technological Effects of Hurricane María on Puerto Rico* (pp. 19-28). Springer, Cham.

Munford, R., & Sanders, J. (2019). Harm, opportunity, optimism: Young people's negotiation of precarious circumstances. *International social work, 62* (1), 185-197.

Nikolaeva, A., Adey, P., Cresswell, T., Lee, J. Y., Nóvoa, A., & Temenos, C. (2019). Commoning mobility: Towards a new politics of mobility transitions. *Transactions of the Institute of British Geographers, 44* (2), 346-360.

O'Brien, J. E., Jordan, B., Honeycutt, N., Wilsnack, C., & Davison, C. (2019). "It's All about Breaking down Those Barriers…": Exploring Survivors' Perspectives on Services and Treatment Needs following Commercial Sexual Exploitation during Childhood. *Journal of Evidence-Based Social Work, 16* (2), 160-177.

Rigles, B. (2019). The Development of Health Lifestyles in

Families Experiencing Disability. *Journal of Family Issues, 40* (7), 929-953.

Ritter, M., & Solt, F. (2019). Economic Inequality and Campaign Participation. *Social Science Quarterly, 100 (3)*, 678-688.

Sniekers, M., & van den Brink, M. (2019). Navigating norms and structures: young mothers' pathways to economic independence. *Journal of Youth Studies, 22* (2), 187-204.

Wheeler, L. B., & Pappas, E. C. (2019). Determining the Development Status of United States Counties Based on Comparative and Spatial Analyses of Multivariate Criteria Using Geographic Information Systems. *International Journal of Higher Education, 8* (1), 92-105.

CHAPTER 6

Brokenness and Transformation

Brokenness is an experience by which one might go through transformation. As noted, earlier brokenness takes different forms, and it impacts people differently. Some people get severely hurt through brokenness to the extent that they remain fixated on the brokenness. Others refuse to remain fixated on the brokenness and decide not to give up. Instead, they get up, dust themselves off and get back on their feet. Every incident or experience of brokenness has a rich reservoir of jewels or lessons that could act as a catalyst for growth. These jewels can only bring transformation in one's life if embraced and diffused into one's being. These jewels can also help in the recovery process. The rate at which people recover from brokenness varies and sometimes can be determined by the extent, scope and gravity of the challenge, problem or hurt. What is critical in this situation is that someone does not remain marooned in a swamp of brokenness but that they translate their experience or experiences into valuable lessons for growth.

Types of problems

In life people go through different types of problems that break them. For example, there are problems involving life issues. These problems pertain to marital conflicts, sexual and intimacy issues, parenting skills, social and relationship issues, and financial issues such as credit problems, debt collections, loss of income, budgeting, and conflict over money (Haggard & Kaufman, 2018). Other problems that may cause brokenness include fear and anxiety over medical conditions, eldercare issues and caregiver stress, loss of a loved one and bereavement and grief issues. Some people may get broken by landlord-tenant issues, homelessness or threatened homelessness; personal relationship and peer conflicts, domestic/partner abuse, and victimization (Day, Casey, Gerace, Oster & O'Kane, 2018).

The other class of type of problems that cause brokenness are emotional problems and mental health issues. These include depression, anxiety, and medication management issues for psychiatric conditions, eating disorders and compulsive eating (Marvanova & Gramith, 2018). Other problem types are social issues and relationship challenges, adult child-parent relationship issues, and parenting concerns over teenagers. Another set of problem types that cause brokenness are alcohol and drug-related problems which include drug-use and drug addiction, sexual abuse, and family members affected by drug or alcohol abuse of another family member (Li, Noll, Bensman & Putnam, 2018). Alcohol and drug related problems sometimes cause relapse issues which lead to abstinence from a program of recovery from addiction and co-dependency (Yang, Perkins & Stearns, 2019).

There are people who get broken by job-related problems. These problems might involve difficulties such as getting to work on time, coworker conflicts, issues in working with a supervisor, job performance concerns, career counseling related matters, difficulties making job related decisions, stress, and exhaustion (Lambert & Hogan, 2018). Other problems might involve work pressures created by downsizing or pre-retirement planning and related concerns including difficulties of navigating a new position with an organization (Lambert & Hogan, 2018). The following suggestions by Edmondson (ronedmondson.com/2016/01/7-values-of-brokenness.html) provide useful lessons for understanding and positively moving forward out of brokenness:

Brokenness keeps one humble. Humility is an attractive quality to others. People do not usually ask for humility, but it comes through a process of self-awareness and taking steps to change. Humility connotes pride and there are no steps to rid one's life of pride except through self-awareness and taking steps to remedy it.

Brokenness teaches valuable life principles. People learn more from the challenging times in life than from the good, in other words being broken is a precursor to growth and development. Life principles are learned consequently from being broken. These are not principles that people willingly choose to learn but come through life experiences of brokenness.

Brokenness brings change and repentance. Being broken sometimes reminds people that they are hopeless and that the only best recourse for them is to change and start afresh on a new path and following the lessons learned.

Brokenness encourages a fresh start. Being broken does not mean the end of the world but it can offer an opportunity to start all over again. For example, if one has been broken through a painful divorce, there will be another opportunity for starting afresh. Starting over is not always as bad as it seems, and it can be a blessing one may not have sought or thought of. When a person who has been broken looks back at what they went through they will see the real reason for the brokenness and perhaps be glad that they had to go through this.

Brokenness invites God's grace. When one is broken beyond measure or hope sometimes the only source of hope is from the Creator and this recognition can bring one to one's knees. As the pain of brokenness increases God's grace increases even more. When confronted with the reality that only God can provide the needed help during hard times, God's favor and protection becomes real and it is a good thing when one's heart longs heavenward.

Brokenness illustrates humanity. Brokenness reminds people that they are frail and that they share the commonality of life's struggles. Every broken person has something to share with others who may or may not be in a similar situation. People who have been broken can help those who are going through hard times with real lessons that may provide hope. People are the same everywhere as they all belong to one humanity. In hard times and in difficult perplexing moments we are in this together. We are all in need of God's mercy and grace because we live a broken and fallen world.

Focusing on lessons learned

Beck, U., & Beck-Gernsheim, E. (2018). *The normal chaos of love.* John Wiley & Sons.

Being broken is not a futile experience. There are always benefits and rewards that come out of being broken. As said previously, broken people make the best conveyors of hope for others. For this reason, it is important to focus on lessons learned from being broken. There are different types of lessons people gain from being broken and these include such areas as marriage, health, money, jobs, poverty, loss, and a host of other challenges. What lessons can be gleaned from being broken through marriage? Marriage is one area in which people struggle a lot and over the years the divorce rate has been increasing over the years (Beck & Beck-Gernsheim, 2018). Divorce has consequences and unless addressed these consequences could have a negative impact on the victims of divorce and their families. The impact can be emotional which can lead to other psychotic problems and depression.

If someone has been broken through divorce, they can analyze their situation and find out what caused their marriage to fail and once they have done that, they could focus on repairing the causes of their problem and, on working on finding pragmatic solutions to the problems. For example, if the divorce was due to infidelity, how can this be addressed so that it does not re-occur and cause further problems in the future. If possible, one would do well to seek treatment through appropriate therapy and counseling. When one has overcome infidelity through treatment and counseling, they might be able to provide the best lessons for other people facing similar brokenness. If brokenness is through health challenges such as cancer and if one survives the cancer through medical treatment and support from family and friends, they might be the best source of help for other people with health challenges. Only those people who have been broken will have the best real-life lessons to pass on to others. For this reason, focusing on what might be learnt from being broken is critical because lessons gleaned from this experience can be life changing to someone else. Focusing on the negative implications of being broken does not do any good. Instead, it usurps life and energy from the subject of brokenness and it sends them into a stream of worry, misery and hopelessness. Being in such a state of despondency does not produce any useful lessons but only aggravates the situation and complicates life for the broken person. Sometimes it may be difficult to draw useful lessons from brokenness but with purpose, focus and perseverance, it is possible. The following suggestions may be useful in helping people draw some lessons from being broken:

1. When one is broken, they need to know and realize that there is a reason why there are going through a particular

challenge. They might not know or understand the reasons and there is no problem with that. However, they should not despair about being broken and what they can do is to assess their situation and see any areas where things are not going right.

2. Brokenness provides an opportunity for introspection and reflection. It is a time for growth and should not be considered as the end of life. It can be the beginning of a new phase of life, one that is filled and loaded with relevant life lessons that may be useful for others.

3. Brokenness should be viewed as a growth opportunity and not as anything negative. This sounds confusing and negative but when seen through a right lens, brokenness viewed from this perspective could be both liberating and enriching and can provide a deeper sense of understanding and appreciation of life.

Striving

Never giving up

Striving is an essential element of recovery from brokenness. Striving amid brokenness means refusing to give in to despair and hopelessness. It means looking beyond brokenness and envisioning a rainbow of hope and recovery. A rainbow reflects many colors that add beauty to the whole. Similarly, brokenness when embraced can produce beautiful colors of renewed and invigorated character manifested in tested growth. Character resulting from brokenness is like a color in the rainbow which like a jewel emanates from those who have successfully endured brokenness. Enduring brokenness means that one does not give up but keeps on striving in the face of hostile or negative forces.

There was a certain man who had a very good managerial job in a reputable bank. However, one day he received a notice to terminate his employment because his bank had incurred continued was downsizing continued losses. The man was broken but unfortunately, he allowed this brokenness to crush him. He gave up and one day went home and shot his wife, then his two children and then turned the gun on himself. This man gave up on life after losing his job he so much cherished and when he lost his job his world had come to end. Sad as his situation might have been, he should not have given up because this was not the end of the rope for him. He was a qualified person with the right credentials that could have possibly landed him another job in the corporate world, but he gave up too soon. Had he not given up and had he fought on he could have curved for himself a rainbow character and many people would have gained from his color-lessons.

A single woman in a certain part of the world was living in abject poverty. She made a living by selling locally grown produce. She had a young son and one day when she went to work in the field she left her son by himself at home. When it was lunchtime and his mother had not yet come back home, the little boy decided to help himself with the only small amount of food the family had for the week. When the mother came back home and found out that that all the last remaining food had been eaten by her son, she got so mad that she poured hot cooking oil on her son. She was arrested for attempted murder. This woman was obviously broken by poverty, but she gave up and allowed her poverty to thrust her into a frenzy of brokenness that cause her to almost murder her son. Although the boy might have healed his scars would later remind him of what giving in to brokenness can do. Although this woman was a hard worker and she tried and did her best to look after herself and her son she failed lamentably by allowing brokenness to break her. She gave in to the pull of poverty and in the process lost her mind and almost killed her son. Had she contained and restrained herself despite what her son did, after all the boy was hungry and needed to eat, she would have moved up into another phase of growth and at the end of the day she would have cultivated a rainbow character. The following suggestions might be helpful for those people who find themselves giving up amid brokenness:

1. Realize that giving up amid brokenness can generate negative energy which can be destructive if left unchecked.

2. Giving up in the face of brokenness can sometimes appear to be the best course of action but it should not. Instead, it should be seen as a platform of opportunity for change and growth. When the first instincts of giving up emerge, every effort should be made to turn these instincts into something good and positive. For example, if one feels any urge to steal, kill or throw a tantrum, they should think first about stopping these negative instincts in their mind and then endeavor to convert this negative energy into something positive.

3. If someone gives up in a broken situation, they should not lose hope and think they world has ended. Life has a tendency to give second chances and, when any second chance for a similar situation arises, they should take it and use it wisely for their benefit. For example, if one loses a loved one such as a child, it is possible that they might get another chance to have another child. If it is divorce, they might get another chance for a second marriage and if it is loss of employment, there might be a second chance for another job.

Connecting with others

There are a variety of ways by which one may overcome brokenness. It is important for anyone broken to always remember that people were not made to live in isolation. We are social beings and our strength to live and purpose for life can be gained from associating and connecting with others (Harasemiw, Newall, Shooshtari, Mackenzie & Menec, 2018). Being intentional about this has several benefits that might include health, stability, and overall satisfaction with life (Grinde, Nes, MacDonald & Wilson, 2018). Isolating oneself during tumultuous times can breed more challenges including illnesses and could eventually lead to psychological breakdown and psychosis (Margolis & Lyubomirsky, 2019). There is power in connecting with others, and this power is unseen yet potent enough to soothe pain, to bring healing, and to create purpose and meaning to life. Today, there are millions of people who are struggling with brokenness. Their lives are empty, lacking direction and value. They are lonely and some of this is by choice while some of it is by circumstances beyond their control. For example, if someone has lost a child they need to connect with others for physical, emotional, and psychological support. If they have lost a sibling, a job, a house, or anything precious to them, they need other people for strength and vitality to live. In almost every brokenness brought about by such disasters as floods, tornados, car accidents, diseases outbreaks, or by anything that impacts people on a larger scale, people are compelled to assist those in need. They do this by their own volition and because it is the right thing to do. They are moved by their compassion for humanity, and their actions reveal the essence of connecting as humans. People who are broken and are not able to connect with others should be reached out to with deliberate efforts. If they are able to they too could do well to reach out to others for encouragement (Storey & Perka, 2018).

The world today has become more like a big village in which people can connect easily using all kinds of methods including a plethora of media platforms. In societies where technology drives human activity, media platforms can serve and be utilized as bridges of helping and connecting with those who may be languishing in the pangs of brokenness. In non-technological societies, people can connect using traditional methods such as personal visits to connect with those in need. Although both methods certainly have merits, the latter method works well because it brings human touch and contact into proximity with those in brokenness. Physical contact by way of a personal visit, a touch, a hug, or any other connection that creates human contact has numerous benefits (Reamer, 2019; Varea, González-Calvo & Martínez-Álvarez, 2018).

References

Day, A., Casey, S., Gerace, A., Oster, C., & O'Kane, D. (2018). The forgotten victims: Prisoner experience of victimisation and engagement with the criminal justice system: Key findings and future directions.

Grinde, B., Nes, R. B., MacDonald, I. F., & Wilson, D. S. (2018). Quality of life in intentional communities. *Social Indicators Research*, *137* (2), 625-640.

Haggard, S., & Kaufman, R. R. (Eds.). (2018). *The politics of economic adjustment: international constraints, distributive conflicts and the state.* Princeton University Press.

Harasemiw, O., Newall, N., Shooshtari, S., Mackenzie, C., & Menec, V. (2018). From social integration to social isolation: The relationship between social network types and perceived availability of social support in a national sample of older Canadians. *Research on aging*, *40* (8), 715-739.

Lambert, E. G., & Hogan, N. L. (2018). Correctional Staff: The Issue of Job Stress. In *The Practice of Correctional Psychology* (pp. 259-281). Springer, Cham.

Li, J. C., Noll, J. G., Bensman, H. E., & Putnam, F. W. (2018). Childhood Sexual Abuse Increases Risks for Eating Disorder Symptoms and Eating Disorder-Related Health Problems in Females. In *Child Maltreatment Research, Policy, and Practice* (pp. 11-26). Springer, Cham.

Margolis, S., & Lyubomirsky, S. (2019). Experimental manipulation of extraverted and introverted behavior and its effects on well-being. *Journal of Experimental Psychology: General.*

Marvanova, M., & Gramith, K. (2018). Role of antidepressants in the treatment of adults with anorexia nervosa. *Mental Health Clinician*, *8* (3), 127-137.

Reamer, F. G. (2019). Boundary issues and dual relationships in social work. *The Routledge Handbook of Social Work Ethics and Values.*

Storey, J. E., & Perka, M. R. (2018). Reaching Out for Help: Recommendations for Practice Based on an In-Depth Analysis of an Elder Abuse Intervention Programme. *British Journal of Social Work, 48* (4), 1052-1070.

Varea, V., González-Calvo, G., & Martínez-Álvarez, L. (2018). Exploring touch in physical education practicum in a touchy Latin culture. *Societies, 8* (3), 54.

Yang, Y., Perkins, D. R., & Stearns, A. E. (2019). "I Started to Feel Better now": Qualitative Findings from Client Narratives on Early Recovery in Inpatient Substance Use Treatment. *International Journal of Mental Health and Addiction*, 1-19.

CHAPTER 7

Reflection and Brokenness

It is important in life to take time to reflect. Reflecting involves assessing one's life in order to see if there are any grey areas that might need fixing (Benn, 2018). It is a type of introspection by which one enters the inner depths of one's heart. This introspection allows one to enter one's inner world and, taking time to deeply search all the different contours and zones of this inner world (Sebeok, 2019). The inner world is tantamount to the human heart in which are stored all sorts of feelings, thoughts, emotions and even pain. These feelings, thoughts and emotions can either be positive or negative. Reflecting may make it possible for one to enter this inner world thereby enabling them to get rid of all the negatives that might be causing self-brokenness (Borysenko, Faulkner, McCormick, Cook & Taegel, 2018). It is almost like cleaning rooms in a house that have been uncleaned for weeks and, in the process, they have gathered dirt. Unless cleaned this dirt can cause illness and disease in the inhabitants of the house.

How can one clean his or her heart to reduce the chances of being broken? This could be done in several ways. First, if one has the capacity to cleanse oneself of the negatives in the heart, then one should do so right away. Second, if this capacity is not available then it is critical that one seeks help from professionals or from friends and other associates. Failure to do so may lead to more brokenness. Thus, reflecting is a good practice that has many benefits, and these benefits can reduce and even heal brokenness (Norcross & VandenBos, 2018). One such benefit is the opportunity to pinpoint the source of brokenness and thereby be in a better position to strategize necessary steps for healing and recovery (Lewis & King, 2019). Another benefit is the realization that reflecting and healing are interconnected in that the former is necessitated by the latter, and when executed, reflecting may lead to healing, growth, and self-discovery.

Surviving

Surviving is an important part of human nature. People always want to survive amid calamity and brokenness. No one wants to live in brokenness forever as doing so could prove detrimental to their human nature. When one is broken, they may not have the fortitude to survive because their lives are disturbed by a negative force that skews their equilibrium. However, this does not mean they do not want to survive and grow from their brokenness. Such individuals need to be supported in every way possible. They need to be affirmed and reassured of their potential to survive. One way this could be done is through helping them attain a beneficial and positive mindset (Weber, 2018). Mindset and attitude are closely interlinked and the two may lead to behavior and actions. If one has a mindset that hinges on hopelessness, then certainly their behavior and outward actions will be that of hopelessness. There are various techniques one may use to assist or help such individuals. Results of applying any of the techniques may take time to show. Continuous effort and diligence is required on the part of the helper to ensure that the broken person attains a positive attitude to life and this is a precursor to recovery, balance and hope. Being broken by life's negative forces such as poverty, a failed political system, health challenges, and natural disasters may cause one to lose a sense of living with anticipation. What is living with anticipation? To live with anticipation is to live with dreams for the future, it is to look forward to a bright and prosperous future. There are individuals who live with anticipation for a better future and this anticipation drives or pushes them to soldier on in the face of storms or barriers. They have a resolve that is unshakeable and solid. They see resolution in the midst of despair, hope in the midst of doubt, strength in the midst of weakness, and focus on the midst of fogginess. Their minds are made up and settled for the best and positive horizon. They do not live in the past brokenness but instead thrive on what the future has in store for them (DeRusha, 2019). Their stamina and determination for life are cemented by a will to overcome. How can this be done or accomplished? One way is through a will to seek out opportunities for growth. These opportunities may not just fall from heaven, they must be sorted out and searched intentionally. When found they need to be fully utilized with one goal in mind, and that is to overcome brokenness and to grow and flourish. Flourishing resulting from the use of opportunities is key to healing from brokenness. For example, if one has lost hope because of homelessness resulting from the loss of a job, they need not sit on their laurels and wish that a job will suddenly appear from the sky. They need to go out and talk to friends, colleagues, associates, and other networks about potential job opportunities. As they make the relevant and needed connection, at the same time they need to sit, write, and submit as many job applications as possible. Their persistence will bring about expected results, maybe a job that may realign their lives again. This approach could be applicable to a plethora of other types of brokenness.

Discussion Questions

1. What are ways one may help a broken person to achieve a level of hope for the future?

2. What are ways of exploring opportunities that might help one to come out of brokenness? What three steps are essential for this to happen?

3. What do you understand by hope and living with anticipation?

4. How can a survival attitude help one to find healing?

References

Benn, M. (2018). *Life Lessons*. Verso Trade.

Sebeok, T. A. (2019). "Tell Me, Where is Fancy Bred?": The Biosemiotic Self!. *The Semiotic Web 1991: Biosemiotics*, *106*, 333.

Borysenko, J., Faulkner, M., McCormick, L., Cook, H., & Taegel, W. (2018). *The Heart Reconnection Guidebook: A Guided Journey of Personal Discovery and Self-Awareness*. Health Communications, Inc..

Norcross, J. C., & VandenBos, G. R. (2018). *Leaving it at the office: A guide to psychotherapist self-care*. Guilford Publications.

Lewis, M. L., & King, D. M. (2019). Teaching self-care: The utilization of self-care in social work practicum to prevent compassion fatigue, burnout, and vicarious trauma. *Journal of Human Behavior in the Social Environment*, *29* (1), 96-106.

Weber, S. (2018). Participatory Visual Research with Displaced Persons: 'Listening'to Post-conflict Experiences through the Visual. *Journal of Refugee Studies*.

DeRusha, M. (2019). *True You: Letting Go of Your False Self to Uncover the Person God Created*. Baker Books.

CHAPTER 8

Strong and Strong

Staying strong and resilient during brokenness is an essential part of bouncing back from it -brokenness. This is not easy especially when the challenges are experiencing are severe and beyond one's capacity to endure. To be strong might mean that one summons all support far and near and it may require development of a solid inner emotional stamina. Emotional stamina might help one to maintain a healthy state of mind in the face of adversity. Although this may not come easily, it can be reached with a correct mindset. It will not come or be realized immediately but with practice, diligence, concentration, and focus, it can come. Emotional stamina will also act as buoyance that dispels or pushes out of one's psychological makeup any traces or elements of negativity. These negative elements are poisonous to the body, and they may compromise the body's immune system to an extent where one becomes subject to psychological stress. If a person is struggling with attaining a useful emotional strength and if they lack the capacity to shift their mind framework, the following points are crucial to consider a) seek friends who are reliable and trustworthy, b) stay connected with a dependable circle of family and friends and c) utilize a teamwork model.

Seek friends close by who are reliable and trustworthy: Friends can be a good and solid source of support and comfort. However, only friends who are serious, good, and genuine and who one knows very well enough to trust should be sought. Some friends may not be a good source of support, and these should be avoided as they could be hindrances who may jeopardize the recovery and healing process.

Stay connected with a dependable circle of family and friends: Once good, genuine, and supportive friends are sought, it is critical to stay connected with them. They should be consulted in emergencies and they should be allowed to participate in the decision making process of healing and recovery. Good friends are like jewels, they should be cherished and appreciated all the time. They may be much more useful and worth than other hostile and negative family members. A person who is struggling with brokenness and has found good, genuine friends should constantly stay connected with them by way of phone, text, and other possible technical connection conduits. Where possible physical visits should be initiated as these tend to foster a strong sense of bonding. A teamwork model described below is a tool that might prove useful for recovery from brokenness. This teamwork model exemplifies the value of connections and relationships at various levels. It highlights the healing, recovery and mending that may result from a deliberate attempt to make the connections alive and active. These connections start at the individual level, then family level, then community level and lastly institutional level. At each of the levels the broken individual will be supported in ways that enable them to move on to the next level. The individual could involve close friends or associates who provide needed support such as visitation, finances, or food. The family level may provide such assistance as shelter, gathering and food. The community level may make opportunities for engagement with the church and other community-based groups. The institutional level will provide the broken person with support from local and state agencies such as food, shelter, transportation, and hospital.

Figure 1 Here [Teamwork Model]

The teamwork model is a good approach that could work effectively when fully understood and carefully implemented with detailed attention and accuracy. If this model is not clearly understood and gets implemented in an unauthentic way, it may not yield the desired outcomes. At that point it may seem murky and could create an unanticipated consequence. A murky state can create messiness to teamwork, and this may present a new layer of challenges. A murky state may also obscure the most promising opportunities for recovery (Gagliardi, 2018). However, even with a murky situation, there are opportunities for growth that may result. If the teamwork model moves beyond the familiar and predictable and creates an environment of uncertainty, it may create opportunities for dialogue and discovery, and that is what teamwork is all about. The rewards of this model may not be immediate. However, they may become evident when collective efforts for support and recovery are made and the model begins to unfold. When this is allowed to happen, positive results will emerge. As a person recovering from brokenness continues to engage with other players in the model, more discoveries, mending, and meaning we'll begin to show on the horizon (Postlethwaite, 2019). With support and collaboration from others in the model, the broken person may begin to show recovery and growth. Further, he or she will need to hold ground as well as demonstrate flexibility in efforts of promoting healing and recovery (Gerber, Loomis, Falvey, Steinbuchel, Leland & Epstein, 2019). It is also important to deal with any barriers that arise as the teamwork model unfolds. These barriers or challenges should be dissected and addressed effectively and acutely. Where possible the healing and recovering person should engage in discourse with other individuals in the model with a view to providing or finding appropriate solutions to his or her problems (Gadamer, 2018). At this stage responses to any identified barriers should be carefully crafted and applied immediately because doing so might eliminate possible hindrances to the healing process (Zackrison, 2019).

References

Gagliardi, J. S. (2018). Unpacking the messiness of harnessing the analytics revolution. *The Analytics Revolution in Higher Education: Big Data, Organizational Learning, and Student Success.*

Gadamer, H. G. (2018). *The enigma of health: The art of healing in a scientific age.* John Wiley & Sons.

Gerber, E. B., Loomis, B., Falvey, C., Steinbuchel, P. H., Leland, J., & Epstein, K. (2019). Trauma-Informed Pediatrics: Organizational and Clinical Practices for Change, Healing, and Resilience. In *Trauma-Informed Healthcare Approaches* (pp. 157-179). Springer, Cham.

Postlethwaite, M. (2019). *Addiction and Recovery: A Spiritual Pilgrimage* (Vol. 9). Fortress Press.

Zackrison, E. (2019). *Christians Are Recovering Human Beings: Returning to God's Reality.* iUniverse.

CHAPTER 9

Navigating Brokenness

Life is a precious gift from God and by it we are given the opportunity of living each day. In addition, life is the source from which we draw our existence and without it we cannot do anything. Further and most important, life is a blessing from God that makes it possible for us to go through the experiences of each day. It is also a blessing that presents us with new possibilities for growth each day at the individual, family, and community levels. When embraced fully and appreciated, these opportunities become conduits through which we navigate, grow, and ultimately appreciate life more and thereby make an impact in this world.

God allowed me to realize how important life is when our dog Rocky was suddenly hit by a car. This happened one Sunday when a friend of mine visited me. As my friend decided to leave, I, as I customarily do, walked him out and down to the street. As we made our way out, Rocky decided to follow us. I turned back and saw Rocky coming. I tried to whistle for him to go back, but he continued to follow, and so I let him accompany us. Dogs are very sensitive to their masters, particularly if they perceive negative commands from them. It appeared that Rocky had realized that I did not want him following us, so he was in an alert state of mind just in case I decided to turn around and chase him away.

As we walked along and chatted, a fast-moving car appeared from behind and at that point I decided to turn to see whether Rocky was walking on a safe side of the road. Unfortunately, as soon as I turned, Rocky thought I was chasing him away. He turned and started running back to the house and he was immediately struck by the car. He was hit so hard that he was confused and took off to my house, entered the yard, crashed against the house, and lay panting on the ground. My friend and I ran back to the house and with my friend tried to inspect Rocky to determine the extent of the pain or injuries that had been inflicted on him by the car. Later that day I took him to the veterinarian. When I returned with him a few hours later, we tried to give him food in the evening and hoped that he would rest and feel better the following day. In the morning I went out early to see him, and just but found that he had passed.

Rocky's passing that night caused me a lot of grief. As we buried him in my house backyard, I was reminded of just how futile life is. It was hard to believe that just a day before a dog that was as vibrant and active as Rocky was, was gone. Without the breath of life in him he was nothing but a "thing." It is the breath of life in each one of us that makes us who we are and that makes us live and function.

When God created man, He breathed in him the breath of life. This is the breath that sustains us daily. In a book entitled *Basic Lessons on Life*, Witness Lee describes the process of life clearly when he suggests that when the "breath of life was breathed into the nostrils of the body of man, man became a living soul, and it is this breath of life that makes us live."

God imbued man with a life-giving breath and it is this breath that makes man live. The first man God created was Adam and when he was created from the dust of the earth, Adam did not have any life in him only until God breathed in him the breath of life. At that point, all his body parts and elements were invigorated by God's power. Within that God breath was the extension of life emanating from God Himself. This life is the eternal energy that touched, impacted and activated all nerve cells in Adam. As soon as the breath of life was imbued in him, Adam became a living soul and had the God given capacity to enjoy God and His creation.

Our bodies have been made in the image of God and are so complex that even scientists today have not been able to fully understand the makeup, including the way it functions. God's word describes how beautiful and yet complex our bodies are by highlighting that we are "...fearfully and wonderfully made" (Psalm 139:14, New International Version). We need to thank God for our bodies and for life and for each day that we are allowed to live. Each day ought to be an opportunity to praise God and enjoy His creation. The body God has made is indeed fearfully and wonderfully made that it would take eons to fully understand it.

For example, the heart is a body organ that is complex and wonderfully made. This is an organ on which life depends. The heart's beats are wonder and unique. They make it possible for us to live and function. They also affirm God's power and wisdom of creation. As we live each day is made possible by the heartbeat, we ought to praise God for His wisdom and understanding in creating us. From the moment the human heart begins to beat until the moment it stops, the beats testify to the omniscience and wisdom of God and the complexity of life.

More recently I went to a doctor's appointment to have a heart imaging and I was in awe to see on the computer screen my heart and heart beats and how the blood was flowing through the ventricles and aorta. In this image on the screen, I remembered God's majesty and creativity in making every organ of our bodies perfect. Every morning when one wakes up it is the heartbeat that keeps him or her alive. It is the heartbeat that makes it possible for the blood to flow throughout the body. It is the heartbeat that helps in the distribution of energy and essential elements throughout all the body and this energy helps us to garner the strength needed to go about each day.

Part of the beauty of life can also be seen in creation, and this is evident when we gaze into the night skies and see the majestic display of the night-lights and their glimmer; the heavenly stars and their magnificence so meticulously expressed in the various star formations. In the animal world, God's wisdom is evident as well. The many and incredible species in nature all testify of God's greatness. All these elements of creation make life more interesting, beautiful and from which we can attain a plethora of blessings and opportunities for enjoying and celebrating life. God is good and His goodness is evidenced daily in our interactions with one another, including those interactions with nature. One day a few years ago, as I was walking out of a Wal-Mart store, I saw a huge rainbow in the sky. As I saw this wonder of creation I was touched by God's love and reminded of His promises and blessings of life. The rainbow's arch shape was a great wonder and as it encircled the blue skies I was reminded of God's love and never-failing promises.

In the summer of 2012, we travelled with some graduate students from the United States to Nairobi, Kenya for a study tour of that country's non-governmental organizations. During one sunny nice weekend of our tour, we decided to visit and tour the Ngong Hills located in the Masai region of Nairobi. Climbing the hills was a breathtaking and exhausting task because we had to climb all the steep contours of the hills to get to the top. When we reached the top of the hills, we got a panoramic view of the East African rift valley that runs from Eastern to Southern Africa. The scenery was gorgeous and the air fresh and exhilarating.

As I sat on a nice smooth rock there on the hills, I contemplated the goodness of God and the life that He has so freely given us to enjoy. As I deeply thought about God's goodness in the hills, it dawned on me that the blessings of life come from many other different sources. They come from getting news of a birth of a child, from news of receiving a college scholarship, from enjoying a vacation at your favorite spot, from getting a good doctor's report, or from marrying a childhood sweetheart.

In all these incidents I was reminded that we experience blessings that make life seem so good, and that push us to higher and more positive heights of existence. Included in the abundance of life are blessings that God wants to bestow upon His children who put their trust in Him.

Every day that God gives us should bring a renewed sense of hope, courage, and positive anticipation for what life's blessings that day God has given us may bring. We should always look forward to the good things that are in store for us daily. Even if we do not fully realize our expectations for the day, we should not lose hope, but remain hopeful that God is faithful and that He always wants to shower His children with the best of blessings. Blessings from God come in many forms and ways and the more we receive them the more we appreciate Him and the gift of life He so generously gives us daily.

Many times, we take life for granted because we usually get carried away by the mundane routines of life, like waking up in the morning and heading for work or school, and then coming back home and the same cycle continues the following day. Yet, within this endless cycle lies the good and beauty of life that God has accorded us. Appreciating God's beauty brings purpose and meaning to our lives and more so as we realize the blessings that come out of these daily routines, we begin to appreciate God more. For example, a good paycheck at the end of a well-worked two-week cycle or month is a blessing, not only for oneself but a blessing from which others may gain as well. Getting good grades that enable one to enter a good college is a blessing that could emerge from this cycle as well. Accordingly, God wants the best for us and He has promised to do so for as long we are obedient and follow His lead and guidance during this earth's life journey. His blessings are immeasurable and can impact every area of our lives such as health, family relationships, career paths, business projects, and many others.

When God blesses us, we too can become conduits of blessings to others. This is one of the purposes of life, to be blessed so that in turn we can become a blessing to others. Perhaps the greatest blessing that one can offer is to be able to come to a point where we are ready to give up anything, even our lives, for others. Jesus said, "greater love has no one than this that he lay down his life for his friends" (John 15:13, New International Version). One of the greatest blessings of life is to be able to give oneself to others. To have a mindset that is driven by this principle requires that we live lives in a different heavenly dimension—a dimension that is universal in nature yet one that reaches out to people from all walks of life. Life at its best becomes a blessing if we can allow ourselves to become a blessing to other people, no matter their backgrounds.

When I was growing up, I had always wanted to become an architect, as different types of buildings and their inherent archeological bearing thrill me. Over the years, however, my career ambitions changed, and God repositioned me to a different professional path where I would best serve Him as well as be a blessing to other people, thereby bringing glory and honor to His name. I became a social worker and since then I have blessed many clients, including seniors, young vulnerable people, and children, in many ways I would not have had I taken a different career path. I remember very well when I was working as District Social Welfare Officer how I diligently worked with orphaned children and how I blessed them in many ways and how they in turn blessed me. In His providence and wisdom God has ordained that life is not only a blessing to us but that we should grow more and more like Jesus. God wants us to enjoy life, not only physically, but that we experience the spiritual realm where we can come to a fuller appreciation of His mercy and blessings as well.

As much as life is a blessing it is not devoid of troubles and storms. The storms of life can come anytime and anywhere. God often allows storms in our lives, and sometimes these storms are engrained within the complexities and intricacies of life. They emerge in various ways and forms. Every child of God faces and endures storms at some point in their life or spiritual journey and these storms may break him or her. Although storms may often be perceived in a negative sense, they could be a blessing as well. To come to this realization involves making a full and total surrender to Jesus who alone can change our minds and perceptions, including the way we look at life including the positive or negative events that life may bring at us.

When I look back at how God has moved me in different locales, I am amazed and just stand in awe of how He has provided for me, how He has sustained and protected me even within the most unexpected of storms. In all the storms that God has allowed to come my way, many blessings have emerged from them. Life, therefore, is not only filled with blessings that enrich our existence but is also imbued with storms that, when looked from God's perspective, bring blessings in ways not fathomed previously. This is very important for social workers to know especially as they work with various types of clients.

CHAPTER 10

Social Work, Life and Wellness

The histories of Christianity and social work have a long-shared background. The history begins in part with the charity organization society (COS) that emerged in the United States in the late nineteenth century. This was inspired by a similar movement in Great Britain (Scales & Kelly, 2011) where these charities practiced almsgiving without investigating the circumstances of beneficiaries. The followers of the movement sought changes in the way charities responded to need-based on three assumptions: that urban poverty was caused by moral deficiencies, that poverty could only be eliminated by the correction of these deficiencies in individuals, and that various charity organizations would need to cooperate to bring about this change (Scales & Kelly, 2011).

The COS flourished in the United States and by the 1890s, over a hundred American cities had charity organization societies. These organizations did not typically give money to the poor who were broken and facing various types of challenges (Graff, 2007). Instead, they coordinated various charitable resources and kept records of those who had received support and charity (Graff, 2007). In this movement privileged middle- and upper-class women volunteered to establish relationships as well as investigate the circumstances of families in need. They visited those individuals who were broken and facing storms using an approach that was driven by their strong conviction that individuals in poverty could be pulled out of their dire situations through association with the middle and upper class (Graff, 2007). These visitors were primarily Protestant women and their focus on lifting struggling individuals out of dire straits was reinforced in Protestant churches by regarding the values of life and faith to the soul and a focus on individuals going through storms of life rather than on the communal relationship to God (Elshtain, 2002).

As this movement expanded a good number of volunteers led the COS agencies to employ agents who were trained staff and who later became professional social workers. This transition highlighted an important connection social workers have with those individuals who are broken and are struggling and facing various challenges and storms of life. Social workers provide hope to those who have no hope and they are a beacon of light to those who as a result of brokenness and storms of life have lost faith and hope. They help people going through storms and assist them in getting a new lease and perspective on life and they empower them to take charge of their lives. Leaders like Mary Richmond of the Boston COS and Edward T. Devine of the New York COS led the movement to train social workers, an approach that led to the professionalization of social work in the early twentieth century (Knight, 2005). If social workers were to be game changers to those who were struggling with challenges of life they needed to be trained. For example, Devin established and directed the New York School of Philanthropy which was the first formal training for social workers. This became the Columbia School of Social Work from which the social work case method, rooted on charity organization philosophies, was promoted. The premise of this method was hope, life and individual restoration through relationship and investigation (Skerret, 2001).

The Relationship between COS and Christianity

Christian social workers were involved in both the COS and the Settlement House movement (SH). These two movements shared a common denominator in that Christian social workers were actively involved in both (Brown, 2004). Leaders of both these movements operated in sync because of their shared belief in the philosophies that drove these movements. While those who favored the charity organization movement highlighted changing individuals, the settlement movement stressed societal reform and attempted to help those in need by changing institutions (Scales & Kelly, 2011). Similar to the COS movement, the SH movement spread very quickly to the united States from England in the 1800s and this occurred in the midst of immigration, industrialization, and urbanization (Scales & Kelly, 2011). Leaders of the SH included Stanton Coit, Robert Woods including Jade Addams who created settlements after visiting London where she had the opportunity to see Tonybee Hall, located in east London.

These settlements and those that later sprung up in the United States followed an approach that emphasized collaboration with local universities (Scales & Kelly, 2011). In this approach students lived among the challenged, broken and poor. Their professors visited while the students lived in the settlements and offered lectures and stimulating discussions. The settlement movement in the United States was not masculine like in Great Britain. It included both men and women and in 1889, a group of women graduates of Smith College founded the College Settlement Association in New York City (Connaway & Gentry, 1988).

Both charity organizations and settlement houses were established in urban areas, and particularly immigrant neighborhoods (Jennissen & Lundy, 2018). The overall goal of the settlement was to create a communication line between the well-to-do and the working class who in most cases were poor (Scales & Kelly, 2011). The settlements did not focus their energies on exclusively reforming struggling individuals but on addressing urban problems as well (Bowpitt, 2000). The social workers networked with residents in assessing and researching economic and social challenges of life that prevented poor individuals from moving forward in life. Their motive was to come up with pragmatic solutions to these challenges. It can be argued that settlement movements were the pioneers of systematic assessment and research into migrant communities and from this they were able to engage in initiatives to reform and change child labor, sanitation, and women's working conditions all of which were in an appalling state (Swanson & Williams, 2010). As way of lifting individuals out of the yoke of poverty, the settlement movement focused on education, recreation, college extension courses, English courses, vocational training, demonstrations of domestic skills, kindergartens, and playground of which were designed to improve the welfare of neighborhoods (Keith-Lucas, 1985). All this was done with a view to bringing hope and appreciation of life to those who were struggling.

As noted above the charity organization society and settlement movement were both important camps that focused on helping individuals who were facing different types of brokenness and life storms. They both actively engaged in macro and micro issues at different levels of society with a view to giving a new lease of life to suffering individuals. Many of the workers in these movements were motivated by Christian values, the desire to help serve the poor (Davis, 1984). Today, social workers who are driven by Christian values aspire to the same standards of helping individuals amid their life storms. These storms may take the form of poor health, lack of food, death of a loved one, lack of a job, poor water and sanitation, lack of health insurance, being homeless, having a chronic disease or suffering from a mental health disease. Individuals experiencing these storms are broken and lose their dignity and their aspiration for life is diminished. It is in this situation that social workers come in to make a difference.

Discussion Questions

1. What philosophical foundations drove the settlement movement and the charity society?

2. Were there gaps in the way the settlement movement and charity society operated? If so what were these gaps? How were clients impacted by approaches used by the settlement movement and the charity society?

3. How did workers of the settlement movement and charity society exemplify their Christian faith? What elements of Christianity were critical to both the settlement movement and the charity society?

Exercise

1. For each of the agencies identified in this chapter– the Settlement Movement and the Charity Organization Society's- list the most significant change brought about by these two organizations. How are these changes relevant for people going through various storms of life such as death of a loved, loss of a job, and disease, today?

Reflect

- What challenges and/or storms have you recently experienced and how have these helped you to grow as a person?

- What are ways in which you have experienced different types of blessings from God? How can you praise Him for these blessings?

- What challenges and storms have you recently experienced and how have these helped you to appreciate God more?

References

Bowpitt, G. (2000). Working with creative creatures: towards a Christian paradigm for social work theory, with some practical implications. *British Journal of Social Work, 30* (3), 349-364.

Canda, E.R., & Furman, L.D. (2010). *Spiritual diversity in social work practice: The heart of helping* (2nd Ed.). New York, NY: Oxford University Press.

Davis, A.F. (1984). *Spearheads for reform: The social settlements and the Progressive Movement 1890-1914.* Rutgers, NJ: Rutgers University Press.

Elshtain, J. (2002). *Jane Addams and the dream of American democracy: A life.* New York, NY: Basic Books.

Graff, D.L. (2007). A study of baccalaureate social work students' beliefs about the inclusion of religious and spiritual content in social work. *Journal of Social Work Education, 43* (2), 243-256.

Jennissen, T., & Lundy, C. (2018). Theoretical research: Radical women in social work: A historical perspective from North America. *Aotearoa New Zealand Social Work, 30* (3), 45.

Keith-Lucas, A. (1985). *So you want to be a social worker: a primer for the Christian student.* St. David's, PA: NACSW.

Knight, L.W. (2005). *Citizen: Jane Addams and the struggle for democracy.* Chicago, IL: University of Chicago Press.

Scales, T.L., & Michael, S.K. (2011). To give Christ to the neighborhood: A corrective look at the settlement movement and early Christian social workers. *Social Work & Christianity, 38* (3), 356-376.

Skerret, E. (2001). The Irish of Chicago's Hull-House neighborhood. *Chicago House, 30* (1), 22-63.

Swanson, E., & Williams, S. (2010). *To transform a city: Whole church, whole gospel, whole city.* Grand Rapids: Zondervan.

CHAPTER 11

Brokenness, Social Work and the Church

Churches and the social work profession share an enduring, long-standing, history of providing social welfare services. This shared history offers a unique opportunity for churches and social workers to collaborate in advancing human needs. Churches and the social work profession retain a long-standing history of providing social welfare services (Ebear, Csiernik & Béchard, 2008; Garland, 2012; Johnson, 2012; Placido & Cecil, 2014). Therefore, a natural relationship exists between these two human services domains (Ebear et al., 2008; Garland, 2012; Johnson, 2012; Placido & Cecil, 2014). These two spheres of influence share this commonality as well as many analogous values and beliefs (Ebear et al., 2008; Lies-Peters, 2009; Placido & Cecil, 2014). Through the collaboration of churches and social work professionals, limitless benefits can viably be acquired to enhance social welfare services (Ebear et al., 2008; Garland, 2012; Lies-Peters, 2009; Placido & Cecil, 2014).

The social work profession focuses on human potential and meeting needs to enhance the wellbeing of individuals, groups, and communities (International Federation of Social Workers, 2012). This profession seeks to empower those broken people facing oppression and alleviates social justice concerns (International Federation of Social Workers, 2012). Social workers identify resources for those in need (Barker, 2003). They are concerned with helping others and enhancing comprehensive well-being (Ebear et al., 2008). Social work draws upon preexisting strengths to assist in resolving problems (Ebear et al., 2008). It is a profession that emphasizes the importance of building relationships, problem solving, and focusing on individual strengths (Placido & Cecil, 2014).

Social Work and Brokenness

As alluded to in earlier chapters, as an evolving profession social work shares similar values with the church. Throughout its history the church has served as a platform from which different population groups have been served. Many of the services provided by the church are meant to not only meet the immediate needs of broken people but to empower them for life as well. Similarly, social work has operated on the same premises and seeks to not only address needs of different population groups but takes a deeper approach that unlocks the potential of broken people by helping them to become functional in society. Groups that are assisted include broken young people who have been affected by HIV/AIDS and have lost one or both parents to AIDS, homeless people, abused women, seniors with no support and others.

Today social work has become an important hub from which relevant services for clients such as broken children orphaned by AIDS are assisted. For example, social workers and the church have a unique responsibility to challenge and broken orphaned children across the globe. Challenges presented by orphaned children create opportunities for both social workers and the church to develop social work practice in other parts of the world (Hoy-Gerlach, Delgado, Sloane, & Arkow, 2019). Morely, 2004). Through these opportunities social workers and the church can meet specific needs of broken children in a tangible way. They can also share resources and knowledge with the church regarding best ways of working with broken orphaned children with a view to enhancing their well-being and overall citizenry (Jonsson, 2010). Further, social workers and the church can work in tandem in finding the best types of assistance that would enhance the well-being of orphaned children. The types of assistance provided is predicated upon the expertise of social workers as this would ensure that relevant and effective interventions are provided.

Just as the church is concerned with the spirituality of its members, social work uses an holistic approach in which physical, emotional, and spiritual needs of needy and broken individuals are met by using different interventions. As social work continues to evolve and become more sophisticated it is possible that new methodologies of dealing with different and broken population groups will emerge. These new methods would strengthen the relationship between the church and social work. Given the shared commitment of both social work and the church it is imperative that efforts are made to find suitable ways of cementing and solidifying the natural bond that exists between the two. There are several studies (Garland, 2012; Johnson, 2012; Placido & Cecil, 2014; Plante, 1999) that have suggested ways in which social work and the church share a common denominator. There is an obvious need to build on the strength of such studies as well as move forward in terms of mapping out a blueprint that can translate the shared denominator between the two into reality.

Church and Social Work

Church social work can be loosely defined as the collaboration of social work professionals with churches to meet social welfare needs (Ebear et al., 2008; Garland, 2012; Johnson, 2012; Placido & Cecil, 2014). In these collaborations, social workers utilize their expertise in offering effective social welfare services in conjunction with the church (Ebear et al., 2008; Garland, 2012; Johnson, 2012; Placido & Cecil, 2014). Armed with biblical faith social workers are concerned for the broken, the poor and with assisting the church in creating corporate responsibility for the well-being of others (Sherman, 2003). Churches utilize social worker's education and training to mobilize congregations (Ebear et al., 2008; Garland, 2012; Johnson, 2012; Placido & Cecil, 2014). Many churches pursue these collaborations for the opportunity to truly impact broken communities while providing service in the name of their Lord (Ebear et al., 2008; Garland, 2012; Johnson, 2012; Placido & Cecil, 2014). Churches who heed the call to follow Jesus are concerned about the role of social work in impacting broken and even non-communities. They are committed to practicing good citizenship by engaging social workers and participating in public discourse about social welfare policies and programs and how these impact poor broken communities (Belcher, Fandetti & Cole, 2004; Boyer, 2006).

The Church and Healing

Churches have long been involved in offering social welfare services and advancing human wellness (Garland, 2012; Johnson, 2012; Placido & Cecil, 2014). In fact, according to the Christian faith, Jesus began with the act of service to others, with ministry following (Garland, 2012). Though Christianity has evolved into the opposite, ministry succeeded by service, and parishioners have often provided substantially to the needs of many (Garland,

2012). Many modern social service programs can be traced back to religious organizations (Placido & Cecil, 2014). Church leaders have often been encouraged to stay active in social services by serving as board members (Johnson, 2012). Church leaders can then easily mobilize church members with their open access to social welfare information on needs (Johnson, 2012). Research on congregational wants and needs revealed that even higher levels of social welfare implementation are desired (Garland, 2012). This information held true throughout a broad range of congregation denominations (Garland, 2012).

As noted previously, churches have provided social welfare services modernly linked to the social work profession since their inception (Ebear et al., 2008). Counseling services, a skill social workers receive extensive training on, is just one example of assistance clergy has provided without preliminary instruction (Ebear et al., 2008). Though the clergy often have extensive skills in other domains, they lack proficiency in the psychological and social dimensions (Ebear et al., 2008). Although social workers possess such abilities, they are not traditionally linked with parish teams (Ebear et al., 2008). While the culture and missions of churches are unique, many religious practices coincide with the social welfare services provided by social workers (Placido & Cecil, 2014). With the rise of social work as a profession in the 20th century the church's involvement in social welfare services declined significantly (Ebear et al., 2008). However, the recent decline in federal funding has decreased the ability for social workers to cover substantial social welfare needs (Ebear et al., 2008). The passage of the Personal Responsibility and Work Opportunity Reconciliation Act of 1996 initiated this parsimonious trend (Johnson, 2012). This shift has led to an increase of church responsibility in this domain once more (Ebear et al., 2008). Faith-based initiatives of 2001 prompted churches to become even more involved (Johnson, 2012). Social work professionals and churches now have a unique opportunity to join in addressing the social welfare needs (Garland, 2012). Collaborations of the two domains are possible with compromising through barriers facing them (Placido & Cecil, 2014).

The Church and Professional Ethics

Churches and helping professions, such as the social work profession, have often faced barriers in collaboration in regard to the varying ethics in each domain (Placido & Cecil, 2014). One such barrier is that of the importance of church teachings (Plante, 1999). In a study completed by Kloos et al. (as cited in McMinn, Chaddock, Edwards, Lim, & Campbell, 1998) clergy members identified a want for collaborator awareness of church theological framework. Another barrier within these professions is the conflicting ideas involving self-determination (Ebear et al., 2008). Social workers believe in every person's right to maintain control of their life whereas churches often believe choices are limited when abiding by religious beliefs and values (Ebear et al., 2008).

Another barrier facing collaboration is the churches' conservative beliefs and values versus the often-liberal view of the social work profession (Leis-Peters, 2009). Churches can be slow to change, where social work is an ever-evolving realm (Leis-Peters, 2009). Clergy is often weary of collaboration with helping professionals due to lack of trust (McMinn, Chaddock, Edwards, Lim, & Campbell, 1998). However, this lack of trust is often a consequence of the lack of interaction between the domains (McMinn, Chaddock, Edwards, Lim, & Campbell, 1998). Churches and the social work profession prove to have a great deal of shared values and beliefs (Ebear et al., 2008). Overlapping beliefs include the importance of human rights and worth and dignity of every individual (Ebear et al., 2008). This also includes economic justice and the provision of adequate physical needs for all (Ebear et al., 2008). Most importantly, the social work profession and churches share a passion for assisting the needy in numerous aspects of life (Ebear at al., 2008; Garland, 2012; Placido & Cecil, 2014)

Benefits of Church Social Work in Brokenness

Social workers can offer an extensive number of benefits to churches as collaboration partners (Ebear et al., 2008; Garland, 2012; Placido & Cecil, 2014). To start, social workers are skilled at forming authentic and effective working relationships (Placido & Cecil, 2014). These relationships are enhanced with theological training and deep self-awareness as a social work professional (Placido & Cecil, 2014). An authentic working relationship can be highly effective in working adjacent to clergy and/or priests (Ebear et al., 2008). Social workers can be a vital partnership in collaborating with priests in addressing a churches or parishioner's psychosocial and spiritual needs (Ebear et al., 2008). A social worker's extensive knowledge surrounding advocacy creates a compelling opportunity for collaboration with deacons, who often provide this service in churches (Ebear et al., 2008).

Due to extensive social work education surrounding systems theory, social workers often have a wealth of understanding to the many factors impacting a person's life (Ebear et al., 2008). This knowledge can be utilized to inform parish or church leaders of the various obstacles parishioners may be facing (Ebear et al., 2008). Understanding clergy's or parishioners' physical, spiritual, psychological, social, and intellectual well-being enhances the churches impact on wellness (Ebear et al., 2008). Social workers can assist not only church leaders in this aspect, but also those providing counseling within the church realm (Ebear et al., 2008). Social workers can provide informed assistance in addressing psychological and social dimensions, information often lacking by priests and other church counselors (Ebear et al., 2008). This assistance would most often lead to increased emotional and social health for clergy and parishioners (Ebear et al., 2008).

Social workers also give congregations opportunities to assist others with the greatest impact (Garland, 2012). As previously mentioned, churches wish to become more actively involved in social welfare provisions (Garland, 2012). These individuals reported not only the wish to be more involved, but also the need to make a deeper lasting effect on broken communities (Garland, 2012). Research has shown that families engaged in service together were more likely to share expressions of faith and attend church services more often than others (Garland, 2012). Social workers in a church setting can also offer the benefit of highlighting the strengths of individual parishioners or clergy (Garland, 2012). Due to social workers' strengths-based practice, these professionals can easily recognize and evoke strengths (Garland, 2012).

Finally, the collaboration of churches and social work offers benefits to the social work professional (Garland, 2012). Collaboration with religious institutions allows Christian social workers to practice two of their passions (Garland, 2012). This is especially true in the social workers holding the belief that their profession was a calling from God (Ebear, Csiernik, & Béchard, 2008). These professionals view their work as an act of service in representation of their faith (Ebear, Csiernik, & Béchard, 2008). Christian social workers can utilize what they believe to be their God given gifts within their career, a precious gift on its own (Ebear, Csiernik, & Béchard, 2008).

Contexts of Church Social Work

In regards to how church social work is defined contextually, it appears that social workers are applying their skills and knowledge to churches on all levels, and the role of church social workers varies by the level of expertise and practice. Increasingly, there is a need for social workers to take a role in program development utilizing their skills in research to assist churches in program planning, implementation, and evaluation (Garland, 2012; Placido

& Cecil, 2014). Furthermore, it is noted that social workers can play a pivotal role in policy development and advocacy for churches (Placido & Cecil, 2014). Social workers are also taking on the role of being educators and learners in churches as they share their knowledge and training with members of the church, while also actively collaborating with church congregants to gain input and insight (Ebear et al., 2008; Placido & Cecil, 2014). In addition, there is a need for social workers in the church to provide direct practice to ensure emotional and social health of congregants (Ebear et al., 2008). Overall, there is consensus that social workers practicing within a church should be culturally competent of the unique attributes of the church, and their role is to be a partner in creating and utilizing customized interventions, programs, and policies for the church (Ebear et al., 2008; Garland, 2012). Therefore, the definition of church social work, including the role of church social workers, is defined by the level of practice the social workers are providing services.

Church and Social Work Services

The need for church social work cannot be ignored. It is rooted in the need for skills and knowledge professional social workers bring to churches including other related instituitons. Hence, church social workers can provide services utilizing research skills such as data collection, management, and analyses, which can be used to develop needs-assessment, provide direction in the planning and implementation of programs, evaluate effectiveness of programs, or provide guidance on how to make current programs more sustainable (Placido & Cecil, 2014). The benefit of church social workers providing these services in churches is that congregants have input in customizing the research through collaboration and are more likely to have positive outcomes from their efforts (Garland, 2012). Garland (2012) emphasizes the need to translate the language of social sciences "into the biblical and theological constructs that are so much the language of a Christian worldview" (p. 95) to make these services more meaningful and applicable to churches.

Furthermore, the social work skill of facilitating group process creates opportunities for social workers to provide services in group work such as team building within churches and facilitating psychoeducational groups (Ebear et al., 2008). Church social workers are also apt to assist churches with services such as uniting individuals with similar concern to advocate for change through education and knowledge of government policy (Ebear et al., 2008). In addition, social workers within churches are also trained in direct practice and can provide clinical services including counseling for individuals and families, crisis intervention, and conflict mediation (Ebear et al., 2008). It appears also that the universal role of church social workers as culturally competent collaborators within churches provide this area of social work with the flexibility to be applicable to most, if not all, denominations of Christianity.

The duty of every social worker is to enhance society by helping broken individuals, families, groups and communities reach their greatest potential individually and collectively (Ebear et al., 2008). According to Ebear et.al (2008), social workers empower broken people by helping them "develop their skills and their abilities to use their own resources and those of the community to resolve problems" (p.179). The church was the first institution to uphold these statues and live by these principles. According to Garland, almost all modern social services can be traced back to roots in religious organization (1992). Johnston (1941) once noted, (as cited in Garland, 1992, p. 1) the church is the "mother of social work."

Many argue that social work practice and church social work are two very different entities (Garland, 1992). However just as the social workers that work in a practice setting, church social workers utilize their skills to bring professional knowledge and values to the church as a resource to help them understand the needs of the congregation, define the needs that are a ministry challenge in regards to the mission of the church, and equip church members for effective service and/or social action (Garland, 1992; Placido & Cecil, 2014).

There is a growing desire to incorporate the professional skills of social work practice into the church setting. According to Garland, the pillars of the church ministry are faith and service and "faith finds expression as action in service as a neighbor to those in need; service is our way of showing our love for Christ" (p.89, 2012). Many congregations have begun to "serve" in a way that goes beyond just providing assistance to charities that provide food, clothes, and shelter to those in need, but are now also engaging their congregations in social action by advocating in behalf of justice for the broken and oppressed (Garland, 1992).

Many denominations within church organizations are seeking the support of direct social work involvement. According to Garland, a research team surveyed 50 congregations that included: "Presbyterian, Lutheran, United Methodist, Southern Baptist, Cooperative Baptist, Unitarian, Episcopal, 'Christian' Disciples of Christ, Church of God, and nondenominational congregations" (p. 92, 2012). The survey indicated that members have a strong desire to engage in social welfare services outside of their family and on a macro level (Garland, 2012). The church leaders within these denominations revealed that they need the professional knowledge and skills of social workers to aid their members in being effective and having an impact that will matter in the lives of people (Garland, 2012).

For example, the Catholic Church has begun to incorporate social workers into their pastoral team. There are a decreasing number of Catholic priests seeking ordination; this has led to creative solutions to meet the needs of parishioners (Ebear et al., 2008). In the Catholic Church, the priest is responsible for meeting the spiritual needs of the congregation; meeting this need may involve providing counseling to those broken people struggling with not only spiritual issues, but psychosocial ones as well. According to Ebear et al. (2008), many priests "do not have the time, let alone the formal training, to fully, properly, and ethically delve into these realms, realms of the social worker" (p. 186).

The Catholic Church now suggests that a parish social worker can be an asset to priests in helping them understand the interrelationship between the parishioners' spiritual and psychosocial issues (Ebear et al., 2008). Social workers can also provide "front line services" by conducting a comprehensive intake interview to assess the issues of parishioners before meeting with priest, to connect members to the appropriate pastoral team (Ebear et al., 2008, p. 186). There are multiple ways that professional social work skills can be incorporated into the church ministry. According to Garland (2012), social workers can work in the mission and ministries of the church locally and globally by helping church leaders and members to become more competent and effective for the "holistic" change in the lives of persons and communities locally and globally (p.94). Churches are now seeking the skills of program evaluation and research to help them find evidence-based models that can be applied to church programs that will "not only feed hungry people, but also help them to own the fishing pond" (Garland, p. 94, 2012).

By utilizing the skills of professional social workers, churches can begin to empower broken individuals, young people, and communities they work with; by enhancing the strengths and gifts they possess (Ebear et al., 2008; Garland, 2012; Placido & Cecil, 2014). Regarding competency, social workers can also provide church leadership by translating social science issues into biblical and theological constructs that represent the language of the Christian church system worldview (Garland, 2012).

According to Ebear et al., social workers can also employ their professional skills and training, by collaborating with pastoral teams to ensure the holistic wellness of church congregants as well as assisting with "policy development, partnering in program development and evaluation, and facilitating the education and training of lay members on the psychosocial needs of individuals for whom they will work with" (p.185, 2008). Social workers are trained to understand the psychosocial functioning of broken individuals and communities. This is an area that many members of congregations work but has not been professionally trained or educated in (Ebear et al., 2008).

Further, social workers can provide services such as data collection and analysis to assist church staff in customizing needs assessments. Needs assessments are critical tools in the planning of any organizations' mission and vision; therefore, social workers can use professional skills to implement useful tools that help to understand areas in "basic research, outcome measurement, and organizational change and motivation" (Placido & Cecil, 2014, p. 81); these tools can heighten the success of needs assessments.

Identifying the benefits of church and social work collaboration is very crucial. Recent studies have shown that congregation's faith is strongly related to service. In a recent study of 35 congregations, surveying 7,300 church attendees revealed that those involved in service to their community reported that they prayed, came to worship services, and gave financially more than those not involved in service (Garland, 2012). According to Garland, many of these church attendees also experienced a heightening sense of self that was contributed by their faith and beliefs in serving (2012).

This working collaboration is also beneficial to the social worker as well. Recent research has suggested that many social work students find the profession of social work "a calling and are inspired to service in the field by their faith and spirituality" (Ebear et al., 2008, p. 181). According to Csiernik & Adams (2003) (as cited in Ebear et al.,2008), spirituality is an important factor in social work student lives as opposed to their peers that practice in other disciplines.

The Way Forward

As alluded previously, the success of social work practice within the church relates to the partnership of professional social workers and the church ministry. Firstly, through this collaboration, social workers will enhance society on a micro and macro level by being able to bring professional knowledge, values, and skills to the church as a resource (Ebear et al., 2008; Garland, 2012; Placido & Cecil, 2014). Church social workers can provide guidance and consultation, through professional leadership and expertise, to the social ministry and social action programs of the church (Garland, 1992). Church social work will also help to create integrated faith-based and science-based professional social work practice (Garland, 1992).

Implementing church social work may open job opportunities in different employment settings. According to Ebear et al. (2008), as a member of a pastoral team, social workers can assist individual parishioners and small groups with the context of *Person-In-Environment (PIE),* while implementing "crisis interventions, short-and-long-term counseling, and psycho-educational group work" (185, p.56). Social workers can also utilize their skills in programs funded by the church such as emergency assistance, prison ministries, children outreach programs, food banks, and homelessness and day care services (Garland, 1992). They can also play an important role in developing resources for churches and helping churches utilize these funds provide more spiritually and religiously sensitive services within their communities (Hugen & Scales, 2008; Scales, Wolfer, Sherpwood, Garland, Hugen, & Pittman, 2002).

There are also overlaps and differences in comparing the social work code of ethics to the church code of ethics. For example, the social work code of ethics does correlate with church doctrine in that both believe in the dignity and worth of human beings, the protection of that dignity through the provision of adequate physical and social resources, and social justice for the poor and economically disadvantaged (Ebear et al., 2008). In contrast, self-determination, a prominent social work value, can create conflict when it relates to fundamental issues of human existence such as life, death, and sexuality (Ebear et al., 2008). Therefore, Christian scholars need to continue to study, record and publish findings that might highlight the important role the church can assume in advancing well-being of their broken or not broken communities. At the same time the church and social workers can play an important role in shaping how they view the communities and how together they can craft the best interventions that can impact communities at a deep level.

They can also act as bulwarks to support those broken individuals who are facing different storms of life. We all face storms, and these can build and strengthen us if we view them in the right perspective.

References

Barker. (2003). *Definitions*. Retrieved from National Association of Social Workers: www.naswdc.org/practice/intl/definitions.asp

Belcher, J.R., Fandetti, D, & Cole, D. (2004). Is Christian religious conversation

compatible with the liberal social welfare state? *Social Work, 49* (2), 269-276.

Benes, K. M., Walsh, J. M., McMinn, M. R., Dominguez, A. W., & Aikins, D. C. (2000). Psychology and the church: An exemplar of psychologist–clergy collaboration. *Professional Psychology: Research And Practice, 31* (5), 515-520. doi:10.1037/0735-7028.31.5.515

Boyer, K. (2006). Reform and resistance: A consideration of space, scale, and strategy in legal challenges to welfare reform. *Antipode 38* (1), 22-40.

Ebear, J., Csiernik, R., & Béchard, M. (2008). Furthering parish wellness: Including social work as part of a catholic pastoral team. *Journal of the North American Association of Christians in Social Work, 35* (2), 179-196

Garland, D. (1991). Church social work: helping the whole person in the context of the church. St. Davids, PA: North American Association of Christians in Social Work.

Garland, D. (2012). Is that church on fire? A unique moment of opportunity for social work leadership. *Journal of the North American Association of Christians in Social Work, 39* (1), 88-99.

Hoy-Gerlach, J., Delgado, M., Sloane, H., & Arkow, P. (2019). Rediscovering connections between animal welfare and human welfare: creating social work internships at a humane society. *Journal of Social Work, 19* (2), 216-232.

Hiilamo, H. (2012). Rethinking the role of church in a socio-democratic welfare state. *International Journal of Sociology and Social Policy, 32* (7/8), 401-414.

Hugen, B., & Scales, T.L. (2008). *Christianity and social work: Readings on the integration of Christian faith and social work practice* (3rd ed.). Botsford, CT: NACSW.

International Federation of Social Workers. (2012). *Definition of social work.* Retrieved from International Federation of Social Workers: ifsw.org/policies/definition-of-social-work/

Johnson, C. (2012). Synergistic Collaborations: Pastoral Care and Church Social Work. *Social Work & Christianity.* 39 (1), 102-104.

Jonsson, J.H. (2010). Beyond empowerment: Changing local communities. *International Social Work, 53* (3), 393-406.

Leis-Peters, A. (2009). Majority church and welfare in Sweden: Some reflections on results from two Swedish research projects: A response to Beate Hofmann. *Christ Bioeth, 15* (2): 147-153 first published online July 20, 2009 doi:10.1093/cb/cbp009

McMinn, M. R., Chaddock, T. P., Edwards, L. C., Lim, B. B., & Campbell, C. D. (1998). Psychologists collaborating with clergy. *Professional Psychology: Research And Practice, 29* (6), 564-570. doi:10.1037/0735-7028.29.6.564

Morely, C. (2004). Critical reflection in social work: A response to globalization? *International Journal of Social Work,* 13, 298-303.

Placido, N. & Cecil, D. Implementing best practices for needs assessment and strategic planning systems: Social work and faith based organization collaboration- a case study. *Journal of the North American Association of Christians in Social Work, 41* (41), 79-94.

Plante, T. G. (1999). A collaborative relationship between professional psychology and the Roman Catholic Church: A case example and suggested principles for success. *Professional Psychology: Research and Practice, 30* (6), 541-546. doi:10.1037/0735-7028.30.6.541

Royse, D. (2011). *Research methods in social work* (6th ed.). Belmont, CA: Cengage Brooks/Cole.

Scales, T.L., Wolfer, T., Sherwood, D., Garland, D., Hugen, B., & Pittman, S. (2002). *Spirituality and religion in social work practice: decision cases with teaching notes.*

Alexandria, VA: Council on Social Work Education

Sherman, A.L. (2003). Faith in communities: A solid investment. *Society, 40* (2), 19-26.

CHAPTER 12

Storms and Brokenness

When I look back at my life, I can vividly see the many storms God has allowed to come my way. I can safely that God has seen me through all of them. Some of these storms have occurred in different areas of my life such as finances, career path development and even health within my family circles. There was a time when my walk with God was not close enough and this, for the most part, happened mostly during my high school and early college years. God used some of the storms and brokenness to redirect and bring me back into a close walk with Him. Until this had happened I thought life troubles just occurred for the sake of occurring and that they did not have any bearing on my character. However, as Jesus Christ began to mold and shape me I soon realized that for a child of God no trouble or storm just happens. Everything has a purpose.

Life is not always a smooth ride. Sometimes it is filled with unpredictable occurrences that strike when we least expect them. As believers and followers and children of God we will face trials and challenges that only God alone can see us through. If a professed Christian has not yet experienced any trials or been broken, they should rest assured that at some point in their life they will. In order to overcome the storms of life and in order to face these challenges squarely in the face, we need the power and presence of Jesus Christ. Though suffering and storms are a promised lot to Christians, we can grow from them. These storms are a platform from which we can grow spiritually and only Jesus can make this possible. It is only by clinging to Jesus and taking refuge in His presence that we can grow from storms of life. The good news is that we can grow spiritually from storms and brokenness and come to a place of full surrender and stability where we begin to appreciate God more.

As we spiritually continue to develop and grow from the storms, a deep sense of daily dependence on God's mercy and grace will emerge in our hearts. Storms are different for different people and perhaps the most important question to ask is what storms are. The Webster's Dictionary defines storms as "a disturbance of the atmosphere marked by wind and usually by rain, snow, hail, sleet, or thunder and lightning," and that a storm is "a serious disturbance of any element of nature-" [Webster's Dictionary, 2013]. In the natural world, storms often cause collateral damage. For example, in the United States the top-ranking storm in terms of property damage was the Great Miami Hurricane of 1926, which created losses between $140-157 billion (Connection. ebscohost.com. Retrieved 08-04-13). This was a colossal sum to offset by the government and other stakeholders. We can note that the key words in Webster's Dictionary definition of storm is that storms are a "serious disturbance" to our lifestyles. These disturbances cannot be predicted, and when they strike they could cause and bring deep pain in our lives.

The pain caused by storms may sometimes be so deep that trying to understand it– pain–could make little or no sense at all. In addition, when it comes to making sense out of the storms of life, we may not truly grasp the motive or meaning behind the storms. The lack of understanding is further made worse when these storms strike in the least expected ways. But no matter what way, conduit, or avenue storms take they always have an impact on those they strike, and usually the impact is negative. Although storms almost always come with negative impacts, for a child of God, the storms always end with positive outcomes. On another level storms may come for various reasons. I look at four.

First, storms could be self-inflicted, and often this could be a result of poor life choices. When I was growing up, as a young boy I went to school with friends of varying interests and persuasions. Some of them had a keen interest in school and looked forward to ambitious careers. However, I also had friends who had a lackluster interest in school and who had no idea in terms of what they wanted to do with their lives. Those friends of mine that did not follow through with school ended up giving up and abandoning school all together. They developed all types of refractory behaviors which consequently landed them into trouble. The end result for these friends of mine was not favorable, as some of them ended up in precarious and challenging situations that could easily have been avoided (Woods, Jeffrey, Troman & Boyle, 2019).

Second, some storms are allowed and initiated by God to fulfill His purpose for our lives. The story of Jesus in Mark 4:35-41 (New International Version) speaks to this point very well. Jesus had asked His disciples to go to the other side of the lake and as they all sailed in the boat a serious storm emerged with strong waves. The waves from the storm broke over the boat, so that the boat nearly flooded with water [paraphrased]. In this story it was Jesus who invited the disciples to go on the other side of the lake in a boat. It was Jesus who initiated and asked the disciples to get into the boat, and it was He who implicitly put the disciples in way of the storm because, as God, He is omniscient and knows everything. He therefore knew that the disciples would face the storm on the lake. In the same manner, God knows our lives more and far above than we do. He knows what and how many storms to allow in our lives.

He knows the end from the beginning and knows all the types, magnitude, scope and gravity as well as the severity of storms of life that will come our way. Although He allows the storms to come our way, He has the ultimate power to stop or adjust these storms as was the case with disciples on the lake. He can lift a standard against them.

Third, storms that are not of our own making are sanctioned by God and may occur only for providential reasons. These types of storms are the most difficult to understand, let alone appreciate, as they can happen when we are at our best and perhaps enjoying our lives at the top of our mountains. Furthermore, storms may take place when we are basking in Jesus' light and enjoying all the blessings that God has poured upon us. For example, Job was taken unawares when he was struck by a barrage of storms in a story that perhaps is one of God's clearest illustrations of Christian suffering as well as blessings amid storms. Job did not anticipate the storms that hit him, nor did he know when exactly and or how they would have stricken him. When they hit, they did so with such ferocity that it is difficult, if not impossible, to imagine the kind of pain and emotional turmoil that Job had to go through. There have been similar stories in the Bible where God has constantly allowed storms in the lives of His people. By learning from these stories from the Bible, and those from real life, we can see that God is constantly refining us. In His wisdom, He uses pain, loss, sickness, and other methods to accomplish His will for our lives. From some of the storm stories in the Bible as well as those from real life experiences God is constantly refining us through His wisdom. He sometimes uses pain, loss, sickness, and other methods as types of storms to accomplish His will.

Fourth, some storms come because God wants to correct us. We all have issues and deficiencies, and without God's help it is impossible to correct these spiritual gaps in our characters. Jesus said that without Him we can do nothing (John 15:5, Paraphrased). He is the true vine, and we are the branches (John 15:5, New International Version). To be what Jesus wants for us, we need to learn to trust Him daily. All of us are sinful fallen beings and our hearts are defiled with all types of impurities. Unless Jesus does a metaphorical heart transplant in us, we risk becoming and remaining contaminated with all types of sins.

Some of us struggle with lifelong and or hereditary sins that may include gossip, entertaining hatred, harboring bitterness, harboring jealousy, engaging in sexual immorality, or getting addicted to pornography. In our futile and fruitless efforts to correct and rid ourselves of these sins, we usually fail. This failure often ends up as precursor to disappointment and frustration.

Unless we come to the cross of Jesus and ask for His grace and mercy to help us in these times we cannot find the type of freedom from these sins. God knows us more than any other person does. He knows our characters, our failures, and knows what we can become if only we allow Him, by faith, to change us. He will break and disentangle every inner body impediment that might be hindering us from growing and becoming more and more like Him. With Jesus, all the storms of life can dissipate. He can give us the full assurance of His presence amidst storms until we attain the joy and peace that attends any child of God who abides in His presence.

Role of Workers in Assisting Storm Stricken Individuals

Christian and non-Christian Social workers have an obligation to help individuals struggling with various challenges and storms of life. In this case the church can play a crucial role helping broken individuals, as alluded to earlier. In order for them to do this effectively they have to be driven by the core values of the social work profession. However, because Christian social workers are also driven by another set of Christian core beliefs and values they have to adhere to these because these values ultimately impact and shape their understanding and practice of social work. People "will act and draw upon their core beliefs and values to help them decide what constitutes an acceptable claim…on the matter under consideration" (Chamiec-case, 2007, p. 503). Separating what is important to us personally from what might be important socially is often difficult (Segal, 2015). According to Segal (2015) "a value is a worth, desirability, or usefulness ascribed to something, and a belief is an opinion or conviction" (p. 10).

Many professions have values that provide parameters for their functionality. Similarly, social work as a profession has a set of core values in which it is rooted. These values reflect "what is unique to the social work profession. These values are found in the National Association of Social Workers (NASW) Code of Ethics. The core values and the principles that flow from them are balanced within the context and complexity of human experience. These core values have been embraced by social workers throughout the profession's history and they are the foundation of social work's unique purpose and perspective. These core values are service, social justice, dignity and worth of the person, importance of human relationships, integrity, and competence. These will be elucidated in the following chapters. For Christian social workers their core beliefs and values about and commitment to the Christian faith should be ultimately decisive in their lives, beliefs to which the rest of their live and thinking are appropriately brought into harmony (Ellis, 2018).

Christian Beliefs and Values

There are several examples of Christian values and beliefs from the literature. Most of these are correlated with the social work core values. Some have argued that a Christian worldview is the soil out of which much of the NASW Code of Ethics has sprung (Sherwood, 2002). Alan Keith-Lucas (1985) was one of the earliest proponents of integrating faith and social work and he developed a Judeo-Christian model from which some of the following examples are highlighted as being critical to faith and social work practice:

1. Human beings are of infinite worth, irrespective of gender, race, age or behavior. At the same time, human beings are created beings, one of whose problems is that they act as if they were not and try to be autonomous.

2. Human beings have been endowed with the faculty of choice and are responsible for the consequences of their choices.

3. Human beings are fallible, but at the same time, sometimes capable, with appropriate help, of transcending themselves and showing great courage or unselfishness.

4. Love is the ultimate victor over evil, including force. Love, understanding, and compassion are the source of well-being and acceptable behavior, rather than the reward for them.

Bowpitt (1989) has largely contributed to integration of faith and social work practice as well. He identifies the following Christian elements as being essential to social work practice:

1. People are the climax of God's creativity and therefore the result of a purposeful act of will, not mere outcomes of an impersonal evolutionary process with its deterministic implications.

2. A facet to the Christianity view of human nature that social workers have traditionally found particularly hard to stomach is the sinfulness of humankind, particularly

the understanding that sin affects every aspect of our humanity at every level (individual, family, community, and society).

3. Because people are made in God's image, they possess many of the attributes of the Creator-intellectual, moral, and aesthetic. Of greatest importance to social work, being made in God's image means people have the capacity for self-determination and moral responsibility. They can make moral choices and are held accountable for them.

4. All persons are potentially redeemed by a re-creative act on the part of the Creator. All persons can be restored by the power of God's grace by a process in which we are active participants, and which transforms every aspect of our beings.

Social workers, both Christian and non-Christian, are obligated to follow the core values of the social work profession. As for Christian social workers, their practice is further driven by Christian values and beliefs discussed above. These Christian values play a significant role in preparing them for service. By integrating these values into their practice, they can work with and address individual storms (Bowpitt, 2000; Douglas, 2018). They are also able to focus on the strengths of individuals and their communities.

Discussion Questions

1. What is the different between Christian social work values and the core values espoused in the NASW Code of Ethics?

2. Why is it important to engage in a value-driven social work practice?

3. Explain the difference between a value and belief.

4. How would you describe what social work core values are to a friend who is not a social worker?

Exercise

1. Ask someone of the same age whether they remember any challenges that might have faced in their life. How did they overcome these challenges? Identify if there are any links between what they endured and what you have faced. List these similarities and draw a conceptual diagram that connects them including how they were overcome.

Reflection

*   Recall any storm that you might have faced in the last few weeks, months, or years. How has God seen you through these storms?

*   Mention one storm that had the most impact on your life. How did this storm help you grow spiritually?

*   Based on how you have overcome past challenges how would you prepare for future storms?

References

Bowpitt, G. (1989). *Social work and Christianity.* Edinburg, Handsel Press.

Bowpitt, G. (2000). Working with creative creatures: towards a Christian paradigm for social work theory, with some practical implications. *British Journal of Social Work, 30* (3), 349-364.

Chamiec-Case, R. (2007). Exploring the filtering of Christian beliefs and values in the integration of Christian faith and social work practice. *Social Work & Christianity, 34* (4), 498-512.

Douglas, K. B. (2018). *What's faith got to do with it? Black bodies/ Christian souls.* Orbis books.

Ellis, R. M. (2018). *The Christian Middle Way: The Case Against Christian Belief But for Christian Faith.* John Hunt Publishing.

Segal, E.A. (2010). *Social Welfare Policy and Social Programs* (2nd ed.): Brooks/Cole Learning.

Sherwood, D. (2002). The relationship between beliefs and values in social work practice:

Worldviews make a difference. In B.Hugen & L. Scales (Eds.), *Christianity and social work: Readings on the integration of Christian faith and social work practice* (2nd ed., pp.9-30), Botsford, CT: NACSW.

Keith-Lucas, A. (1985). *So you want to be a social worker: a primer for the Christian student.* St. David's, PA: NACSW.

Woods, P., Jeffrey, B., Troman, G., & Boyle, M. (2019). *Restructuring schools, reconstructing teachers: Responding to change in the primary school.* Routledge.

CHAPTER 13

Standing Firm
when Broken

Many years ago when I was attending high school, I knew of a certain gentleman who attended the same high school as I did. He came from a decent Christian family. He was my senior by a few years, and when he completed his high school education, he went to the University of Zambia main university campus where he successfully completed his studies. After he completed college, he got a good job, married, and had a child. One day he and his family were travelling to another city to visit his parents and just as they were about to enter that city, they were involved in a fatal car accident that resulted in the loss of his wife and child. Miraculously, he survived. This accident completely broke and devastated him, but by God's grace he was able to go through this storm and he came out strong. He remarried and God blessed and replaced what the devil had stolen from him.

When storms of life strike, we can face them in a firm and strong way as long we have our faith anchored in the power of Jesus. When I was younger, early in my Christian walk, I used to think that being a Christian meant that one would lead a smooth life devoid of problems and challenges. However, as I grew older and as I saw that troubles and problems were a common lot to many of the professing Christians, I soon realized that facing storms and being broken was a normal part of being a Christian and, in fact that is what it meant to be a true and genuine follower of Christ.

Jesus said that in this world we will have trouble (John 16:33, New International Version–Emphasis). Being broken, experiencing trouble and suffering have been promised to followers of Christ and when they come, they strike for different reasons. This means we need to be ready, because Jesus said every Christian will face storms and will sometimes be broken. What do we need to do when storms strike or when we are broken? Responding to the storms of life depends on where we are in our faith walk with Jesus. If our walk with Jesus is close and intimate, then the burden and weight of facing storms by ourselves will be lifted by Jesus Himself. Jesus has promised that even amid the severest of storms He will shield us and give us perfect peace from heaven. This is the peace that passes all understanding, it is a special kind of peace that is heavenly and one that cannot be compared with any form of earthly peace. It is the type of peace that defies all human understanding and that permeates the human heart in a deep way.

This heavenly peace provides us with the needed comfort and the feeling of God's presence. It gives us rest, calmness, and serenity in times of trouble. At another level, it is important to note that spiritually even if the devil bombards us with troubles, we can rest assured that his plans, attacks, and schemes will not have any negative impact on us for as long as we are on God's side.

No storm we will ever face is too big for our God. He is a mighty God, great and awesome, and nothing can compare with His power. He holds the universe and the galaxies in His hands, and He fashions and controls everything that happens in them and to us. If we serve such a might God who controls and manages the universe and galaxies, we need to trust that He can control all the storms that He allows to come our way. We can rest assured that

God will protect us no matter what. However, for us to witness and enjoy His protection we need to have a faith in Him that is solid, firm, and unshakable. This is a faith that should produce evident results in our lives. Exercising a faith of this type will lead to peace and a full realization that Jesus is with us.

Jesus promised that He would be with us during times of storms. Recall the story where the disciples were on the sea, and a great tempest arose. The disciples were so afraid that they thought they were going to sink. However, as soon as their despair sank to its lowest, they saw Jesus appear and coming toward them, walking on the water. They did not call for him but rather He appeared to them because of His grace and wisdom. He also knew that they were in trouble, and they needed him just at that moment. Jesus is everywhere, even in the most severe of storms or challenges. He knows when the storms of life will come and how they will strike and when we are broken. Before the storms strike or when we are broken, He already has plans for our release and deliverance. We need to be encouraged and strengthened by the fact that Jesus is with us in the storms, although sometimes it appears as if He is not. He suffers with us, cries with us, and feels the pain with us. He understands what we may be going through and shares in all that we are going through because He is a merciful God who is full of compassion and grace.

He allows storms because He loves us. How can this be? How can a loving God allow His children to be broken, to suffer and experience pain? The answer is simple— because He loves us dearly. We are precious jewels in His sight. In His wisdom He sees it fit to use pain and suffering to chisel and craft us into His likeness, thereby preparing us for heaven. If He did not care and love us so dearly, He would not bother or pay attention to us. However, that is not His nature. He is love, a God of love who loves deeply and everything He does is driven and shaped by His love. Storms are therefore a sign of God's deep love for us, and we should count them as blessings when He allows them to come our way.

The scope and gravity of storms is determined by our capacity and readiness to face them. Who determines this capacity and readiness? God does, and in His infinite wisdom He knows every phase of our spiritual journey, including the life points at which we can face different storms. He knows exactly the scope, gravity, and nature of storms that will do the best work in us. He knows to what extent we could be broken. Since He knows how much we can handle He sets parameters for these storms and, at the right time, when the specific purpose of the storms has been accomplished in us, He delivers us out of them. Storms dissipate and the brokenness gives way to healing and recovery. Thus, storms of life are allowed for a reason, and when the work in us is done we aren't the same person. The end of storms and recovery from brokenness should deliver and lift us up from the valley of hopelessness to the mountain top.

It is in the storms of life, in the pain, in the brokenness and in the suffering that we begin to experience a wonderful work that God is doing in us. Although the outcomes of this work may vary, the result is untold blessed experiences. For example, all the great men in the Bible that God used had to go through storms, and not until that happened did, they become great instruments of God's plan for the salvation of men. After the storms, these individuals enjoyed a deeper sense of God. They also experienced His intimate presence in their daily lives. The same God they walked with is the same God we serve today. He is the same yesterday, today, and forever. He never changes.

Jesus has given us the privilege of experiencing the same blessings today as did men in biblical days. As mentioned earlier not all storms are the same; some storms are severe and might even involve the loss of a loved one, as was my case when my son died. However, whatever the severity of the storm we are facing Jesus is with us and preparing us for heaven. The pain that comes with storms as well as being broken allows for the process of shaping and developing our characters to flow smoothly. In the end, this makes us special jewels fitted for heaven.

Death and Brokenness

The experience of losing my son in April of 2012 was excruciating, devastating, and deeply painful (Dennis, 2018). It is the kind of pain that chokes you, makes you feel as if your heart is reaping apart, and makes you think that the world is ending. I cannot describe the pain of losing a loved one such as a son.

This type of loss is indescribable an may only be felt and understood by those who have had similar losses.

My son was born in Southern Africa. From an early age, he was an active child in both school and church activities. He was very likeable and, in his own way, made every person that he came into contact with happy. Young people of his age were naturally attracted to him because of his God given gifts of compassion, kindness, and love. When we came to the United States we first lived in Athens, Georgia where he started kindergarten.

After two years of living in Athens we moved to Richmond, Virginia where we lived for six years before coming to Collegedale, Tennessee. While in Richmond he had become very involved in sports and his budding interests in basketball and baseball grew to a different level, and he even tried to play soccer. He went to the Richmond Academy, a faith-based school, where he made many good friends. He was very involved in Pathfinder, a church ministry organization for young people, and he learned a lot of spiritual lessons from being involved with this ministry. I can confidently say that the young man lived and represented Jesus in every aspect of his life. He took advantage of every opportunity to be of service to others, to show true love and courage whenever he found an opportunity to do so. He exhibited a different level of kindness to all his friends. Consequently, he was very well liked at Collegedale Academy, another faith-based school, by almost everyone with whom he interacted or came into contact with.

He reflected Christ in every facet of his life and in all activities, he engaged in and he was a true blessing to all those who benefitted from his gifts. I have no doubt in my mind that he was on a mission mandated from heaven, and he had completed the assignment God had sent him to do. His legacy is reflected in the impact his life left on his friends at Collegedale Academy and in the Collegedale community. At Southern Adventist University they planted a memorial tree in his honor and memory. At Collegedale Academy his basketball jersey was retired and has been placed in a memorial wall placard in the school gymnasium.

His daily life was evidenced, characterized by, and reflected in developing ongoing sincere and true friendships, in honesty, courage, brevity and selflessness. In remembering him I reflect on the goodness of God, His continued presence, and His will as it has unfolded in my life since his passing. It was a beautiful Sabbath Spring morning on April 14, 2012. The birds were singing outside our residence, the breeze was superb, and the morning sunlight was sublime. I woke up early to have my daily devotion and a few hours later my son woke up to prepare for church as he always did.

I often dropped him at church first and then I would join him later. That morning as he prepared for church he looked poised and ready for the Sabbath, which apparently was his best day of the week. After dropping him off at church, I came back home, prepared, and left for church as well. After the sermon ended, he and his friend, the friend he would save and sacrifice his life for later that day, were waiting for me in the lounge. This was rather unusual as I was the one that usually did the waiting for him after Sabbath services. I joined them in the lounge and we stood there for a while chatting, then the two of us headed for the car. On our way outside the sanctuary, my son introduced me to his friends. He always cherished introducing me to his friends. I remember vividly how he and his friends briefly exchanged notes about a Collegedale Alumni basketball tournament that was scheduled that Sabbath evening.

We got home and decided to spend the Sabbath just resting. But after a short while his friend, one he had been in the church lounge, pulled in our yard with his parents and they took my son to spend the Sabbath afternoon with them. As he was leaving, I assured him that when he returned home, I would go with him to the basketball alumni tournament. A short while later he called me, and we chatted for a while without knowing that indeed that was to be my last conversation with him on earth.

A few hours into the day, after talking with him on the phone, I felt a very unusual but strong urge to go out for a drive, I didn't know where. So, I got in my car and decided to drive on to Standifer Gap road. As I was approaching his former school, Standifer Gap School, I received a call from one of his friends. The call was very unusual as his friend seemed to have been crying uncontrollably on the other side. He was shouting that my son was missing. A flood of confusion hit my mind as I tried to figure out what might have happened to my son. At that point I felt compelled to quickly utter a silent prayer in which I asked God to intervene in whatever situation he was in.

This was a big test of faith on my part as I tried to regroup and refocus the composite fears that had engulfed me. I tried to put to rest an avalanche of mixed thoughts that were constantly bombarding my mind. However, I could sense that the devil was busy trying to throw all kinds of confusing and hurtful suggestions into my mind. Later that Sabbath evening we received confirmation that he had died from drowning. As I reflected on his life and death, his death was clearly sacrificial in the sense that he attempted to save his distressed friend on the lake where they had gone for a Sabbath afternoon picnic with friends. At that point during my deep reflection, I concluded that this was it; life on earth can be taken away in a snap, as the Lord deemed fit. Life is a thread and tomorrow is not promised to us as none of us knows or may know what the following day may bring (Proverbs 27:1, New International Version).

My son's death changed my outlook and perspective on life completely. It gave me the opportunity to begin to look at life through a different lens. To this day I have been changed, I am no longer the same person. I look at life differently and each day I thank God for the blessing of life. My son's death has continued to allow me to appreciate this earthly life more and more and has elevated my degree of hope to a whole new level. This level is hope for a better tomorrow and hope for eternity in heaven where "…God shall wipe away all tears from," our eyes; where "there shall be no more death, neither sorrow, nor crying, neither shall there be any more pain, for the former things are passed away" (Revelation 21:4, New International Version). Although my life journey since my son's death has been certainly difficult and painful, I thank God continually for healing and for the continued growth I have gained from being broken. I have gotten closer to God and consequently enjoy a richer and deeper relationship with Him. Based on this journey and on the pain of losing a loved one I have drawn a few lessons that might be helpful to those who are broken in a similar way especially as we walk daily with Jesus. For each day that God allows us to live on this earth we need to:

Know that life is short but eternity is long, long, long: As followers of Jesus Christ we need to live each day with the full realization that our lives on this earth are short. As James says [4:14-ESV], no one knows what tomorrow will bring, for we are a mist that appears for a little time and then vanishes. Yet eternity is long, long, long. Whether one gets to live 16 years, 20 years, 50 years or 100 years does not really matter in the context of eternity. All these are just dots and specks of time compared to eternity. We all need to be ready and live lives that truly reflect Jesus as we do not know when our time and hour will come. Our guarantee for eternity only rests in a genuine, truthful, and daily walk with Jesus, a walk that takes away all fear and worry of death, and a walk that ushers one into Jesus' presence at every moment of one's earthly journey.

Set our priorities right daily: Our earthly lives are a preparation for heaven. Accordingly, heaven ought to be life's priority now more than ever. Nothing on earth can compare with the glory that Jesus is preparing for us as He solidly promises in John 14:1 (Emphasis supplied). No amount of training and education attained, money saved, or accolades attained or accorded can compare with what awaits us in heaven. Whatever one has gained or attained on earth should be used for the sole purpose of praising God and blessing others in readiness for heaven.

What should our life priorities be then? The fundamental life priority should, by God's grace, be to cultivate eternal values that make an impact here on earth and, a lasting impression in heaven. These values need to be provided on an ongoing platform from which we can be trained for heavenly glory. These values include love, care, hospitality, gentleness, meekness, trust, warmness, sacrifice, reverence, happiness, friendship, and humility. They are eternal elements, and they will play a crucial role in shaping and readying us for the hereafter.

Make Jesus the Supreme Commander of your life: Jesus needs to be given the full control and commandership of our lives, particularly as we profess to follow Him. This takes full commitment, genuine surrender, and trust in Him. He needs to be given full space to lead and navigate our lives and He will never disappoint as His way is always the best. He will provide mercy and grace sufficient for our unanticipated or anticipated trials that might include bumps, brokenness, challenges, and other forms of suffering. In all this He will lift us up to a new level where we begin to live lives of glory and praise because Jesus knows what we need, both now and for eternity.

Jesus deeply understands life's complexities that often emerge and unfold when least expected. He has the real-life answers to all life perplexities and according to His unfathomable wisdom, takes care of them volitionally. We need to show our full resolve to trust the Lord and let Him be the supreme commander of our lives. Rest assured that you will not regret your decision to honor Jesus, the supreme commander of your life. Jesus will help you to find meaning and purpose in this chaotic world.

Death is a topic that many shun. The truth is that death is a reality we cannot run away from, it affects everyone, whether Christian or non-Christian, and in its aftermath, it brings with it heartbreaking brokenness, pain and sorrow. It is critical to note that despite the pain and sorrow that death brings, it is in the pain of losing, for example a loved one, that we can experience God in an intimate way. It is in being broken as in the experience of death of a loved one that we get a better glimpse and sense of who is Jesus is. The meaning and purpose of life also undergoes a transformation. It is this experience of brokenness that helps us to fully embrace the meaning and purpose of life. Further, death is a constant reminder of our finite nature here on earth, and that one day we shall all be gone.

Death also reminds us that we are here only for a short while. It motivates us to think about the promises of a better tomorrow in glory and eternity. As such, life does not or need not end with death in the grave but rather it only takes repose through death and will be rejuvenated for eternity at the coming of Jesus. Death then is the true beginning that starts with the end. In death comes life and, this principle is well played out in nature. When we think about death from an eternal perspective and through the promises of Jesus, we can remain confident that death is not the end, it is the beginning of eternity. The good news is that Jesus has conquered death. He died and arose from the dead and ascended into heaven. He is alive today and His victory is our victory and like Paul said, we can confidently anticipate declaring on that day when Jesus comes that "where, O death is your victory? Where, O death is your sting?" (I Corinthians 15:55-57, New International Version–Emphasis supplied).

Jesus exemplified this when He said, "very truly I tell you, whoever hears my word and believes Him who sent me has eternal life and will not be judged but has crossed over from death to life" (John 5:24, New International Version–Emphasis supplied). To Jesus, death is nothing and does not exist in the truest sense of the word. Jesus has already dealt death a severe blow through His resurrection. Although death naturally continues for a little while here on earth, we should always remember that it has been stripped off its power to hold us from attaining our heavenly destiny. In brokenness and in death therefore we have victory and strength.

Strengths Perspective and Brokenness

From a social work perspective, the strength perspective focuses on individual strengths and can provide a sound basis for empowerment (McMillen, & Kline, 2019; Okundaye, & Lawrence-Webb, 2001). Strengths can include client resources, capabilities, intelligence, and other positive qualities that might be used to solve problems associating with for example losing a loved one, losing a job, losing a house, or losing a marriage and, with a view to pursuing positive changes. When social workers use the strengths perspective, they assume that when people's positive abilities and capacities are supported, they are more likely to act on their strengths and ultimately recover from brokenness and storms. As previously stated, to believe in people's inherent capacities for growth and well-being requires that social workers pay attention to people's own resources such as talents, experiences, and aspirations.

In social work practice, the strengths perspective has emerged as the best alternative to the pathology-oriented approach to helping clients (Saleebey, 2002; Saleeby, 1996). Instead of focusing on clients' problems, brokenness and deficits, the strengths perspective centers on clients' God given abilities, talents, and resources. The social worker using this perspective concentrates wholly on identifying and eliciting the client's strengths and assets in assisting them with their problems and goals (Deshpande, 2018). Saleebey (2002) believed that the strengths perspective fits harmoniously with diverse postmodern—narrative, spiritual, and multicultural—perspectives emerging in social work, which favor an interpreted view of reality.

Saleebey (2002) identifies four principles involved in the strengths perspective and that are crucial in working with individuals going through storms. These are:

1. Every individual, group, family, and community have strengths.

2. Difficulties such as illnesses and struggles may be detrimental but can also be a source of challenges and opportunity.

3. Don't undermine your abilities and capacities for growth and change.

4. Every environment is full of resources.

Discussion Questions

1. How can you use the strength perspective principles when working with individuals experiencing loss?

2. Draw a conceptual diagram that shows Dennis Saleebey's different four parts of the strength perspective and explain how these parts are related with each other.

Exercise

1. Find a current daily newspaper or tabloid. How many stories in it are related with individuals dealing with brokenness, death, and loss? How are the issues presented? Does the discussion seem relevant to social work practice and if so, how?

2. How has death and loss affected you, your family, and your friends?

Reflection

- Recall any of your loved ones that you may have lost. How does the anticipation of seeing them in heaven one day shape your thinking?

- How does knowing that one day you will die prepare you for the afterlife?

- What life priorities take preeminence in your life knowing that one day all what we have or have attained will be gone when we die or when Jesus comes?

- What storms or challenges have had the most impact on you?

- How have you grown from these storms or challenges?

- What thoughts come to you when you are in the midst of a storm or challenges?

References

McMillen, D., & Kline, M. (2019). Changing the Trajectory of Life. *Crime, Second Chances, and Human Services: Creating a Pathway to Ordinary Life for the Convicted,* 13.

Dennis, L. R. (2018). *Buried Dreams: From Devastating Loss to Unimaginable Hope.* Abingdon Press.

Deshpande, A. (2018). *Strengths-based approach of caregivers of children with developmental disabilities: A Narrative Inquiry* (Doctoral dissertation).

Wong, D. F., Rose, W. M., & Chan, V. Y. (2019). *A Strength-based CBT Approach to Recovery: From Trapped to Liberated Self.* Routledge.

Okundaye, J.N., Smith, P., & Lawrence-Webb, C. (2001). Incorporating spirituality and the `strengths perspective into social work practice with addicted individuals. *Journal of Social Work Practice in the Addictions, 1* (1), 65-82.

Saleebey, D. (1996). The strengths perspective in social work practice: Extensions and cautions. *Social Work, 41* (3), 296–305.

Saleebey, D. (Ed.). (1997). *The strengths perspective in social work practice* (2nd ed.).

New York: Longman.

Saleebey, D. (Ed.). (2002). *The strengths perspective in social work practice* (3rd ed.).

New York: Longman.

CHAPTER 14

Finding Meaning In a Broken World

When I was young, I had an unquenchable thirst for God, and I always wondered how I could know Him in an intimate way. I always wished that I could walk closely with Him at each moment of life. I also hoped that I would begin to experience God personally and that I would walk and talk with Him just like I did with friends. Further, as a young person I had my own ups and downs, but my greatest desire was to have a deep and rich relationship with Jesus. I wanted to see God, sense His presence, and talk with Him about all my troubles, challenges, and difficulties. I also wanted Jesus to help me find meaning and purpose in life. This same Jesus I so much desired to have as a part of me is the same yesterday, today, and forever (Hebrews 13:8, New International Version–Emphasis supplied). He wants to be our companion who can help us find true meaning and purpose in this broken and chaotic world.

Finding meaning and purpose in a state of brokenness can be a difficult task in this postmodern world. However, in life we do go through experiences that may help us find meaning and purpose. Though it is not easy to come to a place where meaning and purpose of our existence begins to make sense, God always provides opportunities for this to happen. In some cases, opportunities He provides might require us to be acutely aware of the events shaping our lives as they unfold right before our eyes. Sometimes it may be that we will need to search or discern circumstances or situations that might provide clues regarding the meaning of our lives. To do that we need to allow God to move and direct us into situations or experiences that may make this possible.

For this to happen, there must be a deliberate willingness on our part to seek God's wisdom and favor to help us understand what meaning and purpose He has laid out for our lives. This ought to be the kind of deep searching and seeking that invites God to work in our lives. As we seek Jesus more and more, the search and discovery of meaning in our lives will become real as He unveils His plans for our lives. One of the barriers that hinder many of us from discovering the meaning God has planned for us is self. Self stands in the way of discovery and in many cases it is not easy to let go of ourselves completely. We find it difficult to let God take full control of our lives because we are by nature egocentric beings who pride ourselves in living the kind of lives that focuses on self. For example, pride is one obstacle that many children of God struggle with. Pride pushes us to live the kind of lives that embellish self above God.

Egocentrism can be likened to a type of cancer that, unless quickly uprooted out of our system, can destroy us. Unless removed completely it- egocentrism- can spread into every part of our body fiber rendering us vulnerable to all types of temptations (Erle & Topolinski, 2019). Kwame Nkrumah, a great African statesman, once said that the problem with man is the animal that is in him; "him" referring to both man and woman. The animal in man forces him to focus his energies on himself and the resulting effect of this mindset is the unending and insatiable desire to put oneself above anything else. The only way we can be free from the effects and insinuations of self is by letting go and letting God work through us by the power of His Holy Spirit. The task of letting go of self is only possible if we allow God to begin and complete His work in us, and this can be a process.

If we come to that place where we can let go of self, we will find complete freedom, found only in Jesus. We will be able to see the traces of meaning and purpose of life beginning to unfold and take shape in our lives. Moving closer to God and allowing Him to work in our lives will erase the vestiges of egocentrism and self, and obstacles such as fear, pride, and worry will dissipate. In the process of this redemption, we will feel free to trust God more and more. And as God works in us and as our trust in Him unfolds, grows, and solidifies, we will be able to find meaning, tranquility, and peace amid the brokenness and chaos that constantly bombards us every day.

The brokenness and chaos we experience in the world today can only be remediated if the work that God is doing in us enables us to focus on Jesus. Focusing on Jesus will lead us to realize and claim His purpose for our lives. Focusing on Jesus will also provide the answers for our troubled and broken souls, and this is the only way meaning and purpose in our lives will develop. With Jesus on our side, we will begin to experience the heavenly peace during troublesome and tumultuous times. Allowing Jesus room in our lives can transform our chaotic broken situations into precious blessings that we would otherwise not know if we focused on the chaos, fears, and worries of this life.

In this time and age, people are so self-centered that they find it difficult to give up the strongholds that have kept them captive. Part of the reason people allow strongholds to take root in their lives is because of the focus on self, particularly in the face of this world's chaos. We are living in a dangerous period and in a culture that is exposed to all types of attacks, tricks, plots, plans, and schemes from the devil. However, Jesus did warn us that living in this world would not be easy (John 16:33, New Interventional Version—Emphasis supplied). Yes, Jesus has also promised to give us victory and the strength to endure perilous times. The devil is always busy planning against us and throwing missiles at us and creating pressures that lure us into situations where we get hoodwinked, and in the process lose focus on Jesus. When the devil traps us, we become his slaves and begin to worship him, things, and other people who we turn into idols. Many people get caught up in this trap and find themselves at crossroads, trying to satisfy the worldly cultures of insatiable lures while at the same time trying to find meaning and purpose and maintaining an unshakable focus on Jesus. This is a contradiction that makes it hard for many of us to move forward in our journey with God. Consequently, this makes it even harder for us to realize the purpose that God has for our lives.

The world is certainly getting worse and worse by the day. It is getting more and more confused, broken, and chaotic. Given the way worldly events are unfolding now, and unless Jesus comes quickly, this world will become a center stage for all kinds of socio-political and economic challenges, confusion, chaos, and evil. This is all the more reason we need to be persistent and consistent in our search for a closer walk with Jesus—because it is only, He who can bring meaning and purpose to our lives.

God is always here, has always been here, and will always be here for you and me. He is the only one that can provide us with the peace, total security, and hope that we need in this broken, chaotic, and confused world. This is the peace that soothes our hearts and souls amid brokenness and challenges. It is the kind of peace that will bring meaning even when we experience severe tragedies.

There is an African proverb that says, "He who does not mention death is a partner of fear," meaning that in this chaotic life, death is something that we all face. But if we have Jesus on our side and we walk with Him daily and intimately, we will never be shaken by any chaotic circumstance, strategy, or scheme by the enemy, including death itself. For God to be real in our lives and for us to enjoy the serenity that only Jesus can provide, it is imperative that we take the time to examine our circumstances and experiences in the light of Jesus' grace and plans. Every circumstance we face, whether positive or negative, has a purpose and if negative, can be turned into an opportunity to find the meaning and purpose Jesus has planned for us. God loves us deeply now more than ever, and He wants the best for us. He wants to heal all our infirmities and turn our brokenness and chaotic circumstances into opportunities for growth. He wants to bring us to a place where we can experience Him, as well as enjoy the peace and glory of heaven.

If we long to transcend the brokenness and find meaning in the chaos of this world, we need to deliberately grow closer and closer to the Master. For it is only by walking intimately with God that our eyes will be opened to the reality and purpose of life. It is important to highlight that trouble, confusion, chaos and brokenness will come and that this will escalate as we near the end of time. Jesus highlighted this very well when He said that there would be wars and rumors of war (Mathew 24:6, New International Version–Emphasis supplied). The implication of Jesus' statement reminds us that as the world draws closer to its determined end, more chaos, brokenness, and confusion will emerge, the scope of which only those grounded in God will be able to stand. Being grounded in Jesus means that even though we go through brokenness, troubles, and confusion in this world, we will not be afraid of the future.

Fear will not have its grip on our souls because our anchor is Jesus, and He will hold us in His arms as He guides us every step of the way. This world has nothing to offer that can truly satisfy our deepest needs. Our deepest needs are those needs that lie at the bottom of our hearts. These are needs that only God can meet. God knows the best things we need in this world. He understands and knows us more than any other person, including ourselves, and for this reason only He can provide us with the fullest understanding of why we are here. He is willing to provide us with that understanding and the onus and responsibility is on us to let Him do that. Many people in this world are craving something that can satisfy their souls. Their hearts are craving for something bigger than themselves. They are constantly searching for the unknown to fill their emptiness and void that only God can truly fill.

There are days when I have often contemplated Gods infinite power, His unsearchable wisdom, and his incomprehensible love for us fallen and sinful beings. For example, on some nights when I gaze into the skies, completely amazed as I look at the stars, I am in awe as I imagine the size of the universe and its limitless expanse. Yet, I know that there is a God out there whose heart is yearning to provide us with the heavenly blessings He has in store for us. He is in control of everything, and He will take care of us when we are broken and feel confused and numbed by the brokenness and chaos in our lives or, in our children, in our families, on our jobs, and in any situation, we may find ourselves. He will extend His loving arm to pull us out of the trappings of this world's brokenness, chaos, and confusion.

He is always ready to come to our rescue if we call upon Him. We are His children, and we belong to Him. He has given us many blessings, including free choice. He has given us the freedom to choose Him daily, so that He can manifest Himself fully in our lives. I don't know what confusion, brokenness, and chaos you might be facing right now, but this one thing I know. Our God is able and is above any brokenness, problem, or perplexity you might be facing. He has the answers to any perplexing and chaotic circumstances in our lives and for as long we set our eyes on Him and ask Him and allow Him to be in control of our lives, we will never go wrong. Know that "in all these things we are more than conquerors through him who loved us." (Romans 8:37, New International Version–Emphasis supplied).

Cultivating an Essential Faith in Brokenness

Faith is an essential ingredient in the growth and survival of every believer in Jesus Christ. Without faith we cannot grow in our brokenness and our trust and confidence in Jesus will be limited and eventually die. Paul reminds us that followers of Jesus Christ should walk by faith and not by sight (2 Corinthians 5:7, New International Version–Emphasis supplied). I remember my own experience of cultivating faith. When I was young, I used to accompany my grandfather to the fields where we would often spend full days tilling the land and sowing crops. Our favorite crop was maize, or corn, which we planted every year. I enjoyed assisting my grandfather with this seasonal task, although sometimes it was tiresome because of the preparation that went into it. Every day before we ventured out to the fields we would prepare the seeds for sowing, get the food we needed to eat during the day ready, prepare bottles of water for drinking, prepare and check the bicycles, and get work clothes ready.

When the day came, we left very early in the morning for the field. Despite all the elements that went into preparing for work in the field, I always looked forward to when harvest would come and we would harvest all types of produce such as corn, sweet potatoes, beans, cassava, pumpkins, and all types of greens. Faith works in a similar way. It requires the same level of seriousness, preparation, and attention to detail, as well as a closer examination of elements such as prayer, daily reading of the word, spending quality time with God, and listening to His small and still voice. These are the necessary ingredients for spiritual growth, without them there can be no spiritual growth.

A combination and active utility of these elements will, under guidance and unction of the Holy Spirit, produce a spiritual growth and harvest in our hearts. The spiritual harvest will place us on a solid platform from which we can begin to experience God's presence in a much more nuanced and pronounced way. Faith needs to be nurtured because without it, it cannot grow. For example, people that love flowers sometimes make flower gardens that they attend to and look after carefully. They give their flowers full attention and in a meticulous fashion, they make sure the flowers are taken care of, growing, and producing well. They know that with extra attention accorded to their flowers, their efforts will produce the best flowers that will in turn beautify their environments. The flowers in turn will produce gorgeous colors and fragrance that will make their environment sweet and beautiful. Further, for flowers to grow and blossom, they need water. If they do not receive their daily portion of water, they will eventually shrink and die.

In the same manner, if our faith is not tended and watered, it will die eventually. Just like flowers need water, faith needs to be sufficiently watered as well. Watering faith enables it to grow and blossom, and when it does it provides the believer with the buffer needed to counter negative forces, challenges, and circumstances. Faith solidly anchors us in Jesus, and it can shape our paths as well as place us on higher ground. It is a ladder by which we can climb into the heavenly realm and thereby allow God to place in us a heavenly mindset. Faith is also a key that unlocks heavenly treasures, and resources that are ours for the taking.

In addition, faith can help us open the doors of heaven to obtain blessings that God has in store for us. Faith is therefore an essential element of our spiritual walk with God. It holds and keeps us focused on Jesus, the author and finisher of our faith (Hebrew 12:2, New International Version–Emphasis supplied). Each one of us has a measure of faith that God has placed in our hearts. No matter the portion of faith that Jesus has determined for one, one can grow it to an extent where one will be able to use it in doing great and mighty things for God. Not all of us are at the same place of faith. We are all at different levels, and growing and developing spiritually as Jesus enables us and sees fit. No matter what level of faith one may have, one can face and move mountains with it. Even the smallest faith can do wonders in our lives.

Jesus likened faith to a mustard seed and explained that even with faith as small as a mustard seed we can "move mountains" (Hebrews 17:6, New International Version–Emphasis supplied). Faith will help us to deal with mountains. These mountains could be broken, suffering physical pain, or perhaps experiencing an ongoing illness, suffering rebuke or affliction from colleagues or family, or experiencing emotional challenges. We can stand firm in the face of mountains, even with the smallest faith, if Jesus is on our side. We need to constantly grow our faith in these last days because this is our safeguard against the arrows, assaults, tricks, plans, and schemes of the enemy Satan. Satan knows our weakest points and his darts and missiles are often targeted at those weakest points. He is a dangerous foe who "prowls around like a roaring lion looking for someone to devour" and so we should not give him any leeway into our lives (1Peter 5:8, New International Version–Emphasis supplied).

Almost 20 years ago I was at a different place in my faith and, looking back now, I can say that my faith is not where it used to be. We need to have a faith that is constantly growing, maturing and not static. We always need to desire to be at a different place in our faith walk. My deepest desire is to grow spiritually so that I can fully enjoy God. Sometimes I just wish I would walk faithfully with God like Enoch did. Enoch walked faithfully with God and then he was no more because God took him away (Genesis 5:24, New International Version–Emphasis supplied). My wish is that God would transform my life in such a way that I illuminate

His heavenly presence, and that every person that He allows to encounter me will be touched by His presence. Though God may not necessarily take one away to heaven as was the case with Enoch, we should want more and more of Him so that we may experience heaven on earth.

We should ask God to bring heaven down. On the mount of transfiguration heaven came down when Jesus was transfigured before Peter, James, and John. His face shone as bright as the sun. Peter was so impacted by the transfiguration that he said to Jesus, "Lord, it is good for us to be here. If you wish, I will put up three shelters—one for you, one for Moses and one for Elijah" (Mathew 17:1-5, New International Version–Emphasis supplied). We too can have this type of heavenly transfiguration experience and God can make it possible if we truly seek His presence daily. If we ask God to allow us to come into His presence each day, He will transfigure us. He will also, in the process of transfiguration, answer our prayers.

Over the years I have prayed to God and asked Him for specific blessings, and I have witnessed His answers swiftly. The best prayers I have prayed have included an element of a desire to be in God's presence. I know that if we candidly and genuinely ask God to bring us into His presence, we will be transformed, and He will answer our prayers. When Moses met with God on Mount Sinai he was immediately transformed. His face shone with heavenly light, and he had a heavenly aura around him. As he came down from Mount Sinai after spending time with God, Moses' face radiated with God's light and presence. His aura was so evident that people saw it as he came down from the mountain. Similarly, when we spend time with God, we will never be the same, as everything about us will change. We can have the same experience Moses had and God will shine through us a heavenly light that will be witnessed by all.

This is the light that will touch and impact every place we go to, because it is God's presence that will be shining through us. This was the case with the disciples on the mountain of transfiguration. As a result of this experience, they wanted to stay with Jesus forever, they did not want the experience to end because it was so invigorating. When Jesus comes again we will be transfigured for eternity and we will enjoy His presence in the eternal bliss that He has prepared for us. When we are finally there–in heaven–, this earthly life will seem too short, in the context of eternity. Therefore, as we face brokenness, storms and challenges of life, it is faith that will hold us on our path to eternity.

Social workers have a responsibility to the broken people including those struggling with issues of hope and chaos in this world. This responsibility involves promoting and focusing on social justice.

Social Justice and Brokenness

Christian social workers have a responsibility toward individuals struggling with issues of hope and chaos and brokenness. They act as agents of change and facilitators of progress. They give voice to the voiceless, inspire the hopeless and empower the downtrodden. They push for an equal and level ground of social justice, and equal access to resources for all. Social justice is what motivates Christian and non-Christian social workers to do become agents of change and to have a heart for the broken, to the struggling and to those experiencing various storms of life. The Bible is clear regarding the expectation of doing, not just talking, about social justice. This may require that we sacrifice part of we are in the expression of social justice and ultimately love. This is how we know what love is, Jesus laid down his life for us. And we ought to lay down our lives for our brothers and sisters in the name of love and social justice. If anyone has material possessions and sees his brother or sister in need but has no pity on them, how can the love of God be in that person? (John 3:16-17, New International Version–Emphasis supplied).

Edwards (2012) and Stearn (2009) highlighted the same point and called on all Christians to act and not only talk when it came to social justice. Christian social workers are mandated by God to serve individuals dealing with various challenges of life. They have a moral responsibility to focus on the social justice principle of service and equity as well as the promotion of fair accessibility to resources (Sider, 1999). Accessibility refers to the ability of struggling individuals to access resources that are necessary for them to achieve a decent standard of living including crafting a trajectory toward self-actualization (Edwards, 2012).

Similarly, Christian social workers need to care for those facing storms by way of oppression and to support "fairness and common good" (Crethar, Rivera, & Nash, 2008, p. 271). Brady (2006) has posited that Christian social work requires that social workers be ready to work with broken, storm-stricken individuals and that they should advocate for their inclusion and empowerment. This principle calls upon all social workers to collate their voices and make social, financial, political and other relevant decisions that have an impact on their well-being. Social workers are called upon to promote social justice and social change with and on behalf of clients. To do this they need to be sensitive to cultural and ethnic diversity and strive to end such challenges as discrimination, oppression, poverty, and other forms of social injustice (NASW, 2016). Further, the United States Conference of Catholic Bishops has an important publication that pays special attention to social justice. In it the following elements are highlighted:

1. Every economic decision and institution must be judged in the light of whether they protect or undermine the dignity of a human person.

2. Human dignity can be realized and protected only within the community.

3. All people have a right to participate in the economic life of society.

4. All members of society have a special obligation to the poor and vulnerable.

5. Human rights are the minimum conditions for life within a community.

6. Society as whole, including public and private institutions and other stakeholders, have a moral responsibility to enhance human dignity.

Thus, from a Christian perspective, social justice and harmony is God's intention for the world (I John 3:16-18, New International Version). God intended for the world to be one of justice, a place of equitable access, equitable participation, and harmony for all (Wolterstorff, 2008). In the spirit of social justice, God allows for free will, a concept by which individuals who are broken and are struggling with storms of life, are given a voice and choice in their life's path (Ephesians 2:8-9, New International version). Although the current state of the world is one of brokenness, chaos, and injustice, from a Christian social work perspective this is not where the story should and will end. The clarion call is for all social workers to contribute to the change process (Belaire & Young, 2002). Social workers of all faith persuasions should critically consider the social justice foundation of their faith as well as their awareness of social justice principles. They need to be thoughtful about how their faith might inform their professional practice as well as seek out experiences that may challenge their skill, biases and worldviews (Juarez & Hayes, 2008; Parker, 2011).

Discussion Questions

1. How are social justice and faith related? Can you have one without the other?

2. In what ways may social workers help combat poverty, diseases, and homelessness?

3. Do you believe Christian social workers could play a significant role in pushing for social justice? If so explain.

Exercise

1. Identify one faith or religious based agency and find out if it has local office. Visit the office and ask for materials describing the organization's mission and current efforts. Share and exchange information in class.

Reflection

- At what level is your faith walk with Jesus?

- How does being broken and storms of life help you to contemplate and think about eternity?

- What chaotic and confusing circumstances are you or others you know dealing with?

- In what ways has God manifested Himself in these circumstances?

References

Belaire, C., & Young, J.S. (2002). Conservative Christians' expectations of non-Christian counselors. *Counseling and Values, 46,* 175-187.

Brady, J.A. (2006). Justice for the poor in a land of plenty: A place at the table. *Religious Education, 101,* 347-376. Doi:10.1080/00344080600788324

Crethar, H., Torres, R., & Nash. (2008). In search of common threads: Linking multicultural, feminist, and social justice counseling paradigms. *Journal of Counseling & Development, 86,* 269-278.

Edwards, C.N. (2012). Christian social justice advocate: contradiction or legacy. *Counseling and Values, 57.*

Erle, T. M., Barth, N., & Topolinski, S. (2019). Egocentrism in sub-clinical depression. *Cognition and Emotion, 33* (6), 1239-1248.

Juarez, B., Smith, D., & Hayes, C. (2008). Social justice means us White people: The diversity paradox in teacher education. *Democracy & Education, 17,* 20-25.

Parker, S. (2011). Spirituality in counseling: A faith development perspective. *Journal of Counseling & Development, 89,* 112-120.

Sider, R.J. (1997). *Just generosity. A new vision for overcoming poverty in America.* Grand Rapids, MI: Baker.

Stearns, R. (2009). *The hole in our gospel.* Nashville, TN: Thomas Nelson.

Wolterstorff, N. (2008). *Letty Mandeerville Russell.* Retrieved from http://www.yale.edu/divinity/news/070713_news_russell.shtml

CHAPTER 15

Life is short but Eternity is Long, Long, Long

Life is very, very, very short when compared with eternity, and eternity is long, long, long. As the Bible rightly says, life is like dew that is here in the morning and gone by noon day. This reality has finally set as I grow older. It was not long ago that my hair was completely black, but now over the years it has turned grey– a sign of how short life is. I remember not too long ago when I was a teenager, 17 years old to be exact, when my grandfather used to ask me to trim his grey hair using scissors. He loved sitting in the shadow under a tree in his yard and then I would cut and trim the sides of his grey thinning hair. I used to enjoy doing this, especially on nice sunny and dry afternoons. As I trimmed his hair, I was often amused by his grey hair, and as a young man I was not sure as to why his hair was grey and thinning to begin with. Never did I realize that one day my hair would begin to thin and grey as well. My grandfather was a strong Christian man who served as a pastor for many years. As I cut and trimmed his hair, I was quick to conclude that the reason he had grey hair was that he was a senior who was catching up in his years. My concept of senior was vague then, as I did not fully understand what it meant to be an older person, let alone the physical attributes that come with old age.

It is not until now, after my grandfather has long passed, that I have realized that life on earth is indeed short. Over the years I have lost a number of loved ones, and it is only now as an adult that I am beginning to realize how short this earthly life is. The reality of how limited our earthly lives are begins to show as soon as signs of aging begin to manifest. Now, as my own aging signs begin to be more and more evident, I am beginning to fully understand that life on this can be taken away from us in a moment.

Life belongs to God and only He has the overall jurisdiction to take it away from us whenever He determines so. He alone determines when, why and how this is done. I have understood that very well especially when, among other things, I look back at those years when I was younger, cutting my grandfather's hair under that tree, it is just like yesterday gone by. Our days pass so fast that we do not realize when we have reached the zenith of our lives here on earth. We are in most cases taken unawares when we soon realize that we have reached our zenith and have started to descend, a journey that ends in the grave.

The bible is crystal clear when it highlights the uncertainty of life. We do not have surety or guarantee of our lives, and only God does. We can go any time and I realized this truth when my son died in 2012. None of us is exempt from death, we are all candidates of this reality. Then what do we need to do to live lives fully aware that we can go at any time? We need to be always ready for death. How do we get ready? Jesus has given clear and elaborate instructions of how we can be ready. The command is to "seek ye first the kingdom of God..." Seeking the kingdom of God should be our number one priority, and this might mean that we reorganize and prioritize our lives. It also might mean that we focus more on setting aside those things that are temporal, things that trap us and that make us shift our attention away from God to worldly material things. This world has nothing to offer that compares with what the almighty God has in store for us. God "made the earth [and all other planets in our galaxy] by His power... established the world by His wisdom and, by His understanding stretched out the heavens" (Jeremiah 51:15, New International Version–Emphasis supplied). He is an awesome God, infinite in power and wisdom, and therefore we can and should trust Him.

God lives outside of time and holds the universe and all the galaxies out there in His hands. I have always been fascinated by God's power as expressed in His creation. Creation and the universe are what make me wonder at how mighty our God is. For example, I am very intrigued with astronomy as it reveals more of God's creativity. This particularly comes home when I look at the stars in the night. As I see those millions upon millions of heavenly bodies illuminating the night, I am awed at the awesomeness of God. Even in nature I see God's creativity and knowledge everywhere, from butterflies with gorgeous colored wings, to beautiful flowers and plants of all types, to the elegant rainbow in the sky.

All these wonders testify of God's power and grace, love, care, and goodness. It is this same God who holds eternity in His hands, whose magnificence we witness daily, and who has given us the gift of eternity in Jesus Christ. One day I was trying to wrap my mind around the concept of eternity and tried to think about it in terms of one day, two days, three days, and four days and son and so forth. As I went on counting, my finite mind could not fathom counting endlessly, and this is just a glimpse of how mind-boggling eternity as a concept is. Yet it is real. As we live in this world our thinking is shaped and driven by the things we see, but we should also remember that everything comes to an end and only eternal things will last.

Solomon alludes to this very well when he says that there is a time for everything (Ecclesiastes 3:1, Paraphrased). For example, as a day dawns, we know that it soon comes to an end at evening time, when the sun sets. When we go to work, we know that sooner or later the workday will be over, and we will head home. When our children are born it is not too long before we start thinking about the time when they will grow up, become adults, and when eventually they will move out of the house. This cycle of now and then, start and end, continues until we get older, until we die. However, this is only a backdrop when we think about it in the context of eternity.

God wants us to spend time with Him in heaven. He is longing to bestow on us the blessing of living forever in His eternity where we shall enjoy His glory and presence, including all the blessings He has in store for us. As human beings made with finite minds, it is very difficult to fathom eternity. Eternity will only begin to make sense when Jesus comes to take us home to glory. There is so much we don't know now that will be made clearer to us in heaven and, for this reason, our focus needs to be on the things that matter. Things that matter are those things we cannot see now, things that have eternal value.

In the past few years, I have come to realize that material things of this world that people put all their focus on are actually nothing when compared with eternity. Things that matter are heavenly and these have eternal value. Our preoccupation should then be based on focusing on those things that have eternal value and that will last. Although some people find it difficult to shift and preoccupy their minds with things that matter in life, we should be cultivating a liking for those things and traits that will qualify us for heaven. This requires ongoing prayer and reading of the Word of God.

Unfortunately, many people in this era are not interested in heavenly things but are only interested in focusing on things that will give them instant satisfaction. This satisfaction is not heavenly, but earthly and comes from an insatiable desire for material possessions. The focus on earthly material things ends in victims being addicted to fame, popularity, and material possessions which, in themselves, have nothing to offer.

One time I found myself falling into the same trap of expending energy and focusing on those material things that do not have any eternal worth. However, when my son died, my perception changed completely. I now look at life through a different lens of eternity. My son's death has brought me closer to the reality of eternity. My immediate preoccupation and concern now is eternity and nothing in this life will ever compare with that. I have taken a fresh look at life and have examined what really matters and what does not matter. As previously said, Jesus said that in everything we need to "seek ye first the kingdom of God," meaning we should make Jesus and eternity our number one priority.

Anticipation and Expectation

Christian believers have God's promise of a better world which will be ushered in at the coming of Jesus Christ. In this regard our lives need to be lived in great anticipation of Jesus Christ's return, no matter what kind of storms come our way. This world will end one day soon just as Jesus has already promised in His word. God does not lie, and His word and promises are sure and solid, and always come to pass. A better world is coming, and this is the world where there will be no more tears, as God will wipe every tear from our eyes. There will be no more death or mourning or crying or pain, for the old order of things has passed away (Revelation 21:4, New International Version–Emphasis supplied). As we await the second coming of Jesus, we will face storms and sometimes these storms will be severe and painful.

As mentioned earlier it is not easy to stay strong when broken and when in the midst of severe storms, but Jesus has promised to comfort us and to be present with us as He was with His people in the past. For example, Jesus was with Shadrack, Meshack, and Abednego (Daniel 3:16-18, Paraphrased) in their storm, and consequently they were spared and saved from being roasted in the burning furnace. These three Jewish young men were true to Jesus and He was faithful and saved them. This is the same Jesus who is there for us today, He does not change because He is "the same yesterday and today and forever" (Hebrews 13:8, New International Version—Emphasis supplied).

The promises of Jesus are ours for the asking and as such, we need to live with a full realization and anticipation that we can access and claim His promises. God is faithful regarding His promises and the good news is that His faithfulness is renewed every morning (Lamentations 3:23, Paraphrased). Each day can be a new beginning for God's promises and these promises, if claimed, can make a significant spiritual impact in our lives.

When I completed my undergraduate degree, I started working in the Department of Social Services in the Ministry Community Development and Social Services. After working for 13 years, I realized it was time to move forward in my profession, and I started making plans to pursue graduate studies. I started praying about my plans, asking God to open opportunities for graduate education. I claimed God's promises, and, in time, I saw Him begin to answer my prayers.

My answer to prayer came when God opened up opportunities at my workplace. He brought me into contact with international consultants from the United States Agency for International development [USAID]. These consultants visited HIV and USAID funded AIDS projects for orphaned children that I managed (Mbizvo & Hewett, 2018). In less than a year, my professional interactions with this USAID team from U.S. morphed into a series of contacts with contacts here in the United States. Within two years, God had answered my prayer and I was offered a fully paid scholarship to come and study at the University of Georgia [UGA] in Athens. During my graduate studies at University of Georgia I always endeavored to put God first in my graduate studies, and again God proved faithful and blessed me in my schoolwork. I successfully completed my graduate degree and graduated with Honors. From the University of Georgia, God again proved His faithfulness when I was granted a competitive fully paid Graduate Fellowship at Virginia Commonwealth University [VCU] in Richmond, Virginia.

This fellowship made it possible for me to pursue my doctorate studies at VCU without having to pay any tuition including other costs related to graduate education. During this time, I fully focused on Jesus and trusted God's goodness and blessings in moving forward with my graduate education. God was and is faithful.

I can attest to the fact that God is faithful, but sometimes many of us tend to miss this truth. God is there for us and He always challenges us to focus on Him. He will answer our prayers and show us great and unsearchable things that we do not know (Jeremiah 33:3, Paraphrased). God is omnipotent, omnipresent and omniscient and these attributes are the best and perfect panacea for all of our storms.

Are you feeling depressed or emotionally challenged? Look up to Jesus. Are you suffering from an illness that doctors have told you may cut your life short? Look up to Jesus. Have you been angered and frustrated by what your boss or colleagues at work did to you? Look up to Jesus. Are you worried about what your colleagues and other associates are saying about you? Look up to Jesus. Are you frustrated that your efforts at improving and meeting your life goals have not been realized? Look up to Jesus. Are you worried about what tomorrow may bring? Look up to Jesus.

In whatever storm or perplexity of life we find ourselves, remember that looking up to Jesus is the best we can do and we will never be disappointed. Jesus does not and will not disappoint. He knows everything and He is everywhere and has everything under His control. He understands our most intriguing and troublesome situations and only He has the perfect answers to our challenging situations. He eagerly invites and boldly instructs us to take up His "yoke and learn from Me because," He is "gentle and humble in heart, and you will find rest for yourselves" (Mathew 11:29, New International Version–Emphasis supplied). Only Jesus can accord us the serenity and pure rest in these perilous and uncertain times of our earth's history. Let's not drag our feet or be slow in acting and responding to Jesus when He gives the invitation. Jesus is the true sustainer, provider, and protector. While on earth, He fought all spiritual battles and in every case, He won the contest.

Since he was cast out of heaven, the devil has been a defeated foe and is no match for us if only we completely trust and put our confidence in Jesus and learn to focus on Him. When I was in my early thirties my faith in Jesus was fluid, not as solid for a short while. However, and by God's grace I can safely say that I rebounded and have grown, and I am still growing in my spiritual journey. The good news is that I am not where I used to be 20 years ago. In the past few years, I have recognized the significance of fully looking up and focusing on Jesus for anything I need. Whereas 20 years ago, for example, my prayer life was shallow and lacked depth and breadth, now I have made strides in my prayer life. Committing to Jesus and focusing on him has radicalized my prayer life.

I also remember before I came to the United States, when my morning devotionals were not as deep. I would often have very short prayers on the concrete pavement of our house, and I did this as I walked to unlock the main gate to the house. Our house worker lived far from our neighborhood and, consequently, he always reported for work early in the mornings. It was my duty to open the gate for him every morning, and this was the only best time, I thought, I had for morning prayers.

Though I always felt some emptiness in me after my morning prayers, on the other hand, I did have the confidence that Jesus had appreciated my efforts in striving and, as a result, He set me on a trajectory to spiritual growth. He set me on a path I barely knew, yet I had the fullest awareness that He was in control of my situation. His mercy and His grace guided me and led me through all the spiritual meanders that unfolded before me. To this day, I have seen Jesus' good hand continually guide and correct me. He has filled, and continues to fill, my heart with the kind of joy that only God can provide. He has helped me in situations where I have been overwhelmed with doubt, fear, worry, and anxiety as well as other forms of life storms and challenges. He has given me a renewed sense of hope and focus on Jesus. Consequently, I am learning daily that it pays to walk with Jesus.

If one gets grounded in Jesus and enjoys His presence, he or she should encourage others who may be culturally different. One way this may be done is through the use of culture of competency.

Cultural Competency as a Tool for Healing

Social workers have an enormous task of bringing healing, hope to the hopeless and of reminding them of how important it is to strive for self-worth and dignity. Christian social workers particularly bear this responsibility, and they need to do it with care, passion, and compassion. Their goal should be for social workers to embrace inclusiveness as they work with broken people regardless of their backgrounds and ethnicities. For them to do this effectively they need to be culturally competent.

Cultural competence has been defined as a set of cultural behaviors and attitudes integrated into the practice of methods of a system, agency, or its professionals that enables them to work effectively in cross-cultural situations. Cultural competency is achieved by translating and integrating knowledge about individuals and groups of people into specific practices and policies applied in appropriate settings (Chau, 1990; Goicoechea-Balbona, 1997; Julia, 2001; Ronnau, 1994). The National Association of Social Workers (NASW) has highlighted that cultural competency requires that social workers learn new behaviors and techniques that respect, "affirm, and value the dignity and worth of diverse individuals, groups, families, and communities while protecting and preserving the dignity of each" (Workers, 2008, p. 11).

When social work practitioners are culturally competent, they can establish positive helping relationships, engage the people or clients, and improve the quality of services because they can honestly and humbly cross the culture divide. Much of the research on cultural competency has tended to follow a similar path: identifying the characteristics indicative of cultural competency and/or developing a model of how it should be conceptualized. For example, Benson (1978) identified eight dimensions of cultural competency: language skills, communication skills, interactions, reinforcing activities, friendliness, socially appropriate behaviors, attitudes, and satisfaction. All these are critical to helping those individuals who are broken and impacted by storms.

Another study by Hammer, Gudykunst, and Wiseman (1978) found three factors related to successful cultural competency experiences: "the ability to deal with psychological stresses, the ability to effectively communicate, and the ability to establish interpersonal relationships" (p. 389). Furthermore, the study supported a hypothesis that the effective component of cultural competency can be conceptualized "as the degree of third cultural perspective" (p. 384), meaning the perspective or frame of reference used by someone to interpret his or her cultural experience.

This third cultural perspective consists of the ability to empathize with those of the dominant culture and to establish significant relationships with members by being non-judgmental, accurate in perceptions of similarities and differences between cultures, and less exclusive. Spitzberg (1989) and Kealey (1989) extend this idea of establishing relationships and argue that cultural competency needs to be understood from the perspective of interpersonal communication. They both focus on the individual belonging to both the minority and dominant culture, recognizing how people of different cultures strategically construct verbal acts in a reciprocal and compensatory manner to meet interpersonal objectives while in communication with each other. This involves recognizing not only the characteristics, skills, and abilities of each person, but the way they perceive and think about each other.

The process of achieving cultural competency is seen as transformational (Kim & Ruben, 1988). It is a learning and growth process where the individual's "old person breaks up, and the cultural knowledge, attitudes, and behavioral capacities construct a new person at a higher level of integration" (p. 314). Similarly, Mansell (1981) sees the successful cultural competency experience as more than competence in skills, but an essential communication characteristics that create an aesthetic awareness, a "consciousness which transforms an individual's perception of the world and imparts a sense of unity between self and surrounding" (p. 99). In effect, the literature seems to indicate that cultural competency is a transformational process whereby a social worker develops an adaptive capacity, altering his or her perspective to effectively understand and accommodate the demands of another culture. The culturally competent social worker thus does not passively accept the social realities defined by others; instead, he or she is able to actively negotiate purpose and meaning. Moreover, the transformation of becoming culturally competent is anchored within the individual. It is this ongoing process within the individual's internal system that is at the core of cultural competency, which is manifested in definitive behavioral and cognitive abilities such as empathy, motivation, perspective taking, behavioral flexibility, and person-centered communication (Kim, 1992). All these elements are critical in working with broken individuals.

Discussion Questions

1. In what ways might you bring stability to those individuals facing storms of hopelessness, poverty, and lack of direction?

2. What could social workers learn from gaining a deeper understanding of cultural competency?

3. Give an example of a cultural competency driven intervention that might positively impact the lives of people.

Exercise

1. List all possible storms, challenges, or types of difficulties that people may face. Now review the list. How might you address each of the items on your list? What faith-based principles might you use to help you in this assignment?

Reflection

- Focusing fully on Jesus might not be easy in this age and time when we are constantly bombarded with media messages. How might you make sure Jesus becomes your anchor and priority during this age?

- In what ways has prayer shaped your life and how has this moved you closer to Jesus?

- What thoughts come to your mind upon realizing that one day, unless Jesus comes before, you will die?

- How do you react to the idea that you may live eternally with Jesus in heaven?

References

Benson, P.G. (1978). Measuring cross-cultural adjustment: The problem of criteria. *International Journal of Intercultural Relations, 2*, 21-37.

Chau, K. (1990). A model for teaching cross-cultural practice in social work. *Journal of Social Work Education, 26* (2), 124-133.

Goicoechea-Balbona, A. (1997). Culturally specific health care model for ensuring health care use by rural ethnically diverse families affected by HIV/AIDS. *Health and Social Work, 22* (3), 172-180.

Julia, M. (2001). Student perceptions of culture: an integral part of social work practice. *International Journal of Intercultural relations, 24 (*2000), 279-289.

Ronnau, J. (1994). Teaching cultural competence: Practical ideas for social work educators. *Journal of Multicultural Social Work, 3* (1), 29-42.

Hammer, M.R., Gudykunst, W.B., & Wiseman, R. L. (1978). Dimensions of intercultural effectiveness: An exploratory study. *International Journal of Intercultural Relations, 2*, 382-393.

Spitzberg, B.H. (1989). Issues in the development of theory of interpersonal competence in the intercultural context. *International Journal of Intercultural Relations, 13*, 241-268.

Kealey, D.J. (1989). A study of cross-cultural effectiveness: Theoretical issues, practical applications. *International Journal of Intercultural Relations, 13*, 269-286.

Kim, Y.Y. (1992, May). *Development of intercultural identity.* Paper presented at the annual conference of the International Communication Association, Miami, FL

Kim, Y.Y., & Ruben, B.D. (1988). Intercultural transformation. In Y.Y. Kim & W.B.

Gudykunst (Eds.). *Theories in intercultural communication* (pp. 299-321). London: Sage.

Mansell, M. (1981). Transcultural experience and expressive response. *Communication Education, 30,* 93-108.

Mbizvo, M., & Hewett, P. C. (2018). Benchmark assessment of orphaned and vulnerable children in areas of the Zambia Family (ZAMFAM) Project—Brief.

Workers, N. A. (2008). NASW Code of Ethics (Guide to the Everyday Professional

Conduct of Social Workers). Washington, DC: NASW.

CHAPTER 16

Rejoicing in a Broken World

We can learn to rejoice even in brokenness and even as we live each day on this earth. Joy is not something we cultivate but is a gift we receive from Jesus. Only Jesus gives the purest joy and, to receive this, we need to learn to walk intimately with Him every day. The joy that Jesus gives will find room in our hearts and will remain there whether we are going through brokenness. The only requirement to receive this kind of joy is to stay connected with Him. This is the type of joy that erases all negativity harboring in our hearts.

There was a time in my life when I was predisposed to worry. I worried a lot about many things. I worried about school grades, I worried about how people thought about me, and I worried about any negative incidents that happened in my family. Sometimes I could worry for days on end that I developed severe headaches. The only way to overcome worry is by walking closely with Jesus and shifting our minds on Him.

When I fully accepted Jesus in my life, He replaced my worries with joy. This is a joy that I could not explain, as it seemed to have taken root in me. This joy came in different forms, sometimes by way of joyful bursts that occurred anytime and anywhere. Sometimes these joyful bursts would come when I was doing chores in the house, or sometimes it was during quiet times when I would feel a sudden burst of heavenly joy. No matter what I was going through, this joy would surpass all the negative emotions and place me on a different trajectory. However, this does not mean that I don't get worried anymore or that I do not experience challenges. Just like every Christian, I do experience worry and face storms, but in the midst of these, Jesus pours into my heart a special joy that keeps me in a safe place.

In the same manner, God wants all His children to experience joy to the fullest and this can be so even in brokenness. This is the kind of joy that no human therapy or psychosocial counseling can provide. Further, in this life we go through highs and lows and these highs and lows may bring anxiety, depression and fear of the unknown. We are living in an era where many people are just filled with fear, worry, anxiety, and emotional lows. However, the good news is that there is cure for this, and that cure is Jesus, the Master. As mentioned earlier, I have experienced periods of emotional lows which come when least expected, but my buffer has been Jesus. Whenever emotional lows, fear, and anxiety come, Jesus infuses in me a sense of His presence that brings in the fullness of joy. This joy is so sublime that often it reminds me that our destiny is not here on earth. Our destiny is in heaven and if we want to experience the kind of joy that is divine and all encompassing, we need to shift our mindsets to heaven.

Fixing our mindsets in heaven will transform us and consequently, we will be blessed in ways we cannot fathom. Heaven is a place where Jesus is, and where Jesus is there is always peace and joy. Our joy will be complete as we experience the blessings of Jesus daily. Jesus' assurance that He will bless us is as real and definite today as it was when He walked on this earth. Only Jesus has the power to help us face our storms with assurance, peace, and confidence.

He invites us to not "let your hearts be troubled ye believe in God, believe also in me. In my father's house are many mansions: if it were not so, I would have told you. I go to prepare a place for you and if I go and prepare a place for you, I will come again, and receive you unto myself; that where I am, there ye may be also" (John 14:1-3, New International Version–Emphasis supplied).

There are times when I go out during the night and just gaze at the heavens, and I am filled with wonder by the heavenly lights. As I gaze upon these extraterrestrial bodies, I am reminded of God's wisdom and infinite power He so faithfully displays for us all to see. In these heavenly lights I see God's power and love which He wants us to tap into at a personal level. The love that Jesus has for us He demonstrates through the joy and other blessings He gives us. Consequently, in all storms of life I am learning to ask Jesus to grant me the grace to walk with Him, the peace to maintain sanity, the joy to keep me focused on Him, and the happiness to appreciate Him.

Joy is something that we cannot fully grasp, but it keeps us intact when broken or when faced with challenges and obstacles. Challenges may come from different scenarios, but whatever the case might be, Jesus holds us up in His arms and pours into our heart heavenly joy. Many people today are searching for joy and happiness but, unfortunately, they do not get what they are searching for because they search in the wrong places. People are eager and looking for the type of joy that will fill their voids. There is so much fear of the unknown in this world, and Satan is capitalizing on this fear to intimidate and keep in bondage the hearts of many people.

The world has witnessed disappointment after disappointment of crooked individuals who have hoodwinked people's hearts through personal agendas, treachery, and mere tricks. Many people who fall victim to such trickery end up receiving more harm than good, and end up in worse situations. Where can people find true joy and expectancy of what the future holds? Jesus said, "I am the way and the truth and the life. No one comes to the father except through me" (John 14:6, New International Version–Emphasis supplied).

Jesus is the answer to every problem we may face. He is the source of our joy and guarantee of our expectations. The right place to search for joy is in Jesus, who does not fail or disappoint, and walking genuinely with Him is the fullest assurance of joy. Since my son went to sleep in the Lord, I have learned that this world has nothing to offer, and that true joy and happiness is only found in walking closely with Jesus. I think about Jesus regularly and about His goodness, mercy, and faithfulness. I think about His sacrifice for us sinful beings and, above all, I think about the promise of eternal life. I eagerly wait for that day when we shall see Jesus' face to face, and I cannot wait to see my son again on that glorious resurrection day. Each day that passes by awakens in me a great sense of anticipation of what it shall be like during that glorious reunion, when the Master Himself will be in our midst presenting rewards to His beloved ones. As we wait for that soon coming day of final redemption, let's stay focused on Jesus. He will allow His peace and joy to permeate every part of our being.

In my walk with the Lord, I have learned that happiness is a choice that we make because happiness, in most cases, is determined by external circumstances. But unlike happiness, joy is like a seed that one plants in a field and that sooner or later sprouts into a gorgeous plant. That plant might be a flower displaying beautiful flowers, or it might be a plant yielding sweet fruits. Similarly, if we allow Jesus in our hearts, He will sow seeds of heavenly joy in our hearts and these seeds will sprout into streams of unspeakable joy that only our hearts can feel. Experiencing heavenly joy is a promise that we all can claim. The responsibility is ours to approach Jesus daily with full confidence that He will hear us when we trust Him and shift our mindset on Him.

We need to choose to walk with Jesus by our own volition and He will be there for us. Jesus' character and nature is not one that disappoints but one that satisfies every soul is seeking Him. Walking with Jesus will always assure us the grace, peace, joy, and happiness. This walk with Him is the antidote to Satan's tricks and schemes.

The Instigator of Brokenness

Satan is the originator and instigator of all evil in this world. However, I am glad that I serve a God who is powerful, omnipotent, and who, had He wanted to, would have obliterated the devil in seconds. The devil is the enemy of our souls, and his desire is to destroy us at any time. But the devil is no match for Jesus. In His wisdom, Jesus has kept this enemy of our souls on a leash until his time for final obliteration comes. Yet, this same devil was at one time one of the gifted angels in heaven. In the beginning Satan was one of God's closest angels, but pride found a place in his heart. It took root, rendering him a dangerous and cancerous agent in heaven. He was no longer welcome in heaven and God, in His wisdom, deemed it fit to cast him out of heaven. The devil had fallen from his lofty place of abode in heaven and to affirm his exit from heaven Jesus made the following proclamation, "how you are fallen from heaven, O shining star, son of the morning! You have been thrown down to the earth, you who destroyed the nations of the world" (Isaiah 14:12, New International Version–Emphasis supplied). He, who once enjoyed the status of a morning star, became a perpetual curse in heaven and to humanity. He, who once occupied a lofty place in heaven became the son of sin and originator of all of the evil this world has ever experienced.

Satan is the father of all lies and He has hoodwinked this world into believing that he is not the source of evil and of all calamities, upheavals, moral decay, and social vices. He tries to mask himself using all kinds of tricks. However, no matter how much he tries, the truth is that he is the father of lies, he is the "…enemy, the devil," and he "prowls around like a roaring lion looking for someone to devour" (I Peter 5:8, New International Version–Emphasis supplied). He is the "thief" that "comes only to steal, kill and destroy" (John 10:10, New International Version–Emphasis supplied). He is the manipulator who is always attacking families and confusing young people, trapping them in all types of social malaise.

When I was growing up, I was taught that lying was ethically wrong, and every time I lied my parents would punish me. I can vividly remember times when I lied, and how lying was slowly taking root in my heart because I tolerated it. One day as a young boys I was sent to the store to buy some groceries, I was strictly asked to bring back the actual change. However, I bought fewer groceries so I could keep some change. In the end I was caught even after trying to cover this with some lying.

The enemy of our souls is a sophisticated liar, but the good news is that his lies have been exposed and debunked by Jesus. As a young person I often heard of stories told by my grandparents of lions and of how they were fearless creatures that carried themselves majestically. Lions are powerful animals that usually hunt in coordinated groups and stalk their chosen prey aggressively. Their prey consists mainly of large mammals, and they prefer wildebeest, zebras, buffalo, and warthogs in Africa. Many other species they hunt are hunted on availability. Just as the lion is dangerous and often kills its prey, so is the devil. Without Jesus on our side, we cannot stand this foe. He uses schemes, plots, and shrewd plans to attack his targets.

Like a robber planning to rob a bank, he is cunning and takes time to study our behaviors, our eating habits, our most cherished hobbies, our friends, our workplaces, and almost anything that he can exploit to harass and launch an assault on us. The only caveat is that he cannot do these things unless we give room to his advances, and the good news is that whatever the devil does he cannot compete with Jesus.

Just like lions in the jungles of Africa can only pick on prey that makes itself available to them, in the same vein the devil will only attack us if we make ourselves available to him. We should not place ourselves in vulnerable situations where we easily become his targets. He loves to lure his victims into making unwise decisions when they are defenseless. We should flee any insinuations of the devil's tricks, and we should by all means resist any signs of his ideas when they pop up in our minds.

If, by God's grace, we discern his ideas or evil plans unfolding externally or internally in our minds, we should take off immediately and run to the Master, Jesus. We should not linger and play with sin as did Eve in the Garden of Eden (Genesis 3:3, Paraphrased). She lingered with the devil and was caught off guard. We should, instead, be like Joseph who ran away from Potiphars' wife as soon as he discerned what she was up to (Genesis 39:12, Paraphrased).

Satan is a thief and liar. Before moving to the United States, it was common to hear of house break-ins in my former neighborhood. The break-ins became so common that we in the neighborhood decided to form a neighborhood night watch committee in which we actively took turns conducting patrols during designated night hours. We were so vigilant in watching over our neighbors, and in the same manner we should become alert and vigilant in carefully watching and discerning the devil's tricks.

We should be careful not to engage in any behavior that might make us vulnerable and give us away to the devil. Our behaviors should demonstrate a life that is aligned with God's will, and in order for us to do this, we need to fully surrender to Jesus. We need to lay all our burdens at the feet of Jesus and allow Him to control our lives. We should give Jesus full control over every facet of our lives, through his Holy Spirit. His Holy Spirit will give us the power that we need to conquer the challenges that come our way each day. The Holy Spirit will help us to be aware and watchful of the devil, and He will help us to become sensitive to all plans and schemes that the enemy may devise against us.

When my friends and I were teenagers, we used to play soccer in our neighborhoods, and we had different teams that we would play against on different days. Some of these games I remember quite vividly. No matter how many times we played with this one team, we always beat them. This team was always a "defeated foe," at least in our eyes, because even they came to believe that all their games would end up in losses.

In Jesus we do not have to settle for loss, but we do have guarantee of perpetual victory over the devil, and this victory is assured to all those who will claim it in the name of Jesus. The devil has been conquered and his days are numbered, and this he knows very well. Jesus has the final say, total divine power and authority over everything in creation, and with Him on our side and with the Holy Spirit giving us the daily spiritual energy to face each day, the devil is truly a very defeated foe. The Holy Spirit is willing and ready to help and empower us in brokenness if and only when we begin to depend on Him daily. What is empowerment in brokenness?

Empowerment in Brokenness

The concept of empowerment has generally been used to refer to employee involvement initiative which occurred on a larger scale in the 1980s. This initiative focused on task-based involvement and attitudinal change (Wilkinson, 1998). Empowerment is a value orientation which allows social workers to work in the community. It is also a theoretical model for understanding the process and results of efforts to exert control and influence over decisions that may impact life, organizational functioning, and the quality of individual or community life (Zimmerman & Warschausky, 1998). Empowerment does not place the client to the professional level, nor does it let the expert take over the client and run the helping process. Rather, it emphasizes the client's participation and maintains a solid interaction between social workers and their clients. It also takes and treats the clients as individuals who have their own values, and who can set up goals of action for themselves. Thus, the goal of empowerment is to render clients free and strong against a host of challenges (Moreau, 2015).

Social workers can help in the empowerment of broken individuals seeking to live lives filled with hope. It is their responsibility to "raise voices for the voiceless" (Ahac, 2016, p. 25), as well as to empower the powerless. In the end this could lead to an overall blessing to humanity, just like Jesus was a blessing to everyone. As a concept empowerment is a construct shared by many disciplines and arenas including social work, community development, psychology, education, and economics, among others. In recent empowerment literature, the meaning of the term empowerment is often assumed rather than explained or defined (Rappoport (1984). Rappoport (1984) has noted that it is easy to define empowerment as an abstract concept but it is difficult to define in terms of action as it takes on different forms in different people and contexts. As such social workers can use empowerment in their practice to bring hope and purpose to different people broken and impacted by storms of life.

By utilizing the skills of empowerment theory professional social workers can begin to empower individuals, young people, and communities they work with by enhancing the strengths and gifts they possess (Garland & Yancey, 2014). Empowerment theory requires a solid integration of the micro and macro levels to make clear the interrelations among individual, community, and professional empowerment (Placido & Cecil, 2014).

Empowerment is a process of transition from a state of powerlessness to a state of relative control over one's life, destiny, and environment. This transition may manifest itself in an improvement in the perceived ability to control, as well as in an improvement in the actual ability to control. Disempowering social processes are responsible for creating a sense of powerlessness among people, especially those who belong to groups that suffer from stigma and discrimination. A sense of powerlessness leads to a lack of self-worth, to self-blame, to indifference towards and alienation from the environment. This involves an inability to act for oneself as well as a growing dependence on social services and specialists for the solution of problems in one's life. Empowerment is a transition from this passive situation to a more active situation of control. The need for it is part of the realization of one's very humanity, so much so that one could say that a person who is powerless regarding his life and his environment is not realizing his innate human potential (Saleebey, 1992). Since the sources of powerlessness are rooted in social processes that disempower entire populations, the empowerment process aims to influence the oppressed human agency and the social structure within the limitations and possibilities in which this human agency exists.

The empowerment process results in a synergy that encourages the preservation and reproduction of those outcomes that enhance people's lives. As the empowerment process progresses the empowering professional social work practice is reinforced, and from the outcomes of the process and from the process itself it receives proofs of its effectiveness (Katz, 1984). The end product of empowerment leads to an increased degree of autonomy, choice and self-determination. Social workers, Christian and non-Christian, can use empowerment to help broken people and communities in preparing them to fight and face the storms of life. Some of the storms are created by the devil but they can be overcome. With empowerment individuals will be enabled to represent their own interests in a responsible and self-determined way, acting on their own authority. With empowerment they can be enabled to overcome their sense of brokenness, powerlessness, and lack of influence, and to eventually recognize their resources and chances.

Discussion Questions

1. What do you understand by the concept of empowerment?
2. In what ways can social workers use empowerment to work with individuals going through storms?
3. What should be the role and responsibility of social workers in working with families impacted by life challenges?

Exercise

1. You are interested in providing support to a community facing different types of challenges. What might be your first steps?
2. Visit a local social work agency. What types of facilities are available that might empower people?
3. Exercise and recreation are important for optimal health. How might you use these as empowerment tools to uplift the living standards of people facing challenges?

Reflection

*   In what ways has the devil played tricks, plotted, and developed schemes against you?
*   How might you learn to depend on Jesus everyday as you face the attacks of the devil?
*   Think about your walk with Jesus. What might you do to make this walk deeper and richer?
*   What areas in your life are preventing you from enjoying a closer and intimate walk with Jesus?

References

Garland, D.R., & Yancey, G.I. (2014). Congregational social work. North American Association of Christians in Social Work: Botsford, CT.

Katz, R. (1984). Empowerment and synergy: expanding the community's healing resources. Prevention in Human Services, 3 (2-3), 201-30.

Moreau, M.J. (2015). Empowerment through Advocacy and Consciousness-Raising: Implications of a Structural Approach to Social Work. *The Journal of Sociology & Social Welfare, 17* (2).

Rappaport, J. (1984). Studies in empowerment: Introduction to the issue. *Prevention in Human Services, 3*, 1–7.

Saleebey, D. (ed.) (1992d). *The strengths perspective in social work practice*, New York: Longman.

Wilkinson, A. (1998). Empowerment: theory and practice. *Personnel Review, 27* (1), 40-56.

Zimmerman, M. A., & Warschausky, S. (1998). Empowerment theory for rehabilitation research:

Conceptual and methodological issues. *Rehabilitation Psychology, 43 (1)*, 3–16.

CHAPTER 17

The Holy Spirit in Brokenness

When Jesus was on earth, He promised that when He went back to heaven, He would send the Holy Spirit. In His words He said, "I will pray to the Father, and He shall give you another Comforter, that He may abide with you forever" (John 14:16, New International Version–Emphasis supplied). The Holy Spirit plays an important role in our walk with Jesus. He has a comforting presence and personality and has important functions and responsibilities that He performs daily for us. He performs for us a plethora of things by His power. For example, it is the Holy Spirit who gives us strength to overcome brokenness and other life challenges; it is the Holy Spirit who guides us in the right path of this life journey; it is the Holy Spirit who gives us thoughts to think and words to speak, how and where to speak to them when faced with perplexing situations. It is the Holy Spirit who comforts us in times of brokenness, sorrow, and grief. He does these things in His wisdom, and because we cannot see Him, the manifestations of His doings in our lives are the evidence of His work.

The Holy Spirit cannot be seen physically, but His reality is as real as life itself. Similarly, the Bible likens the Holy Spirit to wind. The Holy Spirit is like "the wind that blows wherever it pleases. You hear its sound, but you cannot tell where it comes from or where it is going..." (John 3:8, New International Version–Emphasis supplied). One of the things I enjoy doing when relaxing at home and particularly during early spring is sitting on my balcony. During these days I enjoy the friendly sunshine and breeze. Although I do not see the wind, I feel its gentle touch blowing over me and I immediately know the direction its blowing in.

The Holy Spirit operates in a similar manner. We cannot see Him but if we open our hearts to Him, He will come in, blow over us and take control of our lives. He will manage every part and facet of our bodies. As we can see the physical results of wind, we will also see the results of the Holy Spirit's presence in our lives. Other people will confirm His presence in our lives when they see the manifestations and evidence of His presence. He will be our counselor, our comforter, our guide, our leader, our strength, our friend, our energy, our helper, our peace, our happiness, and He will be everything to us when broken and when faced with perplexing storms.

The Holy Spirit also helps us in shifting our mindset from self to Jesus. Doing this on our own is very difficult because we live in a society that promotes self and self-satisfaction above everything. The philosophy of this society is driven by emphasis on self. We often hear people of all persuasions allude to this by affirming and encouraging others saying, "you can do it," "you can do whatever you set your eyes on," "you can be whatever you want to be." These messages are not only fallacy and deception, but they leave false impressions on people's minds. These are messages that lure people into believing that they can do anything by themselves and are masters of their own destiny. This thinking is very dangerous and antithetical to the word of God. Contrary to this societal belief, the word of God promises that we can only do "…all things through Christ which strengthens me" [Philippians 4:13 New International Version].

If we are not fully anchored in Jesus, we can become vulnerable to attacks from the enemy. Suffice it to say that we are all vulnerable to manipulative and persuasive messages of self-sufficiency and of I can do it by myself. These often end up hoodwinking us into believing that we are our own gods. These messages are deceptive and secular in nature, and unless we are grounded in the Holy Spirit, they can move us farther away from Jesus and from His will for our lives. These messages are a type of storm and sometimes the devil can use them against us, particularly into believing that we can do all things by ourselves, and when this takes root in our hearts we get trapped in a false sense of sufficiency and self-dependency. That is what the devil wants. The devil uses all types of tricks and plots, but we need not fear him because with Jesus on our side the battle has already been won.

During the period immediately following my son's death, the devil launched a barrage of similar attacks. We planned to bury my son back in my home country and, when we started making arrangements to have the body flown back home, we encountered all kinds of attacks from the devil. These attacks included unexplained delays in getting the documentation that was needed to have the body flown out of the U.S., to getting delayed at Hartsfield airport to an extent where we missed our flight from Hartsfield to Dulles airport in Washington, DC. We were scheduled to fly to Africa from Dulles airport, and having missed our flight from Hartsfield, any further delay would have meant missing our African bound flight.

Had this happened, it would have been victory for the devil, because my son's casket would have been flown to Africa unaccompanied. God is good and in all these delay attacks from the enemy the Holy Spirit was at work. He led and directed us and opened opportunities that made it possible for us to jump on the next flight from Hartsfield, the flight had exactly three seats that we needed. I must testify that during this ordeal at Hartsfield, my mind was constantly lifted in prayer to Jesus and I asked Him to allow the Holy Spirit to manifest himself fully by directly intervening in this situation.

The Holy Spirit did intervene, and I was able to see this vividly through the warm and positive actions that the officers at Hartsfield airport accorded us. The officers, after finding out our predicament, resolved to assist us as soon as they understood our situation and the reasons for our travelling to Africa. The Holy Spirit is itching, eager, and waiting to be called upon by God's children anytime and anywhere. He is ready to counsel and comfort those who are in any troubling storm of life. He is ready to provide opportunities where the situation seems impossible. He is the standard that can face, on our behalf, any attacks of whatever scope, gravity and magnitude from the devil. It is only He who can provide us with the kind of counsel and comfort in brokenness and storms that no other person can provide. It is only He who can pour into our hearts the kind of heavenly peace that is able to soothe our souls completely. His counsel is free and incomparable to any earthly counsel.

This counsel can be obtained when we genuinely ask for it. When we fully embrace Him and allow Him to lead us, the Holy Spirit can help us to grow in our spiritual journey. It is only He who can bring sanity to our lives, and it is only He who can give us the strength to live lives each day that are worthy of God's calling. The Holy Spirit can help us to benefit from the providential trajectories that God sets in motion when we are broken and in storms.

For example, when broken, the Holy Spirit can move us from the valley to the mountain top in ways that only He knows. My son's death has further opened me up to the realities of the Holy Spirit's work in the life of a child of God. I have felt Him provide the kind of comfort that I had strongly longed for, and I have also seen Him provide this comfort consistently to struggling and suffering family and friends. The Holy Spirit works in concert with Jesus, and we should know that Jesus wants the best for us. As His followers and children, we are at a vantage point of claiming His blessings every day.

The devil does not want us to enjoy the best of the Holy Spirit including blessings that Jesus wants to bestow upon us. But this can be reversed by our intentional actions. The onus is on us to want and to expect these blessings. These may include health, happiness, peace, patience, and joy. Just like Jesus, the Holy Spirit can help us to reclaim our missed blessings from God, and He can help us regain other losses that we might have incurred. God reaffirms this when He assures us that "I will repay you for the years the locusts have eaten the great locust and the young locust, the other locusts and the locust swarm my great army that I sent among you" (Joel 2:25, New International Version–Emphasis supplied).

The Holy Spirit gives us the privilege of experiencing Jesus daily, and this is the same Jesus who once walked on earth and did so many miracles, signs, and wonders. He is the same yesterday, today, and forever and He is ready and willing to walk with us through the presence of the Holy Spirit. Through the Holy Spirit, Jesus will provide the appropriate healing to our hurting souls. He will provide the needed comfort to our broken and hurtful hearts, and He will provide us with the necessary spiritual growth in all trials and brokenness that He allows to come our way.

I have learned and I am still learning how important it is to allow the Holy Spirit to guide my life. Like everyone else, sometimes I have made mistakes and erred in ways that have not been pleasing to the Holy Spirit. However, by God's grace, I have learned that Jesus is interested in us even when we err or when we are broken or when we fall in our storms. Our salvation is determined by God's grace, and it is not affected by no matter how many mistakes we make or sins we commit. He sends His Holy Spirit to lift us up and to set us up on the right path He has intended for us. He wants to bless us in ways that we cannot fathom, even as Paul testifies when he says, "Now to him who is able to do immeasurably more than all we ask or imagine, according to his power that is at work within us" (Ephesians 3:20, New International Version–Emphasis supplied). If we candidly pray daily, asking Jesus to give us the Holy Spirit, He will answer our prayers, and when the Holy Spirit has come upon us, He will begin the work of shaping and molding our characters.

In my own walk and experiences with Jesus, I have recognized the influence of the Holy Spirit demonstrated and manifested in my life in several ways. Close examination of these experiences has revealed several areas in which the Holy Spirit works, and which areas might work for those brothers and sisters who are struggling with brokenness, storms and life challenges. These areas include the following: (a) I have found that the Holy Spirit will make the presence of God real in one's life during those moments when we are broken or confronted with storms. (b) The Holy Spirit will bring to our remembrance the relevant scriptures that can act as buffers against the schemes, plans, and tricks of the enemy of our souls. (c) The Holy Spirit will reveal to us mysteries and the meaning behind the most perplexing and confusing storms and challenges of life.

There are many other areas in which the Holy Spirit might manifest Himself, depending on individual circumstances and the type of brokenness or the kinds of storms being faced. The areas I have mentioned above are the ones that the Holy Spirit has deemed appropriate to use in my situations, and it is possible He might decide to use the same areas with other individuals facing similar storms. A deeper discussion of the areas mentioned above is provided below:

a) *Holy Spirit will make the presence of God real during those moments when we are confronted with storms and challenges.*

The presence of God is the safest and most ideal place that one can be during brokenness. David attests to this truth when he reminds us that in the presence of God we will be filled with the fullness of joy, as well as enjoy Gods pleasures at His right hand (Psalm 16:11, Paraphrased). God's presence is indescribable and can only be experienced individually. His presence is a place where the heart is at the most peace; it is a place where true pure heavenly joy and peace permeates every fiber of our bodies. It is a place where all worries are arrayed, erased, and replaced by an existential sublime sense of freedom and serenity. These experiences have happened to me when I have least expected them, and sometimes these experiences have taken place when I am alone taking a brisk walk, or perhaps enjoying a quite contemplative quite moment.

b) *He will bring to our remembrance the relevant scriptures that can act as buffers against the schemes, plans, and tricks of the enemy of our souls.*

The word of God is powerful, living, and can work in our lives when we claim it. However, it cannot work unless we read it daily, study and digest it, memorize, and apply it in our lives. The word of God ought to become an essential part of our lives. Jesus testified to this when He said, "man shall not live by bread alone but by every word that comes from the mouth of God" (Mathew 4:4, New International Version–Emphasis supplied). In biblical days God spoke by His word, and whatever He proclaimed by His word came to pass because there is power in His word. The world, including all that is in it, was created by the word of God. The word of God, as found in the Bible, has the same purpose, effect, and power today as in the beginning because God changes not. The word of God can act as buffer against all wiles, tricks, plans, and schemes of the enemy. It can turn dangerous and negative situations into positives.

It can revitalize, it can re-energize, it can refocus, it can realign, it can reposition, it can relocate, and it can reaffirm us in more ways than not. Further, the Holy Spirit will bring to our remembrance the exact words that we need at the right time to come against the assaults from the enemy. He will bring to our remembrance those words that will help us when we are feeling low and down. He will bring to our remembrance those words that will lift us and elevate us spiritually. For the past couple of years, I have purposely read the word every day, studying, memorizing it, and meditating on it and applying it. I have noticed that the Holy Spirit brings up relevant scriptures in my mind when needed, and I have used these scriptures to fend off attacks from the enemy.

c) *He will comfort us when faced with the most perplexing and confusing of storms and challenges.*

It is not easy to fathom the brokenness, storms, and challenges that God allows to come our way, let alone appreciate them. We often ask the "why" questions and wonder whether God is with us or against us during these times. However, we can take comfort in the fact that the Holy Spirit reassures us that God is indeed with us and that He is orchestrating everything. He reassures us that God is directing and keeping control of all the storms and challenges that come our way.

When my son died, I was broken, and a lot of confusing thoughts and questions raced through my mind. Were it not for the Holy Spirit reassuring me that God was present and in control of the situation and circumstances that led to my son's demise, I do not know how I would have survived this trial. I thank God for the Holy Spirit who, time and again, accorded me with the deepest joy, comfort, and stability during those moments. While this was happening, the Holy Spirit was at the same time realigning me with the presence of God in a special way.

He brought a heavenly sense of reassurance that all would be well with me for as long as I continued to walk closely with Jesus. He reminded me that God was able to bless me and that He would set me up on a platform of recovery from my loss. He assured me that storms were not the end, but rather the means to God's end. He further reassured me that God always wins.

Growing and Gaining in Brokenness

God's blessings come in many ways and fashion. God intends that each one of us experience His blessings daily. He is the source of all blessings that He wants to bestow upon His children who trust Him. His nature is good always, and all His actions are driven by the principle of love and goodness. He is good all the time to His children, and He wants to touch every area of our lives. When God created Adam and Eve and placed them in the Garden of Eden, He promised them many blessings for as long as they continued to be obedient to Him in all areas of their lives. They enjoyed a deep sense of peace that culminated from God's presence, and they did not experience any storms only until after sinning. They sinned because they did not obey God. Disobedience leads to punishment.

The consequence of their disobedience was banishment from the Garden of Eden. However, before they sinned God had already prepared a plan for redemption, which resulted in the blessed birth of Jesus Christ. As discussed earlier, sometimes blessings emerge out of storms. When God allows storms to come in our lives, sometimes the blessings are embedded within the very storms or brokenness. God realigns the blessings for us in a way that they have a positive impact on our lives. Understanding this when we are going through storms or when we are broken is not easy, and our only remedy during these times is to trust God. God is all-knowing and even if it may appear that we don't know what is going on in our lives, we need not worry because He is in control. His "thoughts are not our thoughts, nor are our ways His ways and as the heavens are higher than the earth, so are His ways higher than our ways and His thoughts higher than our thoughts and higher than the heavens" (Isaiah 55:8–New International Version–Emphasis supplied).

It is not unusual to discover that in some cases God's blessings are given to us in the most unexpected and most perplexing of ways. When I look back at my own life and reflect on how God has blessed me, I am bewildered by the different types of blessings He has graciously poured on me. I must be quick to point out that I have been undeserving of some of the blessings God has given me, but only for His grace. The extent and scope of some of these blessings has been amazing. For example, when I was in Richmond doing my graduate studies, God blessed me with different opportunities to work on several school related projects. These projects paid all my tuition and fees to an extent that I did not have to spend one cent for my graduate education.

There are different types of blessings that God gives to His children, and only He decide the type or types and extent of blessings befitting of everyone of His children. Some are conditional while others are not. In its report on blessings, the *School of Kingdom Economy* (2013) has highlighted the many blessings that God gives His children. The report identifies the different ways in which blessings come, as well as points out the timing, forms, methods, and quantities of blessings God gives. The report further points out that some of the blessings from God include physical healing: "…I will heal my people and will let them enjoy abundant peace and security" (Jeremiah 33:6, New International Version–Emphasis supplied). God's blessings also include good health: "I will sprinkle clean water–good health–on you, and you will be clean." They include spiritual fortitude: "I will cleanse you from all your impurities and from all your idols" (Ezekiel 36:25, New

International Version–Emphasis supplied). They include a promise of the spirit of prophecy: "I will pour out my Spirit–spiritual blessings–on all people, you sons and daughters will prophesy, your old men will dream dreams, your young men will see visions" (Joel 2:28, New International Version–Emphasis supplied).

Similarly, Dr. Charles Stanley (2013) of the In-Touch Ministries has identified the following as some of the blessings that God bestows upon His children: peace, joy, contentment, spiritual growth, and the eternal blessing of eternal life.

A close scrutiny of these blessings reveals that God's blessings can be placed into two categories: namely, spiritual and material. Spiritual blessings are those that impact us internally and they include peace, joy, happiness, emotional stability, and calmness. Material blessings are external and these might include things like finances, financial stability, good health, a good family, a good job, and maybe a good house in a very good neighborhood.

As I said earlier, God gives these blessings only as He sees fit and to whomever He sees worthy of receiving them. It is important to note that the absence of either of these two types of blessings is not an indicator that one is out of favor with God, or that one's life is full of sin, or that one is engaging in practices that are contrary to the word of God and therefore not worthy of God's blessings.

For example, Jesus did not possess any material blessings when He was on earth, although He was God and had every absolute right to every blessing on this earth. In addition, He is the creator who made everything. Though He lacked material earthly blessings, He was fully spiritually blessed to the extent that His spiritual blessings spilled over to those who came into contact with Him. His blessings were given to those who had the full expectation of being blessed. Paul is another example of a person who was not blessed materially, but yet was powerfully blessed spiritually.

The word of God does present many useful and appropriate narratives and accounts of individuals who were both spiritually and materially blessed, these include Job, David, King Solomon, and many others. I am happy to note that today God is still in the blessing business. However, and, as said earlier, God always reserves the jurisdiction of deciding if, when, and what type of blessings He wants us to receive. He determines our wants, assesses our needs, and decides the best type of blessings for us.

I thank God for how He has blessed me despite the most severe trial of losing my son in April, 2012. He is still God and He is in control of our futures. He knows what is best for us, He knows the end from the beginning and therefore we can rest assured that in all things "God works for the good of those who love him, who have been called according to his purpose (Romans 8:28, New International Version–Emphasis supplied). Even in the most severe of trials, God will bring out blessings that otherwise we would not have received.

If we remain connected and committed to God during brokenness and storms, He will bless us. The bigger the storms or the brokenness we face, the bigger the blessings we can expect from the Almighty God. Blessings are conditional and this might entail that we pray harder, read and study the word daily, and fervently remain in God's will. If we do not read and study God's word, and if we neglect to walk according to the precepts of His word, then He will not bless us. We will not be a blessed people if we fail to live by God's instructions. God intends the best for us, He intends the best blessings and plans for us as highlighted in Jeremiah 29:11, New International Version. "For I know the plans I have for you," says the Lord, "plans to prosper you and not to harm you, plans to give you hope and a future."

If we consciously decide to walk daily in accordance with God's written word, we will be blessed in ways beyond our understanding. God will bless people individually because each person has a different pathway that God has created for them. Some of us will experience blessings triggered by loss, for example through death of a loved one, maybe through loss of employment, or maybe through losing a house in an inferno or from destruction brought about by a devastating hurricane.

Whatever the situation might be, please take heart to know that in all the negative and unpleasant brokenness that God allows, the brokenness might just be another pointer to the eternal blessings He has in store for you. It might be a revelation that in Jesus we have the victory, and that eternal life is fully guaranteed to us. What more can one ask than to wish for the eternal blessings that God has in store for us, and which blessings will usher us into that great and glorious reunion.

Service to the Broken

The Holy Spirit plays a crucial role in the salvation of men and women. His role exemplifies the importance of service. Service is one of the core values of the social work profession. Every social worker should understand service and embrace it through his or her professional path. The late boxer, Mohammed Ali once said that service is the rent we pay here on earth as we prepare for heaven (paraphrased). According to Simmons, Leticia, Vivian, and Takahashi (2008) a social worker's primary goal is to help people in need and to address social problems. Social workers elevate service to others above self-interest and draw on their knowledge, values, and skills to help broken people in need and to address social problems.

The following (http://www.nadadventist.org/) seven principles could be helpful in enabling social workers to effectively provide services to individuals affected by brokenness and other life's storms:

1. Inform individuals affected by brokenness, challenges and the negative effects of storms and offer a hopeful vision. This assures them that their problems are known, that others also experience them and that there is a way out.

2. Work with small groups, especially with negatively impacted children. Gathering five or six youngsters to share their experience and to teach them healthy thoughts and behaviors. This has worked many times in different settings.

3. Provide as many of the following as possible: educational opportunities; presence of family members; a job; cultural identity and traditions; sports and other physical activities; and access to medical and mental health care. Research data has shown that all these contribute to healing and recovery.

4. Facilitate religious shared experiences as this opens opportunities for active individuals to befriend, pray for and even share God's promises.

5. Provide opportunities for creative arts as a form of therapy. Talking, which is a primary avenue for emotional healing, is not always possible because of inhibition and language and culture barriers. Music, painting, or clay shaping can facilitate the avenue for victims to disclose and process their brokenness, storms, or challenges.

6. Where possible equip impacted individuals, families, or communities with self-strategies. This can be ably achieved by both social workers and other mental health professionals such as psychologists and counselors. But when such professionals are not available, there may be astute and good-hearted persons, who can share practical skills and even adaptive behavioral and mental styles that might help broken and storm impacted individuals face their challenges.

Christian social workers can be guided by the Holy Spirit in any practice setting in response to the needs of broken individuals they are working with (Canda, Furman & Canda, 2019). Their role and influence are especially useful as it may lead to improved physical and mental well-being of people facing various storms of life (Rinkel, Larsen, Harrington & Chun, 2018; Idler & Kasl, 1992). For example, their work can help individuals struggling with various challenges to experience decreased depression, increased social support, and increased cognitive functioning (Martin, 2016). They can also become more astute and better prepared to cope with other problems such as substance abuse problems (Fallot & Heckman, 2005).

Both Christian and non-Christian Social workers can work and provide services as therapists, case managers, social justice advocates, policy experts, as well as experts on a range of social problems. As they work in these capacities, they can help brokenness in all dimensions of the client's life (Martin, 2016). For those social workers providing services in employment assistance, they must be aware of economic patterns at the micro and macro levels. They also need to know the impact of globalization on domestic employment as this knowledge might be helpful for those individuals seeking employment (Austin, 2005). As for those social workers working with broken vulnerable children, they need to be aware of different types of theories such as child development theory, child-and family–centered intervention strategies including domestic policy and legislation impacting child welfare on nation and local levels (Abrams, Theberge & Karan, 2005).

Martin (2016) further suggested that social workers keep up with current and ongoing advances in technology. This might include globalization of communication technologies as it could be useful particularly in replicating interventions that have worked effectively in other settings.

Discussion Questions

1. What are some ways you may provide appropriate services to individuals or families stricken by poverty?

2. How can social workers coordinate and network with other helping professionals in combating different types of client challenges?

3. Do you believe religious experiences can bring healing and hope to individuals facing challenges? If so explain how.

Exercise

1. Find any local office of a faith-based or public agency and identify yourself as a student. Spend some time in the agency and take note of how many people are there. Talk to a worker in the agency and collect any information on the programs they have. How effective are these programs and what type of clients do they cover?

Reflection

• What type of blessings have had a big impact on your life?

• Identify any losses that you might have had and think about how God restored your losses and your mental wellbeing. Whether your losses have been restored or not what has been your perception of God in all this?

• In what ways have you witnessed the Holy Spirit work in your life, and how has this strengthened your faith in Jesus?

• Recall any specific times in your life when you have called upon Jesus and the Holy Spirit to come to your aid. What has been the response to your prayers, and how has the response influenced your faith in Jesus?

References

Abrams, K., Theberge, S.K., & Karan, O.C. (2005). Children and adolescents who are depressed: An ecological approach. *Professional School Counseling, 8* (3), 24-292.

Austin, S. (2005). Community-building principles: Implications for professional development.

Child Welfare, 84 (2), 105-122.

Canda, E. R., Furman, L. D., & Canda, H. J. (2019). *Spiritual diversity in social work practice: The heart of helping.* Oxford University Press, USA.

Fallot, R.D., & Heckman, J.D. (2005). Religious/spiritual coping among women trauma survivors with mental illness. *Journal of Behavioral Health Services and Research, 32* (2), 215-226.

Idler, E.L., & Kasl, S. (1992). Religion, disability, depression and the timing of death. *American Journal of Sociology, 97,* 1052-1079.

Martin, M.E. (2016). *Introduction to social work through the eyes of practice settings.* Pearson. NY.

Rinkel, M., Larsen, K., Harrington, C., & Chun, C. (2018). Effects of social work practice on practitioners' spirituality. *Journal of Religion & Spirituality in Social Work: Social Thought, 37* (4), 331-350.

Simmons, Clara S., Leticia Diaz, Vivian Jackson, and Rita Takahashi. "NASW cultural competence indicators: A new tool for the social work profession." *Journal of Ethnic & Cultural Diversity in Social Work* 17, no. 1 (2008): 4-20.

CHAPTER 18

The Blessed Hope

The greatest blessing that I look forward to is the blessed hope and great reunion that will soon take place in heaven. The word of God has promised, without any trace of doubt, that resurrection of the dead will take place. The dead in Christ will be given the privilege of rising first and meeting Jesus Christ in the air when He comes. Those who are alive will join the resurrected in the air, and after that we shall be with the Lord forever (1 Thessalonians 4:14-17, New International Version-Paraphrased)... I am convinced that "Jesus died and rose again, even so God will bring with Him those who sleep in Jesus." (Vs 14). This promise keeps me burning with hope, desire, and great anticipation for that day when I will see my son, friends and other family members who have since gone. Above all, I will be able to see my redeemer Jesus Christ, our Savior who died for me and for all of us so that we spend eternity with Him.

Heaven is real and Jesus will come. Every year we see calamities unfolding in the world right before our own eyes. Natural disasters, epidemic outbreaks, political turmoil, rise of nationalism, extreme acts of violence against the innocent, uncertainty in the global market, general decay in the moral fabric of societies, and general lawlessness in some places of the world, are occurring at an intensity never seen before.

In 2013 a tragedy of unimaginable magnitude struck the Philippines when Typhoon Haiyan hit the mainland. Typhoon Haiyan was one of the most powerful storms ever to hit land and it tore through the Philippines with sustained winds of up to 320 km/h (199mph). Weather projections warned that 12 million people were at risk from Typhoon Haiyan. The death toll from one of the world's most powerful typhoons was staggering. Yet, this is not the only tragedy to have struck in recent years. Incidents of reckless shootings in schools and in various places have occurred simultaneously and are occurring at an alarming rate, thereby further tainting the world social climate.

In all this chaos we should not be taken by surprise, because Jesus did warn that in the last days many various types of calamities and negative events would occur. For example, Jesus did specifically point out that "when you hear of wars and rumors of wars, do not be alarmed. Such things must happen, but the end is still to come" (Mathew 13:7, New International Version–Emphasis supplied). Jesus also said that "in the same way, when you see all these things taking place, you can know that his return is very near, right at the door" (Mark 13:21, New International Version–Emphasis supplied).

As followers of and believers in Jesus Christ, we should not be discouraged by the current trend of world events. All these events are fulfilling Jesus' words; they are a sign that His coming is just around the corner. These events are reminding us that we need to be ready and look up to Jesus, our Savior, for He is coming again.

In these times of earth's closing history, our focus should not be on this earth or earthly things because this world has nothing of eternal value to offer. There is nothing in this world that can satisfy the deep longings of our hearts. There is nothing in this world that can satisfy the emotional vacuum that develops in us when faced with severe storms. There is nothing in this world that can heal our deep-rooted brokenness and pain, or that can fill our emotional emptiness or our loneliness; only Jesus the Master can. He is the creator God who made everything and everything is under His control, and He has determined that all events will only unfold according to His eternal plan. No event in this world will ever happen by chance or by any random act, but only according to God's will and plan. Nothing will take God by surprise. My brother and my sister, as you read this book praise God and give Him the honor and adoration due to Him, because He has allowed you and me to be witnesses of last day events.

As the last day events unfold before us in speedy succession, we should be reminded that eternity is coming and that we need to make every effort to focus on Jesus. Growing up as a child, I always waited in eager anticipation to see my dad return home after he had gone on business trips. My heart would beam with joy as I looked forward to hearing my father's voice as he entered our house. In the same manner we should ask Jesus to pour in our hearts the same kind of anticipation and zeal for His return. Let our prayer be to want to see the Master, and live daily lives that fully reflect our desire for His return. Jesus promised us the resurrection of the righteous dead, and He also promised that one day soon we will be with our loved ones in heaven.

In heaven, we will be with our families forever and ever, and Jesus "will wipe away every tear from their eyes; and there will no longer be any death; there will no longer be any mourning, or crying, or pain; the first things have passed away" (Revelation 21:4, New International Version–Emphasis supplied). Jesus is our only sure guarantee for eternity. His resurrection is the undeniable and irrevocable "verdict" that was made once and for all. We have eternity promised, and this will become a reality soon when Jesus returns. At that point we will be transformed into His likeness.

Therefore, as we await Jesus' return, we should live each day as though it were our last. We should ask Jesus to help us be ready and look forward to His return by living righteously, feeding on His grace and engaging and studying and applying His word. We should also be praying daily and if possible wherever we are. We should be asking God to send us His Holy Spirit, whom He promised to send after He went back to heaven. He told His disciples that "it is expedient for you that I go away; for if I go not away, the Comforter will not come unto you; but if I go, I will send him unto you" (John 16:7, New International Version).

The Comforter, who is the Holy Spirit, is always ready and willing to help us in our brokenness. Ina addition, He is there to help us in our grief, in our losses, in our disappointments, and in our failures. I have had a few disappointments in my life, and in all these the Holy Spirit has been my comforter, always reassuring me not to give up but to totally trust in Jesus. As the Holy Spirit comforts, us He will help and enable us to live one day at a time, and He will give us a new mindset and a renewed focus on life. He will help us to live this life as a preparatory phase for the next one. The next life is far more important than anything we can ever dream of or ever want in this world. The next life is worth every trial, grief, disappointment, challenge, illness, disease, brokenness, or failure that we may encounter in this life. Our preparedness for eternal life in this earthly life needs to be strengthened by the fact that heaven is as real as we are.

Heaven is real and tangible, and we will see and live in it one day soon. As I advance in my earthly years, my focus is shifting more and more toward heaven, and the death of my son deepened my desire for heaven. I thank God that our earthly life is not in vain and that there is purpose and meaning to life, a purpose that God is willing to give to each one who accepts Him.

Jesus is the meaning and purpose of life. We need to be anchored in Him because if we find Him, we find purpose and meaning of life. If we find Jesus and hold Him dear to our hearts, and if we make Him the center of everything we do, then the promise of resurrection and eternal life will become a reality that cannot be dimmed (Darling, 2019). Jesus will give us the hope, the joy, and peace we need as we travail this life's journey. We need to hold on to Him despite the storms that He allows our way. We need to let Him take the forefront seat of our lives and He will be there with and for us even to the end of time.

The Defeated Enemy

The subject of death brings fear and uncertainty in the minds of many people, and many people try to avoid any conversation or discussion that has to do with death. When I was a teenager there was a proverb that elders used often in their stories about death. The proverb says that *he who does not want to talk about death is Mr. or Mrs. fear.*

Today, people are doing all they can to defy the aging process, by doing so they hope to avoid death. The media sends out messages on how to stay young and shows images of the futile promises of longevity made possible by having a young body. Consequently, people get caught up in this frenzy just to stay and look young. They get addicted to all types of cosmetics and surgeries to stay young. The truth is that death will come whether we like it or not, and no matter what we do to avoid it, it will catch up with us. No amount of plastic surgery or cosmetics will prevent or hinder death from striking. The reality is that death is our unwelcome enemy, an uninvited foe lurking always by our side. It will come to all of us in one fashion or another. To some it may come through sickness or a car accident, and to others, it might be as sudden as a heart attack, or drowning, collapsing, or from just falling and dying. In whatever form it comes, it is death.

When God made Adam and Eve, He gave them clear-cut instructions regarding their life in the Garden of Eden. However, much to their chagrin, they disobeyed God and through their disobedience death found its first entry onto earth. Since then, death has become a constant and painful reminder that this life is but a shadow that is here today and gone tomorrow (Lofland, 2019).

At one time in my life, I did not fully understand death and when some family members died it did not really strike me as to what it meant to die. Not until later did I realize that we all must die one day unless the Lord comes before that happens. Death is an enemy we all must face (Lofland, 2019).

As my walk with Jesus has become intimate, my view of death has taken on a new meaning, one that is based on God's word. According to the World Fact Book and the World Almanac and Book of Facts, (2010), there are an estimated 146,357 deaths each day, with 6,098 people dying each hour. These numbers are real and frightening and yet they all suggest that one day we will be part of the death statistics. However, even if death is an unwelcome enemy, Jesus has provided the solution to this foe. It is important to realize that for every negative event God does have an antidote. Jesus came to earth and died and was resurrected, and through His resurrection, we can have the full assurance and confidence that death has been conquered. His resurrection is the heavenly antidote to death.

Jesus knew His mission on earth, and He knew that one day He would have to conquer death on our behalf. When He was with the disciples on earth, Jesus often referred to death as sleep. Yes, that is what it is. Death for a Christian is sleep from which we all look forward to awakening one day soon. When I return home from work after a day's work, the one thing I look forward to is having a good night's sleep from which I will awaken fresh, ready to go for another day. That is what death to a believer is, it is asleep from which he or she will awake in an invigorated state into glory. When Lazarus died, Jesus told His disciples that "our friend Lazarus has fallen asleep, but I am going there to awaken him" (John 11:11, New International Version–Emphasis supplied). In the same manner Jesus refers to His children who die as only sleeping and on that glorious day He will "awaken" (Vs11) all those who have died in His name.

We can learn useful lessons regarding how futile this life is from the seasons. They provide us with vivid lessons regarding death and life. Every time winter approaches, the trees begin to lose their leaves and flowers begin to fall. In the midst of full winter, trees are barely skeletons with most of their leaves dead, and the flowers and grass are also dead. However, when spring approaches, everything begins to come back to life. The dead leaves on the ground provide the nutrients necessary for the tree's life. As spring moves into full gear, the leaves on the trees grow back and flowers bud and display their most gorgeous colors and scents. In the same manner, death is a sign that life will come out of it [death]. It is a sign whose fruition results in the budding of beautiful jewels of resurrected bodies at the return of Jesus.

The Bible assures us that those who are sleeping in Jesus will have the honor of rising from their graves first, and they will meet the Lord in the air. The word of God further says, "for the Lord Himself will descend from heaven with a shout, with the voice of an archangel, and with the trumpet of God. And the dead in Christ will rise first. Then we who are alive and remain shall be caught up together with them in the clouds to meet the Lord in the air. And thus we shall always be with the Lord" (1 Thessalonians 4:14-17, New International Version–Emphasis supplied).

This is the good news that certainly places death in the right context, that it is not the end but rather a one stop over into eternity. Many years before Jesus set foot on earth, Daniel the Lord's servant had prophesized that "many of them that sleep in the dust of the earth shall awake, some to everlasting life, and some to shame and everlasting contempt " (Daniel 12:2–New International Version–Emphasis supplied). Death will be given a final blow when Paul's words "O death, where is thy sting? O grave, where is thy victory?" (I Corinthians 15:55, New International Version) are fulfilled. These are the words we hope to hear on that day when eternity becomes a reality.

If we take God's words seriously and consider that all His promises and words will come to pass, we need not fear death. Yes, it is painful to lose a loved one such as a son or daughter. I cannot imagine the emotional pain faced by those who have lost their sons and daughters, particularly when their loved ones were just at their tender ages. The pain from my son's death pierces my heart every day and I miss him so dearly. However, in the midst of the sorrow and, pain I am comforted by Jesus' words, and I rely on His solid and unwavering promise of one day soon overcoming death. Time and again the Holy Spirit reminds me of this promise and comforts me with the most reassuring of words, "blessed are those who mourn, for they will be comforted" (Matthew 5:4, New International Version–Emphasis supplied). We need not be discouraged by the reality of death. Rather, we need to be strengthened by the fact that death, as far as Jesus is concerned, is no longer an obstacle to glory for He has provided the way of escape.

Jesus is concerned with whether we will make choices that will allow Him to give us His righteousness and victory over death. He is concerned with whether we will get preoccupied with thinking about death rather than thinking about how He has overcome death on our behalf. He is eager and longing to see each one of us in heaven. He has sealed those of our loved ones who have gone before us to sleep, and He will present them to us as gorgeous jewels on that beautiful resurrection morning.

For a believer, death is a bittersweet experience that brings with it stings of pain and sorrow. However, it is sweet in that it is only a sleep from which a believer will awaken to glory. I cannot imagine on that resurrection morning when I see my son in his glorious body, and above all, when I see my Master Jesus and when I bow down and worship Him for all that He had accomplished on our behalf.

A Call for Well-being

Christian and non-Christian social workers have a crucial role to play in making sure that broken clients struggling with life storms are provided with the necessary support for well-being (Dunn, 2018). This is particularly important as we wait for the soon and second coming of Jesus Christ. In order for social workers to support clients who are broken they need to be competent in their practice. This calls for committed social work educators who have an ethical responsibility to assist practicing social workers and social work students in developing professional competence (Burwell, 2006; Seitz, 2014). This competence will make it possible for all social workers to work effectively with those individuals dealing with life challenges. Social work educators can use their understanding of faith and how it can be applied in improving the lives of clients or people facing various life challenges. Research shows that Christian social workers including students may not possess the sufficient competence to address these issues when in practice settings (Furman, Benson, & Canda, 2011).

The social work profession has increasingly recognized that helping practices may play an important in assisting clients coping with life's challenges and, who are working towards self-realization (Furman, Benson, & Canda, 2011). Faith and spirituality are significant bases of how people cope with crisis and oppression and how they access internal and environmental resources for resilience (Holloway & Moss, 2010). Spiritual well-being and a solid faith are useful precursors to positive physical and mental health including improved social relations (Kim & Hill, 2018). Christian social workers can use faith to ensure that their professional practice is compatible with the core social work values such as self-determinism and thereby opening more avenues for improved relationships and general well-being (Hodge, 2003; Hugen & Scales, 2008).

Sheridan (2009) has emphasized the need for social workers to become more competent through appropriate training so they might have a positive impact on people they work with. Similarly, Sherwood (2000) has highlighted that elements such as tolerance, pluralism, and integration of the Christian faith are crucial to social work practice. Hodge and Bushfield (2006) have pointed out that for social workers to work effectively with broken people dealing with life storms they need to pay attention to the following:

1. Self-examination of personal beliefs and biases

2. Development of empathy for and understanding of clients' worldviews; and

3. Relevant skills in creating and employing effective and appropriate practices.

Hodge and Bushfield (2006) further point out that:

> There is an increasing interest regarding spiritual matters among the public, and that this matter is also present amongst clients who desire that their spiritual values and beliefs be acknowledged and incorporated in the therapeutic relationship. (p178).

It is important that Christian social workers are competent to execute their work effectively. This is especially true because many people they will work will believe in God, in life after death, and in heaven and hell. Majority of them want to be saved and live eternally with Jesus in heaven. This means that knowledge about religious beliefs and practices, and skill in addressing those beliefs and practices, are necessary for all social workers, not just Christian social workers (Garland, 2011). Social workers have a moral responsibility toward broken people in crisis, and as discussed earlier, many of the people they might work with could be dealing with storms of life which almost always generate questions about meaning and purpose of human life (Garland, 2011). Every crisis generates questions, for example someone might ask: did we cause our own suffering? How can a loving God let my son die? How can I be depressed if I believe in a loving God?

Some social workers who might not know how to address crucial questions and struggles of faith in times of storms are not equipped to provide culturally competent practice for most broken people. This is whether the setting for practice is a congregation's counseling center or a public mental health center, a Christian nursing home or a public hospital (Garland, 2011). It is very important to know the situation of our clients including their beliefs about God and how they experience God intervening in the storms they might be going through. All social workers should get to know their broken clients, understand the storms they might be facing and be able to work with them in finding pragmatic solutions to their challenges (Keith-Lucas, 1985). As broken people come to realize that all their social workers love them, want to work with them, and that they want the best for them, they become empowered and their faith in God grows (Chikoto-Schultz, Manson, Amiri & Xiao, 2019). They may also live their lives with greater anticipation for heaven.

Discussion Question

1. What skills and values might be necessary for all social workers to work effectively with people facing storms?

2. Why is it crucial for social workers to self-examine their personal beliefs and biases?

3. What role might social work educators play in ensuring that all social workers make a positive impact on their clients?

Exercise

1. Find a nursing home in your area and spend time with a client who has been there for a long time. Build rapport with them and find out from them what storms or challenges they might be facing. What practical steps might you take to address their brokenness? If they are not ready to disclose their storms just spend a few days with them and then reflect on what it felt to spend time with them.

Reflection

- In what ways might you live one day at a time doing what is pleasing to God and walking moment by moment with Jesus?

- Think about loved ones in Christ you might have lost. Dwell on the fact that one day you will see them in heaven. What comes to mind as you dwell on this truth of seeing your loved ones again?

- Pray this week and ask God to help you make Him first in every area your life.

- Think of any areas in your life in which you might be spiritually lapsing and lagging behind and ask God to help you deal effectively with these areas as you prepare for His return.

References

Dunn, J. (2018). *Setting the people free: the story of democracy.* Princeton University Press.

Darling, M. A. (2019). *The God of intimacy and action: Reconnecting ancient spiritual practices, evangelism, and justice.* Fortress Press.

Furman, L.D., Benson, P.W., & Canda, E.R. (2011). Christian social worker's attitudes on he role of religion and spirituality in U.S. social work practice and education: 1997-2008. *Social Work & Christianity, 38* (2), 175-200.

Chikoto-Schultz, G., Manson, P., Amiri, M., & Xiao, Y. (2019). Non-Profit Sector Organizational Actions on Risk Reduction Practices, Policymaking Participation, Community and Social Contributions, and Recovery. In *Oxford Research Encyclopedia of Natural Hazard Science.*

Garland, D.R. (2011). Response to Mark's Chaves: Trends in congregational life challenges and leadership opportunities for Christians in social work. Social Work & Christianity, 38 (2), 133-138.

Hodge, D.R., & Bushfield, S. (2006). Developing spiritual competence in practice. *Journal of Ethnic & Cultural Diversity in Social Work, 15* (3), 101-127.

Hodge, D.R. (2003). *Spiritual assessment: Handbook for helping professions.* Botsford, CT: North American Associations of Christians in social work.

Holloway, M & Moss, B. (2010). *Spirituality in social work.* New York: Palgrave Macmillan. Hugen, B. & Scales, T.L. (Eds.) (2008). *Christianity and social work: Readings on the integration of Christian faith and social work practice.* Botsford, CT: NACSW.

Keith-Lucas, A. (1985). *So you want to be a social worker: A primer for the Christian student.* St. David's, PA: North American

Association of Christian Social Workers.

Kim, G. J. S., & Hill, G. (2018). *Healing Our Broken Humanity: Practices for Revitalizing the Church and Renewing the World.* InterVarsity Press.

Lofland, L. H. (2019). *The craft of dying: The modern face of death.* MIT Press.

Lifton, R. J. (2018). The Apocalyptic Face-Off: The Culture of Death after. *Death, bereavement, and mourning.*

Seitz, C.R. (2014). Utilizing a spiritual disciplines framework for faith integration in social work: A competency-based model. *Social Work & Christianity, 41* (4), 334-354.

Sheridan, M.J. (2009). Ethical issues in the use of spiritually based interventions in social work practice: What we are doing and why. *Journal of Religion and Spirituality in Social Work: Social Thought, 28* (1), 84-126.

Sherwood, D.A. (2000). Pluralism, tolerance, and respect for diversity: Engaging our deepest differences within the bond of civility. *Social Work & Christianity, 27* (1), 1-7.

CHAPTER 19

Spirituality in Brokenness

This chapter is based on content that was researched and written by a graduate student of mine, Jade Chapman. In it she shares very important concepts that are crucial to spiritual development and overall physical well-being. She highlights these concepts by drawing from real life examples that provide a solid contextualization of the chapter. She also discusses and highlights spirituality in the context of brokenness.

There are certain elements that are critical to spirituality and healing. These are particularly necessary when people are experiencing brokenness. This chapter delves into those elements and highlights how they could help broken people heal, recover, and grow from their brokenness.

At some point in time, we have all had a misconception regarding spirituality. For instance, prior to being baptized, I was under the impression that when we give ourselves to the Lord, all of our worries and challenges would be washed away, and we would be new people. From my perspective, only part of that thought is true. Spirituality truly is looking within ourselves. Spirituality is ultimately "a tool to find [our] internal source of joy, thus being able to externally spread that same joy, [allowing us to transform] negative experiences into positive" (Chapman, 2019 as cited by Vanderbilt University, 2013). This chapter highlights a personal spiritual journey in terms of the systems theory, specifically how it assesses the level of spirituality and how the environment affects spirituality. I will also discuss how spirituality correlates with social work. I will also discuss what my parents and other relatives taught me to believe in God, Spirits and other Divine Forces.

Parents, Relatives, Belief or Not Belief in God and Spirits

Religion is an "institutionalized (i.e., systematic) pattern of values, beliefs, symbols, behaviors, and experiences that are oriented toward spiritual concerns, shared by a community, and transmitted over time in traditions" (Canda & Furman, 2010, p. 59). I can vividly recall being a child and going to church every Sunday with my paternal grandma orchestrating the day's events. We would all wake up early Sunday morning to attend the 8:00 service. Subsequently, my dad, mom, aunt, and cousins would commune at my grandma's house for Sunday dinner. This was a ritual up until she passed away in 2009. I say that to say, specifically with my dad, I experienced the religious side of spirituality. I went to church, read my bible, attended Sunday school, and bible study on Wednesdays. My dad would and still stresses to me that without God we are nothing and have nothing. Whenever he feels distressed or uneasy, he always goes to his Bible and seeks God's word for better understanding and salvation. With my mom, however, she always described herself as being "spiritual but not religious" (Canda & Furman, 2010, p. 78). Even more, she did not "participate in a religious group, but [was] concerned about matters of meaning, purpose, and morality" (p. 78). She was raised in church with her grandparents, but as she got older, she grew apart from the church and embraced the spiritual side of religion. When it comes to matters of physiological (i.e., healing), sociological (i.e., looking for a job) or spiritual (i.e., matters of life or death), my mom would always tell me to look within myself and ask the Lord for guidance. She too goes to the Bible to seek God's word, but I recall her relying on spiritual prayer more so than organized religion for salvation and understanding. At this point, I will describe how the religious community I participated in has impacted me.

Spiritual Groups and Religious Community in Brokenness

I grew up in a Christian, specifically Baptist household based on the teachings of my grandma and dad. As I stated in the previous subheading, I would attend Sunday school followed by Sunday [church] service. On Wednesday evenings, I would go to bible study. I remember even attending church events such as Revival services, and church shut-ins, where the youth group would have an evening worship service and sleepover. However, after my grandma died (by this time I was turning 16), I found myself no longer attending church consistently as I had when I was much younger, and I started questioning my faith in God. I remember asking Him why He allowed the very people in my family who said they loved her, treat her so badly to the point she grew weary and sought rest in the Lord. I asked Him why He had not cured her of her long-term diabetes and why had He allowed her to get in such bad shape. I asked Him why He had not allowed her to stand up for herself against her daughter, who manipulated her to not move back to Alabama, as she had been wanting to do for a long time. I guess it is safe to say had my paternal grandma still been alive and in much better health, my faith and relationship with God would be different. As a young adult now, I find myself sometimes confused with where I stand with God. I still seek Him for answers for my questions, even though I was taught to not question God, but how else will we know if we do not ask? Even God Himself tells us to "Ask, and it shall be given you; seek, and ye shall find; knock, and it shall be opened unto you" (Matthew 7:7, King James Version). Biblical scriptures, such as the one previously referenced from Matthew 7:7, as well as stories and rituals have helped me better understand the nature of life and death.

Nature of Life and Death in Brokenness

Births and funerals are symbolic in terms of my explanation of life and death. Whenever a person, a thing, or a thought die, something else is born. For instance, I like to garden, so whenever winter passes over, and the weather breaks something died, in this case the weather, to make room for new foliage to be born. As hard as it is, that is how I had to start viewing beginnings and endings. Another example is when a relationship ends, or dies, a new one is sure to begin. Or when a snake sheds old skin, new skin is waiting right under the old.

Ever since one of my best friends passed away in 2017, I had made it a ritual to go to her gravesite whenever I go home to Chicago. Whenever I go to see her, I feel as if I have been presented with a refreshed mind and attitude; and I feel her spirit overcome me when I talk to her. There is not a day that goes by when I am not thinking about her. Some days are harder than others because there are times when I get stuck on the fact that her body died, but I must remember that each day I am alive her spirit is reborn in me. Every day is a brand new 24 hours I am blessed with to talk to her and ask her to continue watching over me.

Another story that reminds me of life and death is the movie, *The Ten Commandments*, that my parents and I would ritualistically watch the almost four-hour film every Easter. I remember the ending vividly in which the Lord inscribed the Ten Commandments onto the stone plank. I remember seeing Moses' evolution from a man who was adopted into Egyptian royalty, to a man who had learned of the life God destined for him. When I was younger, I had not fully understood the metaphors and symbolism of the film, but I feel since I am older, I have a much better understanding of why Moses had to go through what he went through to recognize not what man wanted of him, but what God wanted of him. In fact, there are times when God may want us to give to others and provide services to individuals or families who may be disadvantaged, such as those stricken by poverty, so that we may in a position to receive more blessings.

Relevant Services to Broken Individuals and Families

Compassion International, Inc. (2019) defines economic poverty as "an inability to meet basic needs because food, clean drinking water, proper sanitation, education, health care, and other social services are inaccessible; and further defines spiritual poverty as a lack of understanding of God's love, which results in difficulty to resist despair; thus leaving children vulnerable "to the emotional and spiritual messages of worthlessness and hopelessness poverty delivers." When impoverished citizens lack necessities needed to care for not only their families, but also themselves, this causes risk factors such as aggressive behavior due to being angry from not being able to afford food, clothing and other needs; impulsivity, which may stem from trying to quickly make ends meet (i.e. selling drugs, prostitution); risky behavior (i.e. using drugs to take pain away, sexual risks); teenage pregnancy (i.e. not receiving family planning aid, which includes birth control); anxiety (from not being able to provide for family); and mood disorders. With all this in mind, three ways in which I may provide appropriate services to individuals or families stricken by poverty are to increase peer and community support; encourage improvement of mental health care systems; and develop effective treatment plans.

Our neighbors and peers are our first methods of interaction in the community. These are the people we say good morning to as we leave our homes, whether on our way to work or school. These are the people who watch us grow from small children to adults that return to the neighborhoods that raised us. Sadly though, when personal challenges arise, these same neighbors and peers are the last people we reach out to, sometimes due to shame and fear of judgement. According to McKenzie and Harpham (2006), "most inner-city neighborhoods have relatively low levels of social organization, as exemplified by a lack of formal organizations, resource-poor social networks, low levels of responsibility for community issues, and minimal involvement in community organizations" (as cited by Anakwenze & Zuberi, 2013, p.54). These low levels of organization stem from a lack of comradery among families and individuals in the community; lack of formal organizations stem from the mezzo and macro levels of government including coalitions, interest groups and parties that fail to take into consideration the needs of the impoverished citizens; and minimal involvement in community organizations such as neighborhood watches and city hall meetings. To improve peer and community support, "social workers can and should play an important role advocating for and building coalitions to generate pressure and political will to create and implement community-based programs" (Anakwenze & Zuberi, 2013).

If no one else knows the ins and outs of a community, the citizens themselves know it and social workers should place themselves in a position where they are accessible to community members and strive to get the best evidence as far as what policies should be made, when they ask the people that those policies will concern the most (Adshead, 2014). Peer and community support can also be increased by using eco-maps as a part of intervention to maximize the strongest connections and relationships that impoverished citizens hold in the community and reach out to those connections as a part of treatment and assistance.

Equally important is to encourage the improvement of health care systems. Hernandez et. al. (2010) explains that economic security can affect the mental health of parents, causing anxiety, psychological distress, and depression (as cited by Anakwenze & Zuberi, 2013). When parents are stressed because of their inability to provide for their family, this causes children to become stressed and worried as well. They may think it is their fault, thus feeling the need to take on the responsibility of or being forced by their parents to work prematurely, when in fact they should be doing what kids do, which is playing and going to school to receive an education. Consequently, "poverty can cause stress and result in depression in children because stressful social environments affect the biology of the brain in ways that can become serious if left untreated" (Hernandez, Montana, and Clarke, 2010, as cited by Anakwenze & Zuberi, 2013). Unfortunately, poverty coupled with crime and unrest in impoverished environments results in imprisonment; when systems fail to take into consideration the emotional and mental distresses families, the degree of poverty is enhanced. "Social workers and policy makers must implement a comprehensive mental health care system that emphasizes prevention, reaches young people, crosses traditional health care provision boundaries, and involves the entire community" (Anakwenze & Zuberi, 2013, p.48). To further explain, we do not need more jails; we need more mental health facilities so that citizens can be provided the proper treatment needed to eradicate depression and lower anxious feelings.

Finally, by developing effective treatment plans, individuals and families stricken by poverty provides families and individuals with a sense of hope moving forward. Social workers can utilize the strength perspective and empowerment theory when working with families who have been impacted by life challenges, including poverty. Perhaps the father is good with his hands, so the social worker could seek employment or even educational opportunities such as welding, construction or HVAC to get the father on his feet and obtaining financial gains. By the same token, social workers do not have to work alone in efforts of assisting and providing services to the disadvantaged. Social workers can coordinate and network with other helping professions to eradicate challenges such as substance abuse and domestic violence.

Combating Brokenness

Three ways in which social workers can coordinate and network with other helping professionals in combatting different types of client challenges such as substance abuse and domestic violence are to work with small groups; provide opportunities of creative therapy; and "offer a hopeful vision" (Chama, 2017, p. 70).

Substance abuse often stems from the desire to escape personal challenges in a person's reality including poverty or illness; and domestic violence includes verbal, physical and/or emotional abuse by a person's significant other. The commonality between both is that they are often cyclic, meaning the abuser was once abused and they continue the cycle until the cycle of abuse has been broken by intervention and treatment. That said, group therapy can be beneficial for both social workers and clients who are combatting challenges such as substance abuse or domestic violence. When there is dysfunction within a unit, group therapy can be very valuable. Opposed to one-on-one sessions, where the counselor, therapist or social worker can only get one person's account at a time of what is going on within the unit and what issues are affecting him or her, group therapy is more likely to draw the stings of isolation, secrecy, and arrogance (which could be defense mechanisms) to the forefront. In group therapy the power has the advantage of "combined power" in which "the instrument of change is the group itself" and not who is running it (the counselor) or only one person (an individual).

Additionally, when people are suffering and enduring life's challenges, we cannot coerce, nor expect people to express openly and explicitly what they are feeling or to outright tell their story. So, this is where creative therapy can be highly beneficial. Depending on the art, it will not require talking and "music, painting, or clay shaping can facilitate the avenue for victims to disclose or process their storms or challenges" (Chama, 2017, p.58). Some of the best art I have seen and heard has come from those who have endured terrible pains. For example, when I was initially diagnosed with Crohn's disease, I found that being in a ceramics class helped combat my anxiety and depressive thoughts. It allowed me to speak through my art by creating some of my favorite things such as vases, flowerpots, and a ceramic version of green eggs and ham. "Talking, which is a primary avenue for emotional healing, is not always possible because of inhibition and language and culture barriers" (Chama, 2017, p. 70). With this in mind, we must find other outlets to allow people to cope with and overcome the challenges they may be facing, and sometimes those outlets are implicit.

By offering a hopeful vision in the mist of skepticism and inconsistencies that plague our society, social workers are assuring clients that "their problems are known, that others also experience them, and that there is a way out" (Chama, 2017, p. 70). Sometimes people do not want materialistic or monetary items to be shown that a person cares. Simply assuring a person who is facing personal trials can be priceless. One of the worst things to do to someone who is facing abuse is to dismiss them, judge their situation and fail to want to understand. None of us are perfect and we all have skeletons in our closets and times that have tested our faith in God. For this reason, by fully embracing religious experiences such as catching the Holy Ghost, crying, shouting, or praying (just to name a few), we can bring healing and hope to individuals facing challenges.

Bringing Healing to Broken Individuals

Religious experiences can bring healing and hope to those who are facing challenges. However, as social workers we must first be in sync with our own views and attitudes about spiritual practices and religious experiences and how we feel they can bring about healing and hope to those facing challenges. When dealing with challenges including being diagnosed with a chronic illness and losing loved ones, crying helped me purge all the unpleasant feelings I experienced during those times. Had I not cried or even shouted my frustrations, they would remain bottled up inside, which is counterproductive to confronting everyday challenges, especially those that are more intense like death or illness. Though I still find myself crying about the loss of my loved ones, it has brought me hope that life goes on. Even though I did not want them to go, and I would rather be anywhere but my gastroenterologist's office every six months, the fear that I once had to confront those intense feelings has been replaced with hope that should I experience future deaths, I will know how to face them. The next section will discuss various things that bring meaning and purpose to my life.

Meaning and Purpose of Life

I consider myself to be much more knowledgeable at this stage in my life. As such the things that matter to me have also become influenced by my experiences and the knowledge gained and appreciation for the little things that experience has taught me. Some of those things that I have come to appreciate and consider meaningful and purposeful are School, Journaling, and Arts/Crafts.

For one, school brings purpose to my life because it gives me structure and the ability to literally learn something new and scholarly every day. I did not want to go to college after graduating high school, mainly because of the exorbitant costs of enrollment, books and numerous other fees. However, I am thankful that my parents strongly encouraged me to go because school is a place where I feel like I belong. I do not feel like an outsider or an outcast.

In addition, Journaling also brings meaning and purpose to my life. As a person who battles with anxiety, I sometimes have a hard time opening to people and verbally expressing my thoughts. For one, I never know who to trust and have found myself venting to the "wrong" people. When I journal, I can talk to myself and reflect. " [Journaling] gives the opportunity to release pent-up negative emotions, keeps [people] in a more positive frame of mind, and helps them build a buffer between their negative thoughts and their sense of well-being" (Positive Psychology Program, 2018). I will say anxiety adds to my overthinking and presuming the worst, when a situation may not even be as big as I am making it out to be. That said, journaling has always served as a healthy outlet for me to express myself, aside from arts and crafts. During those times when I feel unheard and misunderstood, I know the lines and pages of my journal will be there to listen and absorb my limitless thoughts.

Lastly, using arts and crafts I am able to add meaning and purpose to my life through the unabated creative process that arts and crafts invokes from within. I make gift boxes, canvas boards, and frames just to name a few items. Some I have even given away for free to friends and loved ones. Whether I am painting or drawing, I have a sense of peace. Chama (2017) mentioned how "music, painting, or clay shaping can facilitate the avenue for victims to disclose and process their storms or challenges" (p. 70). I agree with this because during my senior year of undergraduate school, I was diagnosed with Crohn's disease that fall. For the fall semester, two of my classes were Art History I and Ceramics, which wound up being two of my favorite courses to date. I had the same professor from both classes which also made me like the class more because he was very vocal and outspoken, but cool and down-to earth at the same time. I had never taken a ceramics course or made any form of pottery prior to taking this course; nor had I been fully educated in art history, only what I learned from my dad and visiting museums. I passed both classes with as, but what I gained mentally is worth much more.

To conclude, while taking these courses I remember feeling drained physically and mentally. Flare-ups and mood swings plagued my body; but being able to listen to my music while working with clay and creating something from my imagination made my situation a little better. Thankfully, the professor left the ceramics room unlocked where students in the class could go to work on our projects outside of class hours; so, there would be times when I just wanted to get out of my room and work on my pottery. I made a flowerpot, green eggs and ham, and a snake in the shape of a flower pot. I learned the process of how pottery is fired; what happens if the clay is overly shaped or manipulated; and the patience required when creating something such as pottery. Likewise, I will discuss the things that help me feel more aware and centered.

Awareness and Centering in Brokenness

People have often complemented me on my sense of awareness and the appearance of a person that is always focused, and goal centered. I am very humble when it comes to complements but I am the first to acknowledge that I wasn't always keen on awareness and centricity. I have had the benefits over the years of being influenced by my experiences and the knowledge gained from some unconventional sources today. Some of those unconventional sources are the library, yoga, and meaningful conversations with homeless citizens that gave me information along with life lessons that college did not provide.

With the availability of the internet, social media via smart phones, the library which is still a vital resource often gets overlooked. For me, the library is a place where I feel more aware and centered in a sense that even when there are many things going on around me, I am still in my own world, free to read and discover what I am curious to know. Not to mention, according to Cannon (2016), visiting the library encourages reading and exploration. It also encourages responsibility because most books (that are not for sale) must be returned or renewed by a certain time or else fees accrue. Libraries bring awareness that we do not know everything, thus there is always some new information to discover.

In addition, practicing yoga also helps me feel more aware and centered. Prior to practicing yoga, I had known I wanted to try it, but I was unaware of the positive effects it would have on my mind and body. Yoga not only stretches and contorts my body into different forms; but also, it stretches my mind, forcing me to tune out the noises of everyday life and center my mind on my innermost thoughts and feelings. When I overthink, I am unable to maneuver my body in the necessary positions that even technique requires; but when I tune out my loud, negative thoughts and focus on the quiet, encouraging thoughts, I execute the technique and my body thanks me for it. It has also helped with my anxiety.

Since being diagnosed with anxiety, I have tried (and failed) to find ways to combat my overactive negative thoughts. Yoga has been Godsend. "Practicing in a group setting, such as a yoga class, stimulates the production of oxytocin, the love and bonding hormone," (McGrath, n.d., as cited by Myers, 2019, p.76). Yoga sessions are very encouraging because you see new and old faces alike; and even more the environment is very supportive and encouraging, which is beneficial for those like me who can be self-conscious or anxious.

In closing, seeing homeless people on the street brings awareness to me. As strange as that may sound, it's not strange at all. I have been volunteering since I was a young girl. Seeing homeless people has always made me even more appreciative of my life and put into context that my personal issues may not be as bad as I make them out to be sometimes.

We all have our trials and tribulations that we may face; but it all comes full circle when I see individuals and families alike holding up signs asking for food, gas money, or anything that can help. For example, there was one lady in particular who really put things into perspective for me. I would always see this lady either at the Office Depot by my house or Walmart, so I would always give her food or hygiene products.

One day I said I was going to stop and talk to her, that day came and so I did. I found out that she had been homeless for a while and sleeping in hotels 1) because her boyfriend (who was now in jail) was physically and emotionally abusive, and 2) she was on the waiting list at Turning Point (Woman/Child shelter for victims of domestic violence). So, I prayed for her and left her with more food and hygiene products, and she thanked me graciously. I am not sure where she is as I no longer see her, but I pray she is safe and out of harm's way. Just as I have described the things that help me centered, I will discuss the places I visit that help me find a sense of deep inspiration and peace, in which I refer to them as my 'happy places.'

Deep Inspiration and Peace in Brokenness

Everyone should have a place to go to get away from it all. Life can be stressful whether it's from a job, school, family, traffic or just everyday struggles. I have found that when I need to get away from it all or un-plug, I find my sense of deep inspiration and peace anywhere near water or in a museum. If the museum is near water that is even better.

Whenever I am feeling overwhelmed by the constant hustle and bustle of everyday life, I take a drive to the Riverwalk here in Tuscaloosa. When I was home in Chicago, my favorite place was downtown Chicago near the beach. It is amazing how soothing water can be to the mind and spirit. I am not sure if it is because I am a Pisces why I love being near water so much (if you believe in astrology), but whether I am near water or drinking water, I feel a sense of relief. It is soothing to just watch the slow, steady water currents flow along. This reminds me it is ok to take a break sometimes. We are living in a world of constant coming and going, where it has been ingrained in our minds to do more, strive for more, and be more, when sometimes the best thing to do is to give our minds and bodies a break. Placing more pressure on ourselves will not help us achieve any more than we would if we did not; and even if we do, by the time we reach the finish line, we are burned out and tired from sprinting through a race called life that is really a marathon (in the words of my parents).

Also, the museum has always been one of my favorite places for as long as I can remember. I remember going to the Museum of Science and Industry located in downtown Chicago being one of my favorite school trips. The museum is like one big real life, panoramic picture still. Each room has a different theme, that focuses on a different topic or subject. The smell of artifacts is soothing. Like the library, the museum is somewhere I know I can go and learn something new that I had not known before and can leave with a deeper knowledge prior to walking inside.

The delicacy of the historical relics reminds me that there are things in this life that still hold value. And most of all, it is always a good thing to stop and take a good look around because you never know what you may see. Just as I can find mental peace in my happy places, I will discuss how the maintenance of partnerships I have with clergy, spiritual leaders, and religiously affiliated organizations in my community also provide me with spiritual and religious peace.

Role of Clergy, Spiritual Leaders, and Organizations in Brokenness

I have been attending church since I was a young girl; but I was not baptized until August 2014. As a long-time, member and attendant of my church I have developed and maintained the following relationships in my church: church member, youth leader, and sister in Christ.

As a member of my church back home in the south suburbs of Chicago, I would attend church every Sunday, as well as attend bible study on Wednesdays. I enjoyed bible study, because our group would sit at round table, begin with prayer, and proceed with the session. The pastor would often present a theme for us, followed by bible scriptures to refer to that would supplement the topic. It was a judgment free environment, meaning no one could judge or talk about someone because of a challenge they were facing or issue they were dealing with; and our jobs were to support one another and introduce possible solutions for each other. On first Sundays, I would partake in church communion as well.

As a youth leader I would help with hosting church events such as revival ceremonies; usher church services; and speak during programs including Black History Month and Father's Day programs. Most recently, while at home in Chicago, I recited a poem entitled 'We Wear the Mask' by Paul Laurence Dunbar at the church's Black History Month program.

Prior to being baptized, I had always been known as 'Brother Chapman's daughter' and being in my dad's shadow as a strong, Christian (Baptist) man. The title did not bother me, but not having my own identity in church did. My dad had been asking me for quite a while when I was going to get baptized, but I would either put the idea off for another Sunday or ignore his question. Underneath it all, I felt being baptized was something I had to *feel* and was not something I could rush and complete. One day, while we were at church, the sermon had touched me in a weird way, and when it came time for the pastor to call those to the alter who wanted to give their life to God, something overcame me (which I think was the holy spirit), telling me to go to the alter. This started the process which would result in me being baptized. Since being baptized, I am still known for being my dad's daughter, but I now have my own identity in the church as Sister Jade Chapman, and I feel good because it lets me know that I am officially a member of the church.

Furthermore, as a sister to church members in Christ, this affirms that whether I am facing a challenge or rejoicing, I know I can go to my other brothers and sisters in Christ at church. This has been helpful, especially being away from home and sometimes feeling alone. I have received cards, text messages and phone calls from fellow church members at home, providing words of encouragement and this is very helpful in terms of my motivation. Hearing from my brothers and sisters, as well as reaching out reminds me that I need to do my part to maintain close relationships. It also reminds me to keep going and even when I am having a bad day or bad week, there is always someone there praying for me and hoping things get better. I will discuss the positive effects of maintaining strong religious relationships in my community that provide cooperation amongst community members and provides a means of future referrals or communal collaborations.

Cooperation, Referral and Collaboration in Brokenness

I mentioned before that my dad is a strong and prominent member of the neighborhood church and community overall. As a probation officer, he works with troubled youth (boys and girls), to keep them off the streets and out of the [jail] system. My dad has worked with parents in our church who may have troubled sons or daughters in an attempt to get them back on track before it is too late. By referring the client, in this case the church member's son or daughter, to my dad, the outside spiritually based social support system, this allows church members "to utilize a current support system more effectively, to restore connection with a support that has been discontinued, or to create a new support system" (Canda & Furman, 2010, p. 295). As soon as people find out that my dad is a probation officer, they begin to tell him stories of their children or loved ones that are facing challenges and going down the wrong paths. I have seen firsthand the positive effects my dad has on troubled youth, in which some go to college; some develop trade skills; and some go on to become leaders in their communities. I will discuss the extent to which resources of spiritual diversity are utilized in my community.

Extent to Which Resources of Spiritual Diversity are Utilized in My Community My home church in Chicago, as well as the church I attend in Tuscaloosa are both come as you are" churches, meaning the pastors do not pass judgment for how someone may praise God; or a person's personal beliefs. Specifically, in my hometown community, it is predominately African-American with Christian believers; but due to gentrification, there are more Hispanics moving into my neighborhood and neighboring communities. There are also a few Islamic families that live down the street from me. This means that the neighborhood is becoming more colorful in terms of ethnicity and religiosity and spirituality.

Both churches stress the importance of giving back to the community. My home church hosts lunches and dinners that proceed church, recognizing that not everyone has the luxury of going home to home-cooked meals, so they provide food for members after service. They also have a church closet, in which members donate delicately used clothing they no longer want; and the church has days in which less fortunate members can come shop so that they may have something nice to wear to or outside of church. My home church has also hosted back to school drives, in which church members and community members donate school supplies; and before the school year begins, they host a barbeque in which families can come eat and collect free backpacks filled with supplies for their children. In a similar manner, the next section discusses the importance of maintaining levels of trust, mutual understanding and practicing cooperation between social workers and religious personnel and organizations.

Level of Trust, Mutual, Understanding, and Practice Cooperation between Social Workers and Religious Personnel and Organization

Maintaining strong levels of trust, mutual understanding, and cooperation between social workers and religious personnel and organizations is critical because social workers will often have to refer clients to and collaborate with religious groups in the community. Canda and Furman (2010) further support this by explaining how spiritually based clergy, healers, and helpers cross-train can and meet with social workers to learn one another's perspectives and procedures, facilitate cross-referral collaboration, and establish on-going partnerships that can be easily activated on a case-by-case basis (p. 309). By including religious groups and encouraging a cooperative and collaborative relationship, this strengthens communal relationships as well. This can cut down on crime in the community; encourage citizens to speak out about issues they may be seeing going on; and takes the pressure off social workers who feel they have to have all the answers, when they in fact may not know all the ins and outs of the community, they are servicing. Equally important are the practices of spiritual transformational practices, which can help social workers build self-trust and self-awareness. That said, in the next section I will discuss practices including intentional breathing, equipoise, [maintaining] consistency, focused systematic relaxation, and focusing on our purpose.

Intentional Breathing

When Canda and Furman (2010) mentioned in the intentional breathing section of chapter ten that "taking periods through the day to watch the breath and settle into it can instantly relieve stress and clarify the mind" (p. 335), I thought of the Breathing feature that is on Apple Watch. I am not sure if the feature is correlated with the wearer's heartrate, but it pops up various times during the day when it feels the wearer needs to take a moment to breathe. The breathing exercises can be completed in one-minute intervals, and it is required that the wearer sits down or is still when participating. I like doing them, especially when I am feeling stressed because it gives me a moment to "get out of my mind" and to not worry for a minute or two. Thus, I agree with their statement that "it is easier to be mindful when our breathing is smooth and peaceful" (2010, p. 335), because when we are mindful, we can pay more attention to what we are doing, rather than aimlessly performing tasks.

When I am not wearing my Apple Watch to participate in the breathing exercises, if I am at home, then I will sometimes turn the TV off, put my phone and other electronics away so that I can have a moment to simply breathe; and I am better able to pay special attention to my inhalation and exhalation. It is surprising to see just how many distractions take our attention away from something as menial as breathing. When I do take these quiet moments to myself to breathe, I sometimes notice that my heartbeat is at a steady pace or at a quicker rate. Quicker heartbeats mean that something is either worrying me or I am overthinking; while a steadier heartbeat means that I am calm.

Equipoise

Along with intentional breathing, there are times when I will sit in silence in my room, or at the park and let my body just be. From being hunched at the computer doing homework, to constantly moving at work, it can be hard to be still and take strain and stress away from my body. Canda and Furman express that equipoise can also be done "while walking, jogging, and engaging in other postures and activities" (2010, p. 336). That said, I enjoy dancing to balance my body in an unstrained, coordinated posture. Dancing allows me to be flexible and it lifts my spirits, especially when I am feeling under pressure or in a dull mood.

One thing that I have struggled with for a long time is not allowing the actions of others to influence my emotions. For instance, at one of my jobs, the store manager tends to press buttons of those she knows she can get a reaction from: one of those people, being me. For a long time, I struggled with ignoring her when she would antagonize me and fell victim to her deviations. Until one day, because of not being able to ignore her, I wound up blowing up on my mom out of frustration. This called for intervention. My mom sat me down and basically told me the trick to not feeding into her antagonizing and that was to not pay her any attention and remain in control of my emotions. By not allowing her to sense my emotions or see how I was really feeling, she would not be able to move me. And it worked! Oh, how awesome it felt to be able to remain unmoved by her annoyances and to be "unreadable" as she calls it.

I learned that when I allow annoyances and frustrations to get to me, that is when I am swayed. I also learned from my parents that patience was a virtue I had not quite fully developed. Although, since I am a little older, I have found that while my patience has gotten better, it still has a long way to go. Not to mention, I honestly think that patience is a journey, not a destination. There is always something that requires patience, whether with people or daily situations. With patience breeds consistency, in which I will next discuss how I consistency engage in transformational practices such as walking.

Consistency

Every day I walk. Prior to getting diagnosed with Crohn's disease I was an active runner, whether at the park, on a track or around my neighborhood. Since being in remission though I have yet to start back running; but thankfully walking is still adequate exercise. Dr. Melina B. Jampolis explains that "going for regular walks is one of the best and easiest things you can do for your health" and it is the number one exercise she recommends because "it is very easy to do, requires nothing but a pair of tennis shoes, and has tremendous mental and physical benefits" (Prevention.com). According to Meghan Rabbitt (2018), some of the health benefits of walking include but are not limited to mood improvement, creative juices will start flowing, a decreased risk of chronic disease and improvement in digestion. I am not sure if walking counts at work, but I can say I do a lot of it; but when I am off work, I will take out the trash or go check the mail just so I can have a reason to get up, go outside and walk and get some fresh air.

As Canda & Furman stated, "in order to become proficient in any practice, consistency is necessary" (2010, p. 336). In other words, consistency is key. If I were not always working, active, or just overall enjoyed going outside, I would not worry about walking. However, knowing how beneficial just a simple 10–20-minute walk is to my mental and physical well-being is all the motivation I need and aids in my consistency. Sometimes even when I am driving, I will pull over at the park to get out and walk so I can stretch my legs and get some sunlight (Vitamin D) on my skin.

Focused Systematic Relaxation

Anything artistic allows me to let go of anything negative, whether it is writing/journaling, listening to music, engaging in arts and crafts, or even reading or taking a drive to clear my head. Being aware and paying attention also helps me let go of negativity. Canda and Furman (2010) gave an example that when "someone makes a comment [I] find irritating or disagreeable" to "just notice the comment and [my] reaction. But do not react to [my] reaction" but to instead "just be aware and let it go. Only respond after [I] can accept the moment and the person with clear awareness" (p. 335). During one therapy session, I had a dilemma at work that I had been holding onto and my therapist told me three simple words: Let it go.

Moreover, I go with the flow by no longer allowing situations or people's behaviors and attitudes that are out of my control affect me. I must understand that the only person I am in control of is myself. I have had to learn that some situations and people are not for me to fix and that is why God is in control because He knows more about what goes on behind the scenes than I could ever understand.

Canda and Furman assert that it is important "that paying attention be done gently and nonjudgmentally." What we focus on and what we allow is what will continue. That said, when we allow negativity to brew and grow internally, that is what will externally manifest and continue. On the other hand, if we notice something negative, but instead shift those negative thoughts to something positive, then that is what will manifest. That said, I strive to attain a nonjudgmental awareness toward others by doing two things:

1. Praying to God in all matters. As an example, before I go to work, I always pray before I leave. I pray for a good shift, for Him to keep negative energy and spirits away from me, and to only allow positive people and spirits in my presence. I pray that I can do all that while I am at work (and I also pray for the shift to go by promptly).

2. While I do not know who originally said this quote, "Be kind, for everyone you meet is fighting a hard battle," I try to keep this in mind to attain non-judgmental awareness towards others. Most of the time, how others behave towards us is not personal and that is something I must keep in mind. Everyone has lives behind closed doors that we do not know about. We do not know what they are going home to, leaving behind, or overall enduring. This does not mean we should allow others to treat us poorly or disrespect us, but it does put into perspective that this world is bigger than just us and that every person in this world is truly enduring a battle, no matter how big or small. What may be small to me, may be significant in their life and vice versa.

Purpose in Brokenness

I set sincere intentions to achieve a calm state of mind by engaging in self-care. Self-care "promotes overall well-being and helps to prevent stress" (Canda & Furman, 2010, p. 340). Thus, I can focus on my purpose which is to achieve a calm state of mind. Taking bubble baths with Epson salt or hot showers are very therapeutic. Yoga also helps me achieve a calm state of mind and find my purpose; and it allows me to pay attention to parts of my body that I may have been ignoring. It also allows me to remove distractions such as cell phones, the outside world, and overactive thoughts that cloud my mind.

I focus my attention inward by praying to God or talking to my guardian angels like my best friend Diamond or grandma; and asking them for continuous guidance and protection. For outward focus awareness, I journal or engage in "artistic expressions such as poetry, drawing, dance, or musical performance" (Canda & Furman, 2010, p. 339). In between allows the advantage to prepare for either inward or outward focused awareness, so I focus which direction needs the most attention on a given day. Though spirituality has its advantages in the field of social work, with regard to practitioners and clients, apprehensions regarding personal issues in working with religiously affiliated organizations must also be discussed.

Faith Organizations in Brokenness

Although the potential arises that helping professionals can disagree on matters regarding religion and spirituality, there are ways to address professionally and logically said issues. One is to enhance spiritual and religious education of social workers. Those who are in helping roles, including social workers, should be required to undergo training that will teach them how to appropriately and competently address a client's belief in religion or spirituality. For example:

> Social workers may often work on treatment teams with other practitioners including pastoral counselors, nurses, physicians, and other health care professionals. These professionals also need to understand the importance that religion and spirituality may play in the client's ability to cope with their physical or mental illness. (Heyman, Buchanan, Marlowe, & Sealy, n.d).

Unfortunately,

> Social workers may feel more comfortable in interviewing clients about their physical, emotional, or social circumstances but remain reluctant to ask about matters of faith because such topics may be considered private. Venturing into this area may also raise uncomfortable feelings on the part of the worker should the worker be unclear about his or her own views and attitudes about their spiritual practices. (Heyman, Buchanan, Marlowe, & Sealey, n.d).

Apprehension to new, unfamiliar territory is normal; but rather than run from unfamiliar territories, we must face them head on and religious and spiritual education are those topics of discussion that social workers should be required to face head on to be culturally competent when working with clients who may rely on spirituality or religion as their strength. Another one is to "compare diverse perspectives for similarities, differences, and mutual understanding" (Canda & Furman, 2010, p. 7). This is one way to open discussions about religion and spirituality without being insensitive to the thoughts of clients who may or may not utilize spiritual practices when facing challenges. For instance, I view spirituality as a person being open and honest with self, letting go of any emotional inhibitions than maybe holding them back to reach their full spiritual potential, while my client may have a completely different view. Rather than disregarding their definition of spirituality, this will open the conversation to ask how they reached their definition and how do they incorporate their definition into their everyday life. In this case, I will discuss more ways these issues can be improved.

Additionally, these issues can be improved by preparing workers to address or refer and collaborate with clergy in terms of clients' preference; creating clear definitions and conceptual models; and engaging in diverse ideological and spiritual perspectives in dialogue, along with avoiding negative stereotyping (Canda & Furman, 2010, p. 7). The goal is to create a space where clients are free to express themselves and to focus on their strengths. If the basis of their strengths involves engaging in spiritual or religious practices that build on those strengths, then it is our job as social workers to be competent of said practices. We want to empower clients, not judge them for their spiritual or religious beliefs.

Implications for Spiritual Growth

I hope that based on the transparency of my autobiography, I will have engaged social workers to further their education in spirituality and religion in relation to the social work field. I have gained an immense amount of knowledge pertaining to spirituality and I was unaware that spirituality and religion can be included in social work practice, depending on the comfortability of my clients. It is unfortunate that the field of social work has not further delved into knowledge of these practices due to "judgementalism;" focus on maintaining status quo regarding religion; separatist views of social work and religion; and efforts to combine spirituality and religion in social work not being adequately developed (Canda & Furman, 2010, p. 7). This course has shown me another side of social work. Social work is not just answering questions or providing services. It is a field that requires vulnerability in the micro level, allowing social workers to being able to emote with clients. How can we help and be honest with others if we are not honest with ourselves? We must be one step ahead in this field in terms of empowerment and strength perspectives in order to empower our clients, who may come to us in during a time when they are disadvantaged.

I cannot stress enough that spirituality is more than stereotypical connotations that plaque this concept. This course alone has allowed me to be vulnerable in ways I was unable to before. I have been able to explicitly address feelings that I harbored inside for over two years and not to mention, I found myself praying, walking, and taking deeper breaths than I could ever recall. By embracing our spirits, tapping into what guides and moves us as social workers and individuals, and ultimately able "to find [our] internal source of joy, thus being able to externally spread that same joy, [allowing us to transform] negative experiences into positive" (Chapman, 2019 as cited by Vanderbilt University, 2013). By marrying "Religious patterns of values, beliefs, symbols, behaviors, and experiences" (Canda & Furman, 2010, p. 59) with spiritual concepts such as intention breathing, equipoise, focused systematic relaxation, focusing on our purposes, praying, and worshipping, we can address spiritual concerns shared by a community and answer the questions that seemed unanswerable within ourselves.

References

Anakwenze, U & Zuberi, D. (2013). Mental health and poverty in the inner city. *Health & social work. 38* (3), 147-156. doi: 10.1093/hsw/hlt013

Canda, E. R. & Furman, L. D. (2010*). Spirituality diversity in social work practice: The heart of helping.* New York: Oxford University Press, Inc.

Cannon, A. (2016, Feb. 12). *7 modern reasons to visit your local library today.* Retrieved from *https://www.wisebread.com/7-modern-reasons-to-visit-your-local-library-today*

Chama, S. (2017). *Navigating the storms of life: Critical lessons for Christian and non-Christian social workers.* New York: Nova Science Publishers, Inc.

Chapman, J. (2019). *Depending on the holy spirit* [Unpublished manuscript]. Alabama A &M University.

Chapman, J. (2019). Spiritually oriented transformational practice [Unpublished manuscript]. Alabama A &M University.

Chapman, J. (2019). *Spiritual sensitive and culturally appropriate practice* [Unpublished manuscript]. Alabama A &M University.

Chapman, J. (2019). *The meaning of spirituality* [Unpublished manuscript]. Alabama A &M University.

Compassion International, Inc. (2019). *Children and poverty: What is poverty?* Retrieved from https://www.compassion.com/poverty/what-is-poverty.htm

Djokić, D. & Lounis, S. (2014). *This is your mind on grad school.* Retrieved from http://berkeleysciencereview.com/article/mind-grad-school/

Heyman, J.C., Buchanan, R., Marlowe, D., & Sealy, Y. (n.d.). Social workers' attitudes toward the role of religion and spirituality in social work practice. *Journal of Pastoral Counseling* (PDF). Retrieved from https://aamu.blackboard.

com/bbcswebdav/pid-792902-dt-content-rid-13374662_1/courses/201910.11252/ContentServer.pdf

McInerney, C. & Adshead, M. (2014, Oct. 31). "*'By the people, for the people'*" *bringing public participation back to politics* [Video file].Retrieved from http://www.youtube.com/watch?v=_oNmNUdvx_g

Myers, W. (2019). *11 unexpected health-promoting benefits of yoga.* Retrieved on February 18, 2019 from *https://www.everydayhealth.com/fitness-pictures/10-surprising-health-perks-of-yoga.aspx*

Positive Psychology Program. (2018, Aug. 27). *83 benefits of journaling for depression, anxiety, and stress management (PDF).* Retrieved from *https://positivepsychologyprogram.com/benefits-of-journaling/*

Rabbitt, M. (2018, Sept. 28). *7 incredible health benefits of walking 30 minutes a day.* Retrieved from *https://www.prevention.com/fitness/a20485587/benefits-from-walking*-every-day/

Treviño, J. (2019, Jan. 8). *How is a rainbow formed?* Retrieved from https://www.popsci.com/how-rainbows-form

[Vanderbilt University]. (2013, Mar. 22). *Black women's spirituality and the Oprah effect* [Video File]. Retrieved from *https://youtu.be/b8J9R44UYEU*

CHAPTER 20

Inspirational Insights

As you purposively read and ponder these inspirational insights, I hope you will be drawn closer to God. I also hope you will be armed with hope, resilience and spiritual ammunition to navigate brokenness and other life obstacles on a daily basis.

January 1ˢᵗ

Psalm 17:3

You have tested my heart
You have visited me in the night
You have tried me and have found nothing
I have purposed that my mouth shall
not sin

Comments

God wants you to have a heart that is pure and holy. How will you attain this? Begin by praying that He gives you strength to do this. Constantly pray for the Holy Spirit to help you in this task because if you do it from the bottom of your heart God through his Holy Spirit will help you redirect your thoughts so that you can start to dwell on those things that are important to Him. As your thinking changes under Gods inspiration even the words you speak will begin to take a different path and meaning. This might include thinking about those things that have heavenly virtues such as humility, gentleness and meekness. The more you allow the Holy Spirit to change your thoughts, the more you will begin to see the world differently and appreciate God and his goodness for your life.

January 2nd

Psalm 17:5

Uphold my steps in your paths
That my footsteps may not slip

Comments

You may not know what lies ahead of you today. You may not know what challenges, difficulties, disappointments, or frustrations are awaiting you. But one thing is sure, if you set your eyes on Jesus and stay focused on His presence today, He will give you grace, mercy and strength to overcome all hurdles and brokenness. Your victory as in staying a victor is dependent on totally relying on Jesus. Do that today and see how God carries you under His wings.

January 3rd

Psalm 18:30

The word of the Lord is proven
He is a shield to all who trust Him

Comments

Do not neglect to read and digest Gods Word every day. His Word is the only solid shield for living a life that reflects Jesus' character. Jesus is alive today and he is *"the same yesterday, today and forever."* Trust Him today and claim His promises for your life. God has never failed in any one of His promises and you have every right to claim them if only you trust Him and take Him seriously at his Word. By the power of the Holy Spirit run away from all doubts that the Devil may throw at you. Ask Jesus to protect you from the arrows of the adversary.

January 4th

Psalm 18:36

You enlarged my path under me
So that my feet did not slip

Comments

Only Jesus will guide you today if you trust Him for anything. You may find that your path is getting smaller as you face certain disappointments and frustrations unexpectedly. Your secret to victory over brokenness is for you to let Jesus handle the situations for you. He will make a way where you experience hopelessness, and He will guarantee you victory.

January 5th

Psalm 18:35

You have also given me the shield of
your salvation
Your right hand has held me
Your gentleness has made me great

Comments

Jesus has promised you salvation free of charge. His right hand is ready to save you anytime, anywhere. Allow Him to do this for you today. He is as gentle as a Lamb and is willing to do the best for you beyond your best possible imagination. Just give Him a chance and you will be amazed at how He'll carry you through the day.

January 6ᵗʰ

Psalm 3:5

I lay down and slept
I awoke for the Lord sustained me
I will not be afraid of ten thousands of
people who have set themselves against me
all around

Comments

When we sleep at night, we do not know what is happening. There is always a possibility that one may awake the following morning, or one may not. But if you surrender your life to Jesus He will keep you safe throughout the night. Make sure before you go to sleep you say a prayer surrendering your life to Jesus. He owns your life and if He desires to take it so be it because after that He will give you a much greater promise of eternal life. Give your life to Jesus and trust Him in everything and see how He is going to sustain you even in the night.

January 7ᵗʰ

Psalm 16:11

You will show me the path of life
In your presence is fullness of joy
At your right hand are pleasures for
ever more

Comments

Only Jesus can reveal what is best for you. Only He is the meaning and purpose of life. Embracing Him into your life will give you the opportunity to experience joy at its fullness. Jesus has in store real pleasures that you need. He knows the best paths you need to walk. Allow Him to do this today and you will be amazed.

January 8ᵗʰ

Psalm 24:7

> Lift up your hands, O you gates
> And be lifted up you everlasting doors
> And the King of glory shall come in

Comments

Open your heart to Jesus and He will work His will in your life today. He is the King of Kings and Lord of Lords. He does not disappoint anyone who comes to Him, and once you put Him first in your life, He will not fail you. He wants to take your heart so that He can change it for a new one. Once you have Jesus in your heart life will become more meaningful and you will be able to make a difference in lives of others God brings in your path.

January 9ᵗʰ

Psalm 24:8

> Who is this King of glory?
> The Lord strong and mighty
> The Lord mighty in battle

Comments

Jesus is stronger than any evil force you face. He has already won the battle for you on Calvary and all you need to do is trust Him with your whole heart. He will fight all your battles and struggles today and, He will give you success because with Him there is no failure. There is never been a battle He has failed and you can rest assured that whatever problem today you are facing Jesus will handle it.

January 10th

Psalm 24:10

> Who is this King of glory?
> The Lord of hosts
> He is the King of glory

Comments

You need to acknowledge that Jesus is far and above any earthly king, power, or authority. That is why He is worthy of all praise, worship, and honor. Remember He is the creator who holds the earth and the entire universe in place. We serve a mighty King and therefore just praise Him today with all your heart and mind.

January 11th

Psalm 27:1

> The Lord is my light and my Salvation.
> Whom shall I fear?
> The Lord is the strength of my life
> Of whom shall I be afraid?

Comments

When Jesus is on your side you need not fear any difficulty, challenge, or problem that may come your way today. He will and can handle any problem or obstacle that comes your way today if you give Him a chance. Nothing is too hard for Him, just trust Him, sit back, and see how He solves all your problems.

January 12th

Psalm 27: 4

> One thing I have desired of the Lord and
> this will I seek
> That I may dwell in the house of the Lord

All the days of my life
To behold the beauty of the Lord
And to inquire in his temple

Comments

Make it your desire to dwell in the presence of the Lord every moment. There is nothing desirable and wonderful as to want to abide in the presence of the Lord. In His presence is the fullness of joy and in His presence, you will feel most secure and your happiness will be at its highest. This should be your goal today, to want to walk with Jesus and to experience His presence.

January 13th

Psalm 28:6

Blessed be the Lord because he has heard the voice of my supplications

Comments

Whatever it is that is bothering you, do not hesitate to take it to Jesus. He cannot fail you because He specializes in winning battles. Why don't you try Him today and see how He handles your situation. We often fail in our battles because we rush to find our own solutions. Yet Jesus is waiting with His arms open to receive you in His presence today, He is the guarantee for victory and eternal security.

January 14th

Psalm 25:15

My eyes are ever toward the Lord
For he shall pluck my feet out of the net

Comments

Focus on Jesus today. Think about His goodness and what He can do for you today. Think about Him and what He has done for you by dying on the cross of Calvary. Trust Him and take advantage of His presence and your mind will be blown as you see at how He moves you out of your difficulties and unseen challenges.

January 15th

Psalm 25:8

Good and upright is the Lord
Therefore he teaches sinners in the way

Comments

Jesus wants to teach us His ways and He wants us to walk with Him daily. Walking with Him daily means trusting Him and committing all our burdens to Him. As you do this today He will constantly guide and teach you the way you should walk every day.

January 16th

Psalm 26:1

Vindicate me o Lord
For I have walked in my integrity
I have also trusted in the Lord
I shall not slip

Comments

Trusting Jesus is the most important honor one can bestow upon Him. God wants His children to constantly trust Him so that He can prove His faithfulness. He does not disappoint those that put their trust in Him. Throughout His word are precious and infallible promises that are ours for the asking. Take Him at His word today because His word is solid and never changes.

January 17th

Psalm 29:4

The voice of the Lord is powerful
The voice of the Lord is full of majesty

Comments

God speaks to us every day and we need to pay attention to His voice. He speaks to us quietly sometimes and to hear His voice we need to be still and enjoy those moments when His voice penetrates the silence. Make some quite time today and just listen to God speak to you. His still and small voice will bring into your heart a peace that cannot be matched by anything this world has to offer.

January 18th

Psalm 30:5

For his anger is but for a moment
His favor is for life
Weeping may endure for a night
But joy comes in the morning

Comments

God gets annoyed when we fail to follow His commands. But His anger is always imbued with love and does not last forever. When you follow His will for your life, don't worry about what you are going through. Today, just know that at the end of the day He will give you victory and joy.

January 19th

Psalm 28:8

The Lord is their strength
And he is the saving refuge of his anointed

Comments

In every situation you face today make Jesus your strength. He will save you and give you the strength you need to go through different trials you might face. Run to Him and be safe.

January 20ᵗʰ

Psalm 28:9

Save your people
And bless your inheritance
Shepherd them also
And bear them up forever

Comments

Jesus Christ will save you today if you trust and commit all your burdens to Him. Let Him bless you and your family and allow Him to guide your steps. He will bless you beyond measure if only you trust Him and demonstrate your faithfulness in Him. God wants to pour His heavenly blessings on you. Take advantage of His offer.

January 21ˢᵗ

Psalm 28:2

Give unto the Lord the glory due to his name
Worship the Lord in the beauty of holiness

Comments

You have been created to worship God as well as to give glory due to His name. No one deserves praise and glory than Jesus does. He is the creator, He made you and He understands every detail surrounding your life. God lives in glory and therefore praise Him every moment of today and you will see how many blessings you will get in return.

January 22nd

Psalm 28:10

The Lord will give strength to his people
The lord will bless his people with peace

Comments

True strength, peace, and blessings come only from Jesus. He is
the powerful one and He only can bless you with what you need.
In any challenging situation you face today run to Him and get
the strength to see you through the day. Be obedient and trust in
His unfailing grace and mercy and you will enjoy the blessings
He has for you.

January 23rd

Psalm 31:19

Oh how great is your goodness which you
have laid up for those who fear you
Which you have prepared for those who
trust in you
In the presence of the sons of men

Comments

God has in store the best for you. You cannot imagine what it
means to get the best from the creator of the universe. Only trust
God with your whole heart, mind, and soul and He will respect
your trust. Fear for God is showing reverence for who He is. His
goodness is beyond measure and all you need to do is to trust Him
and He will prove His faithfulness. Do that today.

January 24th

Psalm 31:24

Be of good courage and he shall strengthen your heart
All you who hope in the Lord

Comments

Sometimes Jesus will allow certain negative situations to affect and move you beyond what you can bear. In doing this He will give you the strength to overcome. Just be reminded today that Jesus has already won the battle for you and all you need to do is trust Him

January 25th

Psalm 24:15

My times are in your hands
Deliver me from the hands of my enemies
And from those who persecute me

Comments

Put your life in Jesus' hands and he will protect you. You don't have guarantee for tomorrow because tomorrow may not be yours. Therefore lay your life in Jesus hands today because only He can protect and assure you eternal life. No matter what difficulty comes your way, He will give you freedom and victory.

January 26th

Psalm 36:5

Your mercy O Lord is in the heavens
And your faithfulness reaches to the clouds

Comments

God's grace and mercy are incomprehensible, reaching to the heavens of heavens. Take advantage of God's mercy today and enjoy His presence. Lay your life into His care and He will direct all your steps every second and minute of the day.

January 27th

Psalm 37:7

> How precious is your loving kindness
> O God?
> Therefore the children of men put their
> trust under the shadows of your wings

Comments

Put your trust in God today and He will not disappoint you. It is your privilege to trust God and He will show you mercy. You cannot go wrong by depending on Jesus because that is what he wants you to do. Obey Him today and reap the benefits of totally depending on him.

January 28th

Psalm 37:37

> Mark the blameless man and observe the
> upright
> For the future of that man is peace

Comments

If you totally trust God, you will not be forsaken. All your physical and emotional needs will be met by Him, and you will enjoy such peace as can only be experienced by those who trust in God. All those who have entrusted their lives in Jesus experience a peace that no one can understand. This peace is yours for the asking today. Take it by faith.

January 29th

Psalm 37:40

> But the salvation of the righteous is from the Lord
> He is their strength in the time of trouble

Comments

Trouble is the lot of everyone who believes in Jesus. Trouble will make you grow stronger if you put your trust in God and let Him lead you all the way. Jesus did say that suffering and trouble will be part of our lives. He also promised victory for those who place all their trust and confidence in Him. Invite Him into your heart today and enjoy the victories He'll give you.

January 30th

Psalm 38:9

> Lord all my desire is before you
> And my sighing is not hidden from you

Comments

Let all your needs and desires be known to God and He will fulfill them according to His bounties. Only God can meet and address all your needs and wants. He has never failed anyone who comes to Him. Just try Him today and your life will never be the same.

January 31st

Psalm 38:15

For in you O Lord I hope
You will hear O Lord my God

Comments

Put your hope in God and He will not forget you. Let your hope be anchored in Jesus because only He can answer and supply your needs. Jesus is alive and He wants to meet all your needs, go to Him in prayer and lay all your burdens before His throne. Trust Him today and experience His faithfulness.

February 1st

Psalm 39:4

Lord make me to know my end
And what is the measure of my days
That I may know how frail I am
Indeed you have made my days as handbreadths
And my age is as nothing before you
Certainly every man at his best state is but vapor

Comments

Be reminded that your earthly days are numbered, and Jesus holds them in His Hands. Compared to eternity your life on earth is but a breath. Invest your life in Jesus and eternity is yours. You cannot imagine what it means to spend eternity with the creator of the universe. Let your life be grounded in the son of God today and eternity will start right now for you.

February 2nd

Psalm 40:5

Many O Lord my God are your wonderful
works
Which you have done
And your thoughts which are toward us
cannot be recounted
If I would declare and speak of them
They are more than can be numbered

Comments

God thinks the best for you, and you have the privilege of claiming His promises for your life. You cannot imagine the exceedingly wonderful things God has prepared for you. Trust Him and claim every promise in store for your life. Jesus wants the best for your life and the onus is on you today to claim all that He has in store for you. Start claiming your promises today and your life will never be the same.

February 3rd

Psalm 41:11

By this I know that you are well
pleased with me
Because my enemy does not triumph
over me

Comments

If you completely trust God all your enemies, no matter what they plan against you, will be defeated. God has given us a test and that is if your enemies do not gain any triumph over you then you know that God is happy with you. There is no trouble that God has failed to overcome. Let Him have control of your life and all your troubles will be overcome through faith in Jesus.

February 4th

Psalm 42:1

As a deer pants for the water brooks
So pants my soul for you, O God

Comments

Crave God's presence every day and you will find meaning for your life. Let your mindset be focused on Jesus today. Let Him become your air and breathe Him in every moment. Your life can only find full purpose in Jesus.

February 5th

Psalm 43:5

Why are you cast down O my soul?
And why are you disquieted within me
Hope in God
For I shall yet praise him
The help of my countenance and my God

Comments

No matter what you are going through today put your hope and trust in God. Praise and worship Him and He will see you through every troubling situation you may be facing. Don't forget that God is the creator and there is nothing impossible with Him.

February 6th

Psalm 44:8

In God we boast all day long
And praise your name forever

Comments

If there are accomplishments, you have made in your life praise Jesus for these because only He has made this possible for you.

Praise Him all day today and think about His goodness and what He has done and can do for you.

February 7ᵗʰ

Psalm 44:20-21

> If we had forgotten the name of our God
> or stretched out our hands to a foreign God
> Would not God search this out?
> For he knows the secrets of the heart

Comments

God knows the deepest parts of our hearts. Whatever you are thinking about today you must not set your heart on idols such as the car you drive, the house you live in, the clothes you wear or the amount of money in your bank. God knows every thought you conceive and if you want His approval let Him control your mind and thoughts today. Let Him run your life.

February 8ᵗʰ

Psalm 46:10

> Be still and know that I am God
> I will be exalted among the nations
> I will be exalted in the earth

Comments

Take time to be still and just think about God's goodness and mercy and grace for you. Take time today to contemplate the goodness of Jesus and His sacrifice for you. No person in this world can be compared to Jesus. He is the King of Kings and Lord of Lords. He is the everlasting, the eternal God, the almighty God. Invite Him to be your friend today.

February 9th

Psalm 46:1

God is our refugee and strength
A very present help in trouble

Comments

Jesus cannot fail to handle any troubling situation you are facing. Claim this promise and cast all your cares and worries on Him. He will always be there to see you through. Just trust Him and do not run to friends or family members to solve your problems. Bring every problem you may be facing to Jesus and He will not disappoint you.

February 10th

Psalm 47:8

God reigns over the nations
God sits on his holy throne

Comments

No country, government, authority, or any earthly power can be compared with God. He owns this universe including you. Why don't you make Him your God and personal savior today? No one can match Him because he owns everything.

February 11th

Psalm 48:14

For this is God
Our God forever and ever
He will be our guide
Even to death

Comments

Let Jesus be your guide today. Let Him direct every path to take today. He knows your past, present and future. He knows the best paths you can tread. He is the best guide one can ever have. Let Him navigate your life today and you'll not be disappointed.

February 12ᵗʰ

Psalm 49:15

> But God will redeem my soul from the power of the grave
> For he shall receive me

Comments

Don't be afraid of death. Jesus has already overcome death on your behalf and the gift of eternal life is yours for the asking. What marvelous glory awaits His saints and all those who have put their complete trust in the master Jesus. When you make Jesus your anchor you do not have to worry about death or what tomorrow may bring. Today make Jesus your personal savior.

February 13ᵗʰ

Psalm 52:8

> But I am like a green olive tree in the house of God
> I trust in the mercy of God forever and ever

Comments

If you trust in the mercy of God, He will bless you and keep you. You will be surprised at what God can do for you. Trust is crucial to drawing on God's promises. Exercise genuine faith today and you will be amazed at what Jesus will do for you.

February 14ᵗʰ

Psalm 50:14

Offer to God thanksgiving
And pay your vows to the most High

Comments

If you make any vows to God keep them. Praise Him and give thanks to Him today for every vow you fulfill and He will do His part. Do not make any promises you may fail to keep. Follow through with any promise you make today and give Him thanks for helping you to this.

February 15ᵗʰ

Psalm 50:15

Call upon me in the day of trouble
I will deliver you and you shall glorify me

Comments

No amount of trouble is too big for God. Claim the promise of victory today. If you are going through any difficulty or any troubling situation, bring it to Jesus. With God on your side victory is guaranteed.

February 16ᵗʰ

Psalm 50:23

Whoever offers praise glorifies me
And to him who orders his conduct aright
I will show the salvation of God

Comments

God lives in praise because he is worthy to be praised. Give Him thanks and praise Him because He is God. Let your conduct today show Gods glory and Jesus will be praised. Others will see this and give glory and praise to God.

February 17th

Psalm 51:10

Create in me a clean heart O God
And renew a steadfast spirit within me

February 18th

Comments

Jesus wants to give you a new heart because this is what he specializes in. Allow Him to do so today and let Him give you His Holy Spirit to guide and strengthen you. Start today.

Psalm 51:11

Do not cast me away from your presence
And do not take your spirit from me

Comments

God's presence is always with us. To enjoy it you must allow Him to become your personal savior. Ask Him to fill your heart with His presence and let His spirit take charge of your life. You will be blessed.

February 19th

Psalm 51:17

The sacrifices of God are a broken spirit
A broken and contrite spirit
That O God you will not despise

Comments

God is interested in your heart. When you feel remorse for whatever wrong or sin you commit or have committed just come to Him and confess all your wrong doings and, He will not turn you away. He will comfort you and give you peace and joy.

February 20ᵗʰ

Psalm 54:4

> Behold God is my helper. The Lord is with those who uphold my life

Comments

No one can help you as God can. No one can give you strength as God can. No one can comfort you as God can. He will even bless those who bless you. Let him be your helper in every situation and you will not be disappointed.

February 21ˢᵗ

Psalm 54:7

> For he has delivered me out of all trouble
> And my eye has seen its desire upon
> my enemies

Comments

No trouble is too big for Jesus. Whatever obstacle you are facing let Him handle it and He will give you victory. If you want to see and experience a life of victory allow Him in your heart today.

February 22ⁿᵈ

Psalm 55:16

As for me I will call upon God
And the Lord shall save me

Comments

Call upon Jesus in every difficulty and He will save you. Don't rush to finding your own solutions or to consulting friends and relatives when faced with troubling situations and danger. Just call upon Jesus with all your heart and He will help you.

February 23ʳᵈ

Psalm 55:17

Evening, morning and at noon
I will pray and cry out at aloud
And he shall hear my voice

Comments

Prayer is your privilege. Prayer is the best communication pathway God has given those who trust in Him. There are no barriers and conditions to fulfill before you pray. Live in prayer and let Jesus know all your concerns, problems, and praises. Make prayer your number one priority today.

February 24ᵗʰ

Psalm 55:22

Cast your burden on the Lord
And he shall sustain you
He shall never permit the righteous to
be moved

Comments

When you cast all your burdens on Jesus, He will not fail or disappoint you. Every small or big burden you are facing is important to Him. Claim this privilege and let Jesus handle every obstacle in your life. Tell Him in prayer.

February 25ᵗʰ

Psalm 56:3

Whenever I am afraid I'll trust in you

Comments

Fear is one of the biggest weapons Satan uses to intimidate. Don't allow him to break you with his lies, just let Jesus handle it on your behalf. When fear begins to pop up in your mind ask the Holy Spirit to help shift your mind and focus on Jesus. Only Jesus will give a spirit of calmness.

February 26ᵗʰ

Psalm 56:11

In God I have put my trust
I will not be afraid
What can man do to me?

Comments

Once you trust God and put Him first He will take care of every burden and obstacle standing in your way. Even your friends or relatives cannot harm you if you put your trust in Jesus. Jesus will shield you from all kinds of weapons the enemy may place in your path.

February 27th

Psalm 56:9

When I cry to you
Then my enemies will turn back
This I know because God is for me

Comments

Crying and bringing your burdens to God is your privilege. Let Him know all your anxieties and allow Him to give you the victory you need. Once you make Jesus first in your life all your enemies will be defeated.

February 28th

Psalm 57:2

I will cry out to God Most High
To God who performs all things for me

Comments

It is Jesus who does everything for you. He will feed, clothe and house you and meet all your emotional needs. All this is possible if you make Him the anchor of your life today.

Psalms 57:11

February 29th

Be exalted O God above the heavens
Let your glory be above all the earth

Comments

Nothing is as important as worshiping and praising God. You were created to praise and worship God. Remember that He is the creator of the heavens and the earth, and nothing can equal His power and authority. Let praise and worship be your todays and minute to minute activity.

March 1ˢᵗ

Psalm 59:16

> But I will sing of your power
> Yes, I will sing aloud of your mercy in
> the morning
> For you have been my defense
> And refugee in the day of my trouble

Comments

You have been created to worship and praise God. Somebody once said that God "survives in worship and praise.' To some extent this statement is true because God is worthy to receive honor and praise and worship. God will protect you in times of trouble and He will protect you in danger. Trust Him for this and give Him glory and honor when he demonstrates His faith. Whatever situation you are going through just let Him work on your behalf.

March 2ⁿᵈ

Psalm 60:12

> Give us help from trouble
> For vain is the help of man
> Through God we will do valiantly
> For it is he who shall tread down
> our enemies

Comments

No amount of help or support from friends, family or relatives can supersede the help that Jesus has for you. Today tap into this reservoir of promises and you will be amazed at what God will do for you. Although it is important sometimes to get help from folks and relative, the best person to run to for help when in trouble is Jesus. He will never disappoint you.

March 3ʳᵈ

Psalm 61:1

Hear my cry oh God
Attend to my prayer
From the end of the earth I will cry to you
When my heart is overwhelmed
Lead me to the rock that is higher than I

Comments

When you find yourself in all kinds of trouble let Jesus the rock, refugee and deliverer come to your rescue. Jesus has never failed any battle and He will never. He is your fortress, your high tower, and your refugee. Go to Him today when perplexed by this world's difficulties and He will give you rest and peace for your soul beyond measure.

March 4ᵗʰ

Psalm 62:5

My soul waits silently for God alone
For my expectation is from him

Comments

Whatever your needs are only Jesus has the power to fulfill them. Go to him in prayer and let all your requests be known to Him and sit back and see how He will address your requests, needs, or wants. Remember, He wants the best for your life, claim this promise.

March 5ᵗʰ

Psalm 62:6

He only is my rock and my salvation
He is my defense
I shall not be moved

Comments

When you put all your trust in Jesus rest assured that everything
will go well, at least according to His will. His will for your life
will prevail and He will provide all your needs according to His
grace and bounties and as He determines. He is your defense and
rock. You can run to Him and not get disappointed at all. Do
that today!

March 6ᵗʰ

Psalm 63:1

O God you are my God
Early will seek you
My soul thirsts for you
My flesh longs for you in a dry and
thirsty land
Where there is no water

Comments

Make it a point to seek God early this morning when you open
eyes from sleep. If you persist in this practice, you will find total
joy as well as experience the presence of God in your life every
moment of the day. Remember that the essence of life is to seek
God and do His will. Let this be your number one priority in life.

March 7ᵗʰ

Psalm 20:1

> May the Lord answer you in the day
> of trouble?
> May the name of the God of Jacob
> defend you?

Comments

When in trouble of whatever magnitude run to God and He will save you. No power is above God, and you can rest assured peacefully in His presence. Jesus is the creator, and He holds all things in His hands. He wants to give you the best and He'll do this if you allow Him to.

March 8ᵗʰ

Psalm 20:4

> May he grant you according to your
> heart's desire?
> And fulfill all your purpose

Comments

Only God can fulfill all your dreams and desires. Let Him do this for you today, trust Him and depend on Him daily and you will never be disappointed. Bring all your cares one by one and just watch how God in His infinite wisdom fulfills each one of them.

March 9ᵗʰ

Psalm 20:7

> Some trust in Chariots and some in horses
> But we will remember the name of the
> Lord our God

Comments

You can never go wrong when you put your trust in Jesus. Never be tempted to trust friends, relatives, or colleagues when under temptations. Jesus is honored when we put our trust in Him and guess what, He will never, never let you down. Try Him today.

March 10ᵗʰ

Psalm 21:2

> You have given him his heart's desire
> And have not withheld the request of his lips

Comments

Only Jesus can grant you all your desires. Make your specific requests known to Him and see how these are fulfilled. Recall that He wants the best for your life and all He needs is your request and invitation.

March 11ᵗʰ

Psalm 22:28

> For the Kingdom is the Lord's
> And he rules over the nations

Comments

God owns the world including all nations, countries, and everything in them. He has the prerogative to do whatever He wants. No one can stop Him. He is sovereign and He does whatever He pleases. So if God is on your side then you are in the most comfortable and secure zone today.

March 12th

Psalm 19:1

> The heavens declare the glory of God
> And the firmament shows his handiwork

Comments

Take time to wonder outside and look at the heavens and see the glory of God. Gaze at the stars during the night and look at their splendor. The universe and its entire host speak of the glory of God. Join in the praise and worship of God today whenever you see Gods glory revealed in His creation.

March 13th

Psalm 19:12

> Who can understand his errors?
> Cleanse me from secret faults

Comments

We are all vulnerable to sin. We all have our own weaknesses and faults. But no one can cleanse us from these vices any better than Jesus. He only has the power to give us the true freedom we need. Allow Him to come into your life and you will be amazed at how He works out everything for you.

March 14th

Psalm 19:13

> Keep back your servant from
> presumptuous sins
> Let them not have dominion over me
> Then I shall be blameless
> And I shall be innocent of
> great transgression

Comments

Ask God today to keep you from committing deliberate sins. Sometimes these sins are so subtle that you may commit them unknowingly. Only Jesus can give you the victory over of these sins. Jesus does not condone any type of sin, small or big. To Him sin is sin. If you sin, confess and repent and you will receive pardon and peace from Jesus.

March 15th

Psalm 22:10

I was cast upon you from birth
From my mother's womb you have been my God

Comments

God knows you from the time you are conceived. He knows you from your youth up. He is interested in your future, and He wants to give you the best in life. Allow Him to do this today.

March 16th

Psalm 22:11

Be not far from me
For trouble is near
For there is none to help

Comments

When you are in trouble let Jesus come to your rescue. Apart from Him no one else can guarantee you the victories you need that are so crucial to your faith. Pray for His intervention when you reach a dead end, and He will see you through.

March 17ᵗʰ

Psalm 104:33

I will sing to the Lord as long as I live
I will sing praise to my God while I
have being

Comments

God wants His creatures to praise and worship Him because He is the creator. Praise Him today, every day and moment of your life and you will be amazed at how refreshing this experience can be. When you do this, you will be immensely blessed.

March 18ᵗʰ

Psalm 105:19

Until the time that his word came to pass
The word of the Lord tested him

Comments

Remember that as long you are in this world you will be tempted. Temptations, trials, and all kinds of difficult situations are necessary for faith and growth. God will use these to strengthen your faith and trust in Him. When in trouble be happy and look to Jesus for deliverance. Doing this may not seem easy at first but with endurance and trusting Jesus you will be victorious.

March 19ᵗʰ

Psalm 105:1

Oh give thanks to the Lord
Call upon his name
Make known his deeds among the people

Comments

It is good practice to give testimony of what God is doing in your life. Others get saved through testimonies shared and ultimately God is gloried. Take note of your blessings today and next time at worship or with friends or family testify of these so God can be glorified.

March 20th

Psalm 103:2

Bless the Lord O my soul
And forget not all his benefits

Comments

Always make it a habit to look back and see what God has done in your life. God is gloried in this way if you express gratitude and appreciation for His good deeds in our lives.

March 21st

Psalm 103:13

As a father pities his children
So the Lord pities those who fear him

Comments

Jesus loves you and He wants to do the best for you. His love for you is more than the love an earthly father has for his children. Whenever you are in trouble, He is there with you and He will share the sorrows you may face today with you. Be comforted to know that Jesus will always stand with you no matter what you are facing or going through.

March 22nd

Psalm 103:29

> You hide your face, they are troubled
> You take away their breath they die and
> return to their dust
> You send your spirit they are created
> And you renew the face of the earth

Comments

God oversees creation. Everything and all things depend on Him for life and survival. He waters the earth and provides food to all. He gives you strength to work and earn a living. He provides you with good health to enjoy life. Any blessing or anything positive in your life that you may think of comes from Him. Trust Him today and you will enjoy many more of these blessings.

March 23rd

Psalm 106:8

> Nevertheless He saved them for His
> name's sake
> That He might make his power known

Comments

Whenever God does something remarkable for you, He wants to make His power and grace known to others thereby creating opportunities for salvation of those who are not saved. Today if God does something special for you do not be silent, testify and make His power known.

March 24th

Psalm 107:6

> Then they cried out to the Lord in
> their trouble
> And He delivered them out of
> their distresses

Comments

Are you in debt, in poor health, looking for a job, or having family problems call on Jesus and He will never disappoint you. Let your cries be genuine and bring them to God and He will genuinely answer you.

March 25th

Psalm 107:7

> He calms the storm
> So that its waters are still

Comments

Whatever storms you may be facing right now take them to Jesus and He will resolve them for you. No amount of trouble is too much for Jesus because with Him all things are possible. Take Him by his word and see His power in action.

March 26th

Psalm 108:12

> Give us help from trouble
> For vain is the help of man

Comments

Whenever you find yourself in doldrums do not put your trust in fellow men. Only Jesus has the power to solve all your problems.

So why don't you take advantage of his power today, remember He is God and He knows every detail of your life.

March 27th

Psalm 108:13

> Through God we will do valiantly
> For it is He who shall tread down
> our enemies

Comments

When God is on your side, all your battles will be won. Let Him fight your battles today. Call upon Him in genuine prayer and trust Him for victory and, sit back and see how He works out your situation. Nothing is too hard for Him.

March 28th

Psalm 109:22

> But you O God the Lord
> Deal with me for your name's sake
> Because your mercy is good, deliver me

Comments

God's grace and mercy is beyond our imagination. We have the privilege of taking advantage of this grace and mercy every day. Ask God to show you His mercy in whatever situation you are in today.

March 29th

Psalm 13:13

> Consider and hear me O Lord my God
> Enlighten my eyes
> Lest I sleep the sleep of death

Comments

Whenever in trouble today or indeed any other day plead your case with God. If you need to fast do that and cry out for His mercy before His throne. He will forgive and restore you and guarantee you the gift of eternal life.

March 30th

Psalm 71:20

> You who have shown me great and
> severe troubles
> Shall revive me again
> And bring me up again from the depths of
> the earth

Comments

Remember that in this life God will allow you to pass through suffering, brokenness, troubles, and difficulties. Sometimes you may not understand these, but trusting in God no matter what, will always guarantee you victory in this life or the next.

March 31st

Psalm 65:5

> By awesome deeds in righteousness
> You will answer us
> O, God of our salvation
> You who are the confidence of all the ends
> of the earth
> And of far off seas

Comments

When you make genuine requests to Jesus, He will answer you. Sometimes His answers may be quick and sometimes they may take longer than expected. Sometimes they may come as requested and sometimes they may come in different ways. Sometimes they may not come. Not receiving an answer to your prayer is itself an answer. But no matter the case know that God will answer you in His own time and His answers are always the best.

April 1st

Psalm 109:23

I will greatly praise the Lord with my mouth
Yes I will praise him among the multitude

Comments

It is important to praise God because essentially, we were created with a view to praising God. Every creation praises God and you, the crowning work of His creation are no exception. Praising God brings a sense of joy that cannot be imagined. Begin praising God today by speaking to Him, praying to Him, singing songs about His greatness, and living and moving in Him every day.

April 2nd

Psalm 100:5

For the Lord is good
His mercy is everlasting
And his truth endures to all generations

Comments

God's mercy is everlasting, it has no end. He is Truth with a big T and he wants the best for you. As is said, "God is good all the time". You will experience his goodness if you trust Him completely and allow Him to dwell in your heart.

April 3rd

Psalm 102:2

Do not hide your face from me
In the day of my trouble
Incline your ear to me
In the day that I call answer me speedily

Comments

When facing any kind of trouble call upon God today. Pray to Him and ask Him to deliver you from all your problems. Tell him that He is faithful and remind Him of the good things he has done in your life and proclaim that He is God and that all things are possible with Him.

April 4th

Psalm 100:27

But you are the same
And your years will have no end

Comments

God is the same despite the passage of time. He lives outside time and time has no effect on Him. He never changes His character which is based on love. He will always love you if you come to Him and accept Him as your personal savior.

April 5th

Psalm 97:6

The heavens declare his righteousness
And all the peoples see his glory

Comments

All creation including the heavens declares the glory of God. We are part of His creation, and we are supposed to praise Him as well. Praise Him today through your work, through your family engagements and through everything. Remember He is God.

April 6th

Psalm 97:9

For you Lord are the most High above all the earth
You are exalted far above all gods

Comments

Nothing in creation can match the power of God. He is God and he is above every power and authority. Exalt Him and continue praising Him and declare that He is above every god.

April 7th

Psalm 98:7

Let the sea roar and all its fullness
The world and those who dwell in it

Comments

The seas roar and declare the glory of God. Even the world and all those who inhabit the earth should praise and worship God. They are blessings that come when you offer praise to God. Make Jesus the centerpiece of your life and give Him praise, glory and honor.

April 8th

Psalm 99:9

Exalt the Lord our God
And worship at His holy hill
For the Lord our God is holy

Comments

Praise, praise, praise is what we are supposed to do. Let worship and praise become central to your life and God will shower you with blessings beyond your imagination. Create opportunities every day for quite time to commune with God and to praise Him.

April 9th

Psalm 94:10

He who instructs the nations, Shall He not see
He who teaches man knowledge

Comments

God directs nations because He is sovereign, and His plans always work out. He is the source of knowledge and if you want knowledge know God first. When you put God first in your life he will not disappoint you. He will put you first as well and His blessings shall follow you wherever you are.

April 10th

Psalm 95:6

Oh come let us worship and bow down
Let us kneel before the Lord our Maker

Comments

Set time each day to worship God. Remember that he is the creator and maker of the earth and heavens. Start your day each day with bible and prayer time. Make this practice your habit and allow God to speak to you as you seek Him and see how He will bless you.

April 11th

Psalm 96:4

The Lord is great and greatly to be praised
He is to be feared above all gods

Comments

Always remember that God is to be praised and worshiped because he is God and there is no other. Fear for Jesus demonstrates reverence and the more you do this the more you will feel closer to God.

April 12th

Psalm 96:5

For all the gods of the peoples are idols
But the Lord made the heavens

Comments

God is the creator, and it is he who made the heavens and everything in the heavens. Nothing that man has made can compare with Him. Do not let anything come between you and Jesus.

April 13th

Psalm 92:2

To declare your loving kindness in the morning
And your faithfulness every night

Comments

Pray every morning and ask Jesus to walk with you during the day. If possible, you can ask for specific prayers and see how these are fulfilled. At the end of the day thank God for His faithfulness even if your prayers may seem not to be answered. Thank Him in advance and declare that you know that He will answer you in His own time and way.

April 14ᵗʰ

Psalm 93:3

The foods have lifted up O Lord
The floods have lifted up their voice
The floods lift up their waves

Comments

Whenever you face floods of all kinds run to Jesus and he will fight all the battles for you as well as give you the victory you need in every situation. Jesus has not failed any person and even you today can take advantage of His blessings.

April 15ᵗʰ

Psalm 93:4

The Lord on high is mightier
Than the noise of many waters
Than they might waves of the sea

Comments

God is mightier than any of all your problems. Do not worry when you are confronted with all kinds of problems. Ask Jesus to fight the battles for you.

April 16th

Psalm 94:9

> Ho who planted the ear shall he not hear?
> He who formed the eye, shall he not see?

Comments

Remember that Jesus can hear and see everything you are going through because it is He who created the ear as well as the eye. So, when you are feeling low remember that God is seeing you and He is listening to your cries.

April 17th

Psalm 86:7

> In the day of my trouble I will call
> upon you
> For you will answer me

Comments

When you are in trouble today call upon Jesus and He will answer you. Bring all your burdens to His feet and He will handle them for you.

April 18th

Psalm 86:17

> Show me a sign for good
> That those who hate me may see it and be
> ashamed
> Because you Lord have helped me and
> comforted me

Comments

God wants us to test Him sometimes. Ask for a sign from Him that demonstrates His faithfulness to you. Wait and see how that sign gets fulfilled and praise God for it.

April 19th

Psalm 88: 13

But to you I have cried out Lord
And in the morning my prayer comes
before you

Comments

Every morning bring all your requests to God through prayer. Cry out to Him for any burden on your heart. He will help you and give you the joy and peace you need.

April 20th

Psalm 88:1

O Lord God of my salvation
I have cried out day and night before you

Comments

Every time, whether day or night, is the best time to confer with God. Bring all your special requests to God and He will address them as he sees fit. Start that today.

April 21st

Psalm 88:2

Let my prayer come before you
Incline your ear to my cry

Comments

When you pray to God be certain that your prayers are ascending to His throne. God will incline His ears to your genuine prayers and will answer you accordingly. Trust Him for this and He'll not disappoint you.

April 22nd

Psalm 84:10

For a day in your courts is better than
a thousand
I would rather be a doorkeeper in the
house of my God
Than dwell in the tents of wickedness

Comments

There is nothing better than having worship where you fellowship with fellow believers and have special time with God. There are blessings in worshipping with brothers and sisters. Enjoy your worship every time you are in the sanctuary and experience the presence and blessings of God.

April 23rd

Psalm 84:11

For the Lord God is a sun and shield
The Lord will give grace and glory
No good thing will he withhold from those
who walk uprightly

Comments

If your walk with God is genuine, He will not keep any good thing from you. He will honor you with untold blessings if only you put Him first. He will bring you favor and grace which sometimes will scare and surprise you.

April 24ᵗʰ

Psalm 85:10

Mercy and Truth have met together
Righteousness and peace have kissed
each other

Comments

God is the God of mercy and righteousness. He does not allow anything less than this. Today pray that He helps you to become righteous and enjoy His mercy.

April 25ᵗʰ

Psalm 8:1

O Lord, Our Lord
How excellent is your name in all the earth
You who have set your glory above
the heavens

Comments

God's name is to be revered in all the earth. He is powerful and His glory extends far beyond the heavens. He is God and praises Him today in all your actions.

April 26ᵗʰ

Psalm 12:7

For the Lord is righteous
He loves righteousness
His countenance beholds the upright

Comments

God is righteous and He wants all His children to be righteous. When you are a child of God you cannot mix light and darkness, you cannot be righteous and at the same time remain in darkness. Make the choice to stay in light and grow in righteousness today.

April 27th

Psalm 34:8

> Oh taste and see that the Lord is good
> Blessed is the man who trusts in Him

Comments

You can test God for His goodness. This is His challenge to us. All you need to do is to trust Him in all things and He will never let you down. Try Him by asking specific things and see how these get fulfilled. Your part is to be obedient and live a righteous life.

April 28th

Psalm 12:6

> The words of the Lord are pure words
> Like silver tried in a furnace of the earth
> Purified seven times

Comments

God's words are true and never fail. They have been tried and tested and none of them have failed. Try to Read the Bible every day and take every word in His book to be true. The Bible is full of promises which are yours if ask and claim them. Ask Jesus to give you the Holy Spirit to help you put into practice what you read. Your character will change because only the word of God can change you.

April 29th

Psalms 12:3

Consider and hear me, O Lord my God
Enlighten my eyes
Lest I sleep the sleep of death

Comments

Whenever you are in trouble plead with God to help you overcome whatever trouble or pain you are going through. God will never turn away a humble request from a humble heart. He will hear you and save you.

April 30th

Psalm 13:1

I will sing to the Lord
Because he has dealt bountifully with me

Comments

Praise God for any victory He gives you. Worship Him and let His grace and mercy cover you. Jesus is waiting to shower His blessing on you to help you in any troubling situation you find yourself. Take Him by His word and He will deliver you out of all your doldrums.

May 1st

Psalm 16:8

I have set the Lord always before me
Because he is at my right hand I shall not be moved

Comments

When you set God before you in everything you do, you will never go wrong. He will fight the battles for you and victory is assured. Jesus is the answer to all human problems, and He is the only one who can guide and lead you in the path you are supposed to walk in. Trust Him and place Him first in all that you do including today.

May 2nd

Proverbs 29:23

A man's pride will bring him low
But the humble in spirit will retain honor

Comments

God hates pride. Pride is a cancer and if left alone can devour you. Pray to Jesus that He gives you victory over pride and allow Him to teach you humility through His own timing and methods. Several times in the Bible God mentions that He hates pride. Ask Jesus to teach you humility and when He is done with you, you'll begin to see life from a different perspective. Ask Him today.

May 3rd

Proverbs 29:24

The fear of man brings a snare
But whoever trusts in the Lord shall be safe

Comments

God wants His children to trust Him always. When you trust God you will be honoring Him and He will not let you down. He will show you His goodness and faithfulness in every situation that challenges you if only you trust Him.

May 4ᵗʰ

Proverbs 30:5

For every word of God is pure
He is a shield to those who put their trust
in him

Comments

It is crucial to read the Word of God every day. Reading His Word makes you growth spiritually and it also prepares you to face life battles. Make time early each morning to commune with Jesus by praying and reading His word. In the beginning this may not be easy but with practice and perseverance Jesus will see you through and the results will change you.

May 5ᵗʰ

Proverbs 30:7

Two things I request of you
Deprive me not before I die
Remove falsehood and lies far from me
Give me neither poverty nor riches
Feed me with the food you prescribe
for me
Lest I be full and deny you
And say who is the Lord or lest I be poor
and steal and profane the name of my God

Comments

Jesus provides for His children every day. He gives food, clothes, and shelter through His daily providences. Thank Him for this and by faith claim the many promises found in His word. God does not want you to be poor and beg. Rather He wants to see you prosper and succeed in all that you do because in the end it is He who will receive the glory.

May 6th

Proverbs 30:1

I will both lie down in peace and sleep
For you alone, O Lord makes me dwell
in safety

Comments

During sleep it is God who keeps you safe. His angels will surround
you to protect you from the enemy. A lot of things happen when
you are sleeping and if it is not for the love of God you may be
destroyed by the many dangers we face while asleep. But through
His grace He allows you to wake up every day and enjoy what
He has in store for us. Remember to commit your life to Jesus
before sleeping.

May 7th

Psalm 4:8

But let all those rejoice who put their trust
in you
Let them ever shout for joy because you
defend them
Let those also who love your name be
joyful in you

Comments

Trusting in Jesus brings rewards including happiness and joy. God
is honored when we do this and He uses every occasion when you
express trust in Him to demonstrate His power and authority.
Trust him today and you will enjoy His blessings.

May 8ᵗʰ

Proverbs 5:12

For you O Lord will bless the righteous
With favor you will surround him as with
a shield

Comments

Every child of God who is righteous will be blessed. Total trust
and surrender to Jesus means that God will favor and bless you
beyond your imaginations. He will protect you and shield you
from all harm if only you place your total and unwavering trust
in Him.

May 9ᵗʰ

Psalm 24:7

Lift up your heads O you gates
And be lifted up you everlasting doors
And the king of glory shall come in

Comments

Jesus wants to dwell with you forever, but He cannot do this unless
you invite Him in. Remember that He is the King of glory and
there is no other King or authority mightier than Him. Praise Him
today and always and allow Him into your heart. If you do so He
will direct and guide, you every day of your life.

May 10ᵗʰ

Psalm 24:10

Who is this King of glory?
The Lord of hosts
He is the King of glory

Comments

There is only one King of glory and that is Jesus Christ. Bless Him, Praise Him and Worship Him. He is the creator God who is supposed to be gloried because He is worthy.

May 11ᵗʰ

Proverbs 24:8

Who is this King of glory?
The Lord strong and mighty
The Lord mighty in battle

Comments

The Lord will fight all your battles for you. Whatever problem you might be going through today take advantage of Jesus' presence and you will be blessed. Jesus does not disappoint anyone who trusts in Him.

May 12ᵗʰ

Psalm 73:17

Until I went into the sanctuary of God
Then I understood their end

Comments

It is in the sanctuary where you find the presence of God. When you come into the sanctuary you have to be reverent and always being mindful that you are in the presence of the almighty God.

May 13ᵗʰ

Psalm 73:23

Nevertheless I am continually with you
You hold me by my right hand

Comments

Jesus Christ will always be with you for as long as you let Him lead you. Allow Him to do so and He will carry you with His right hand. His right hand is powerful. It will shield you from all harm, difficulties or problems you may encounter.

May 14ᵗʰ

Psalm 73:24

You will guide me with your counsel
And afterward receive me in glory

Comments

Let God guide you today and let Him be your counselor in all matters. One of the greatest things in life is to let God lead you all the way. You will never go wrong when you do this. At the end of your life is the eternal promise of glory.

May 15ᵗʰ

Psalm 73:25

Who have I in heaven but you?
And there is none upon earth that I desire besides you

Comments

There is nothing that can compare with heaven. On this side of creation heaven should be your focus and vision. When you have Jesus by your side you have all that matters, and heaven is guaranteed.

May 16th

Psalm 70:5

But I am poor and needy
Make haste to me, O God
You are my help and my deliver
O Lord, do not delay

Comments

Only Jesus is the surest deliverer and helper. When you are in need today call upon Him and He will come to your rescue. He loves you and He wants to do the best for you. Trust Him and He will never fail you.

May 17th

Psalm 71:5

For you are my hope, O Lord God
You are my trust from my youth

Comments

Put your trust and hope in God. God takes care of you from the time you are born until you die. Let Him lead, guide, and protect you every moment of your life, even beginning today.

May 18th

Psalm 71:9

Do not cast me off in the time of old age
Do not forsake me when my strength
fails me

Comments

Jesus will always love you no matter how old you are. If you are young continue trusting Him until you're old. He loves you too much to leave you alone. The key is to keep on trusting Him and allowing Him to lead and guide you. Consult Him in everything and at every stage of your life.

May 19ᵗʰ

Psalm 71:18

Now also when I am old and gray headed,
O God do not forsake me
Until I declare your strength to
this generation
Your power to everyone who is to come

Comments

Jesus will keep you safe until your head is gray. Give Him the opportunity to work marvelous things in your life and declare these blessings to the younger generation. Every day starting today should be an opportunity to let Him shine in your life so others might see the mighty acts of God in your life.

May 20ᵗʰ

Psalm 67:1

God be merciful to us and bless us
And cause His face to shine upon us

Comments

Every day beginning today your prayer should be to let God extend His mercy and blessings on you. Always pray daily and ask Him to let His face shine on you. People will see that there is something different about you when you let Jesus shine His face upon you.

May 21st

Psalm 68:19

Blessed be the Lord
Who daily loads us with benefits?
The God of our salvation

Comments

It is God who gives us everything we have. Your job, strength to perform your job, material possessions and everything you may have now or in the future come from Him. Even our lives belong to Him. We move and live in Him, so let your desire be to bless Him every day of your life.

May 22nd

Psalm 69:13

But as for me my prayer is to you
O Lord in the acceptable time
O Lord in the multitude of your mercy
Hear me in the truth of your salvation

Comments

Let your prayer be always to praise and bless God. When pressed with this world's problems and anxieties let Jesus handle these on your behalf. He never fails, so why don't you try Him.

May 23rd

Psalm 69:34

Let heaven and earth praise him
The seas and everything that moves
in them

Comments

The essence of life is to worship God. Worship Him when you are working, worship Him when you are sitting, walking, or just about doing anything. Let the thoughts of continual praise spring out of your mind and mouth always. You will be happy, fulfilled, and joyful when you do this.

May 24ᵗʰ

Psalm 65:11

> You crown the year with your goodness
> And your paths drip with abundance

Comments

If you want God's blessings, ask Him, and trust Him. God's Word is full of promises that are ours for the asking. Continual trust and dependency on Him are crucial in this process. You will be surprised at how the blessings of God will overtake you if only you trust Him completely.

May 25ᵗʰ

Psalm 65:5

> By awesome deeds in righteousness
> You will answer us
> O God of our salvation
> You who are the confidence of all the ends
> of the earth
> And of the far off seas

Comments

Today, pray for anything you need and in His own time, will and way God will answer you. The key is to believe and that He will answer you.

May 26th

Psalm 66:7

He rules by his power for ever
His eyes observe the nations
Do not let the rebellious exalt them

Comments

God is sovereign. He is much more powerful than anything in creation. He holds this world by His power, and nothing can stand in His way. He does whatever He pleases, and no one can question whatever He does.

May 27th

Psalm 66:18

If I regard iniquity in my heart
The Lord will not hear

Comments

Do not give room to sin in your heart. This might block God's blessings from reaching you. Confess every sin that you may be harboring and, today ask Jesus to give you strength to overcome.

May 28th

Psalm 80:3

Restore us, O God
Cause your face to shine
And we shall be saved

Comments

Let God's face shine you. If people see Jesus' face shining on you, they may be drawn to Him. If you are in trouble, ask Jesus to help you and He will deliver you from your situation. He will place you where you need to be, even in a higher position you may not be expecting.

May 29th

Psalm 81:10

I am the Lord your God who brought you
out of the land of Egypt
Open your mouth wide and I will fit

Comments

God's promises are sure and true and always come to pass. It is God who takes care of all your needs. Let your needs be known to Him and He will fulfill all of them, He does not fail.

May 30th

Psalm 82:3

Defend the poor and fatherless
Do justice to the afflicted and needy

Comments

If you get an opportunity to serve the poor or any one broken or suffering, do so in the name of Jesus. You must promote social justice for all if is within your means and capacity to do so. In so doing you will be answering Gods call for salvation of all mankind.

May 31st

Psalm 35:18

I will give you thanks in the
great congregation
I will praise you among many people

Comments

Praising and worshiping God should be your number one priority. Do this when you are alone, or when you are in the congregation, or when you are with your family, or when you are working. God is worthy of all praise and worship and let praise continually spring from your heart, mouth or lips.

June 1st

Psalm 83:13

That men may know that you whose name alone is the Lord
Are the most High over all the earth?

Comments

God is God and He must be praised by all creation. His creation is unfathomable, and no one can measure His greatness. Praise Him today with all your heart and soul.

June 2nd

Psalm 78:35

Then they remembered
That God was their rock
And the Most High their redeemer

Comments

The greatest privilege you have today is to bring all your burdens to Jesus. He is the rock who will never let you down. He will bring you out of all your troubles and He will redeem you from all your wrongs and inequities.

June 3rd

Psalm 78:39

For he remembered that they were but flesh
A breath that passes away and does not come again

Comments

God knows that you are breath and dust and that at a stroke of a second you could lose your breath. But if you believe in Jesus you can rest assured that eternity awaits you even after you pass away. Start believing today.

June 4th

Psalm 79:8

Oh do not remember former iniquities against us
Let your tender mercies come speedily to meet us
For we have been brought very low

Comments

The Lord will forgive your sins if you genuinely repent. Jesus wants to extend His mercy to you today and even tomorrow. Come to Him and drink from the cup of His tender mercies.

June 5th

Psalm 76:11

Make vows to the Lord your God and pay them
Let all who are around him bring Him presents to him who ought to be feared

Comments

It is easy to make vows. But be careful that whenever you make vows to Jesus you stand ready to keep them. Jesus is worth of receiving your blessings, praise and worship. Do not hesitate to praise Him through vows that you will keep.

June 6th

Psalm 76:1

I cried out to God with my voice
To God with my voice
And he gave hear to me

Comments

Whenever you are in deep trouble run to Jesus and put your burdens at His feet. He will never let you down or send you away. Claim His faithfulness.

June 7th

Psalm 76:12

I will also meditate on all your work
And talk of your deeds

Comments

God is the creator, and His creation is revealed in nature every day. Take time to contemplate God's greatness by looking at the stars, the moon, and other heavenly bodies at night. Look at these in the context of Gods greatness.

June 8th

Psalm 74:12

For God is my King of old
Working salvation in the midst of the earth

Comments

Only Jesus can guarantee you salvation and eternal life. It is free and all you need to do is to claim it. God wants every person including you to be saved. Take Him seriously at His word and He will never disappoint you.

June 9ᵗʰ

Psalm 74:16

The day is yours, the night also is yours
You have prepared the light and the sun
You have set all the borders of the earth
You have made summer and winter

Comments

Everything in creation has been made by God. The day, night, and the seasons are made by Him. When you go through your day today remember God is in control of your life because He is the creator.

June 10ᵗʰ

Psalm 75:6

For exaltation comes neither from the east
nor from the west, nor from the south
But God is the judge
He puts down one
And exalts the other

Comments

Only God will promote you. Exalt and worship Him and walk in His steps every day beginning today and He will never let you down.

June 11ᵗʰ

Psalm 90:1

He who dwells in the secrete place of the
most High shall abide under the shadows
of the Almighty

Comments

Let today draw you closer to God. Pray that His presence goes with you wherever you go. Ask Him to bring you into His presence where you will experience true peace and joy.

June 12ᵗʰ

Psalm 91:15

He shall call upon me and I will answer
I will be with him in trouble
I will deliver him and honor him

Comments

Whatever trouble or obstacles you may find yourself in today always take your burdens to Jesus. He can handle whatever problem you are facing. He never fails and He is always faithful.

June 13ᵗʰ

Psalm 91:16

With long life will I satisfy him and show him my salvation

Comments

Your life belongs to Jesus. Acknowledge this to Him and let Him lead you and guide you because only He knows what is best for you.

June 14ᵗʰ

Psalm 89:7

God is greatly to be feared in the Assembly of the Saints
And to be held in reverence by all those who are around Him

Comments

Remember that God is holy and is above everything. When you talk to Him in prayer do so with fear and trembling because you are coming into the presence of the creator of the universe. Even at the mention of His name you should be careful not to misuse it. He is a holy and awesome God.

June 15ᵗʰ

Psalm 89:11

The heavens are yours, the earth also is yours
The world and all its fullness you have founded them

Comments

God owns everything including you and whatever you own. He takes, gives and, takes away and therefore you must be thankful for everything you have and even just for the life you are breathing today.

June 16ᵗʰ

Psalm 89:16

In your name they rejoice all day long
And in your righteousness they are exalted

Comments

Full joy can only be found in offering worship and praise to God. Let this day be a blessing to you and praise Jesus at every moment of your day.

June 17th

Psalm 90:4

> For a thousand years in your sight are like
> yesterday when it is past
> And like a watch in the night

Comments

God is not limited by time. He lives outside of time. When you make Him your God today you are assured of eternal life. This is your promise today.

June 18th

Psalm 118:6

> The Lord is on my side
> I will not fear
> What can man do to me?

Comments

If you make Jesus your comforter and guide today, He will protect you and give you peace n the midst of problems. Trust Him today and experience His joy and peace.

June 19th

Psalm 118:8

> It is better to trust in the Lord
> Than to put confidence in man

Comments

Don't trust friends, family, relatives, or colleagues for any problem that you are facing. These individuals will fail you, but Jesus will never.

June 20ᵗʰ

Psalm 118:10

All nations surrounded me
But in the name of the Lord I will
destroy them

Comments

Whatever obstacle you may be facing, in the name of Jesus you will overcome it. Take Jesus at His word and see what happens. Jesus has won all battles for you so just trust Him and let Him address all your challenges.

June 21ˢᵗ

Psalm 118:18

The Lord has chastened me severely
But he has not given me over to death

Comments

Sometimes God will see it fit to discipline you. This may happen by way of problems, troubles, family tensions, sickness and so forth. If this take place recall it means that Jesus loves, you and He is fashioning your character so you can become more like Him. Rejoice amid trouble and affliction because God is chiseling and pruning you for His glory.

June 22ⁿᵈ

Psalm 119:37

Turn away my eyes from looking at
worthless things
And revive me in your way

Comments

Ask God to direct your steps today so that you don't waste time on worthless things. Let Him direct your focus so that you concentrate on things that matter in life. Your life will be more fulfilling this way and you will be a happy and joyous person.

June 23rd

Psalm 119:67

Before I was afflicted I went astray
But now I keep your word

Comments

God will use illness and other kinds of challenges to redirect you, prune you, clean you up, develop you or sharpen your character. If you go through this process remain faithful and trust Him. He will never let you down.

June 24th

Psalm 119:71

It is good for me that I was afflicted
That I may learn your statutes

Comments

After you have trusted Jesus amid your afflictions, He will give you peace and joy to endure. In the end you will become a better person filled with joy.

June 25th

Psalm 115:16

The heavens even the heavens are the Lords
But the earth he has given to the children
of men

Comments

God is creator. He made the heavens and all heavenly bodies. The earth is a special planet in the universe because this is where He placed mankind whom He made in His image. When you look at yourself in the mirror, rejoice because you are a special creation placed on a planet that is highly regarded in all creation.

June 26th

Psalm 116:1

I love the Lord because he has heard my voice and my supplications

Comments

Whatever problems you may be facing today take them to Jesus in prayer and He will answer you according to His abundant grace.

June 27th

Psalm 116:2

Because he has inclined his ear to me
Therefore I will call upon him as long as I live

Comments

God will always be there for you. Tell Him of all your issues and concerns and He will hear you if you take Him at His word.

June 28th

Psalm 116:13

Precious in the sight of the Lord is the death of His saints

Comments

Jesus has already conquered death. If you die today, you are safe in His arms and eternity awaits you. Let your mindset be imbued with the presence of God every day and eternity will start right now for you.

June 29th

Psalm 113:3

From the rising of the sun to its going down
The Lord's name is to be praised

Comments

Praise God every moment of your life. He is worthy of being praised. Talk about Him and sing songs of praise to Him whenever you have time.

June 30th

Psalm 113:4

The Lord is high above all nations
And his glory is above the nations

Comment

God resides in the heavens of heavens, and He is above all nations. No one can get to the heavenly realm where God resides. But one day when Jesus comes you will be there. Let this hope encourage you today.

July 1st

Psalm 115:3

But our God is in heaven
He does whatever He pleases

Comment

God is the ultimate creator of everything. He does not need any person's permission to do whatever He wants to. He is God and He is only one God. If He blesses you no one can thwart your blessings. If He curses you no one can reverse the cursing. Ask Him for blessings today and rest assured that if He answers your prayer your blessings will come no matter what they devil may try to do against you. Further, remember that whatever situation or experience you may find yourself in today remember that God is in control. He will see you through if only you trust Him. God has promised that help is only a prayer away and if you focus on Him the devil will have no chance. Take advantage of His presence and bring all your burdens to Him.

July 2nd

Psalm 115:12

The Lord has been mindful of us
He will bless us
He will bless the house of Israel
He will bless the house of Aaron

Comment

Jesus will never forget those who trust Him. He is there for them day in and day out. He wants to bless you to the extent that you recognize His goodness and faithfulness. His blessings are free and available if only you claim by faith. His Word never fails, and it has always been tried and tested. He wants to bless you today with victory, joy, and peace and with much more.

July 3rd

Psalm 115:13

> He will bless those who fear the Lord
> Both small and great

Comment

Fearing God is the beginning of wisdom. As you demonstrate your fear and reverence to God, make Him first in your life and He will show you His goodness on you. Jesus does not segregate between the young and old when it comes to blessings. He will bless both alike. Do not forget that you are precious in His sight and always be mindful of His presence as you go through this day and know that He got you.

July 4th

Psalm 111:10

> The fear of the Lord is the beginning
> of wisdom
> A good understanding have those who do
> his commandments
> His praise endures forever

Comment

True wisdom does not lie in the amount of academic knowledge one may possess or in one's intellectual capacity. The best thing you can do today and going forward is to fear God and give Him glory. Fear for God will enable you to tap into His wisdom. Keep His commandments because these are important for your life. Further, as this day unfolds do not forget to always send praises to Jesus because He is worthy to be praised.

July 5ᵗʰ

Psalm 112:6

Surely he will never be shaken
The righteous will be in
everlasting remembrance

Comment

You occupy an important place in God's heart. Whatever may happen to you today or tomorrow remember that you will always be in God's plan for salvation. God will make this possible because He loves you and He wants to demonstrate His faithfulness to you even now. Focus on Him and on His goodness.

July 6ᵗʰ

Psalm 112:7

He will not be afraid of evil tidings
His heart is steadfast trusting in the Lord

Comment

When you fully fix your eyes on Jesus nothing will come against you. He will protect and deliver you from all kinds of obstacles and trials you may face. You sole responsibility is to trust Him completely and totally depend on Him today and every day. God wants you to trust and depend on Him so that He can show and prove His goodness in your life.

July 7ᵗʰ

Proverbs 9:10

The fear of the Lord is the beginning
of wisdom
And the knowledge of the Holy One
is understanding

Comment

Fearing and worshiping God is the most important responsibility you can have in your life. Make Jesus the center of your life. Acknowledge His presence and let Him handle all your problems whether it be marriage, financial, health, relationship problem, He will take care of it. You will never be disappointed when you walk with God.

July 8ᵗʰ

Proverbs 9:11

For by Me your days will be multiplied
And years will be added to you

Comment

Your life is in the hands of God and He knows the number of all your days. It is He only who can multiply or reduce them. But remember He wants you to have the best of life at its maximum. When you walk with Him every day and when you totally trust Him even today, you will enjoy your life and Jesus will add more years to your life.

July 9ᵗʰ

Proverbs 10:22

The blessings of the Lord make one rich
And He adds no sorrow with it

Comment

God wants to bless you. His blessings are sure and will last as long you trust Him. When God blesses you no one will stand in the way of His blessings. He will make sure that the devil does not jeopardize the blessing that he pours on you. Trust Him.

July 10th

Proverbs 10:24

The fear of the wicked will come upon him
And the desire of the righteous will
be granted

Comment

When God is pleased with you be certain that your desires will be granted. Although sometimes they may not come as expected they will be fulfilled. Even your enemies will not be able to stand against God's blessings for your life. Just trust Him today and follow His lead in your life.

July 11th

Proverbs 11:8

The righteous will be delivered
from trouble
And it comes to the wicked instead

Comment

God is on your side, and He wants the best for you. He will deliver you from all trouble and guess what? He will let your enemies bear the brunt of your troubles and their faces will be filled with shame. They are the conditions for this promise though. You need to wholly place Jesus as first in your life and then He will be your provider and protector.

July 12th

Proverbs 11:28

He who trusts in his riches will fall
But the righteous will flourish like foliage

Comment

Do not trust your material possessions. Material possessions including earthly riches will pass away but God's Word and promises will not. If you trust God with your life and all that you have you will never go wrong and you will find true meaning for your life.

July 13th

Proverbs 12:13

The wicked is ensnared by the transgressions of his lips
But the righteous will come through trouble

Comment

Every trouble, obstacle or challenge that comes your way today will be defeated if you trust in Jesus. Ask Him to give you victory for every battle you may face today. The key is to trust Jesus and focus only on Him. Do that and you will not be disappointed?

July 14th

Proverbs 12:22

Lying lips are an abomination to the Lord
But those who deal truthfully are his delight

Comment

God does not like lying, He hates it. Be truthful in all your dealings and He will reward you. Lying is of the Devil. The devil will do all he can to make you lie. Just trust Jesus and ask Him to keep you from lying. When under pressure to lie send a prayer to Jesus to intervene on your behalf and rest assured, He will be faithful.

July 15th

Proverbs 6:16

A proud look, a lying tongue
Hands that shed innocent blood
A heart that devises wicked plans
Feet that is swift in running to evil
A false witness who speaks lies
And one who sows discord among brethren

Comment

God does not like pride, lying, or heart that devises wicked schemes. Let the Holy Spirit help you overcome these ills if you are a victim of any one of them. It is not possible to deal with these issues on your own. Only Jesus can help you overcome them. Let Him do that today and you will be blessed.

July 16th

Proverbs 8:18

For riches, honor is with me
Enduring riches and righteousness

Comment

Do you want to enjoy a blessed life? Do you want to gain true riches in your life? Do you desire real honor? Jesus can provide all these blessings because He is God the creator. He will lavish these promises on you if you let Him rule over you. Your life will never be the same and you will shine like stars in the sky.

July 17th

Proverbs 8:35

For whoever finds me finds life
And obtains favor from the Lord

Comment

Finding Jesus means acquiring eternal life. It is the most important thing one can ever do. Make Jesus the most important person in your life, even today. Allow Him to be Lord of your life and He will bless you beyond your wildest imagination. Contemplate on the blessings you might have if you let Jesus take total control of your life. He is a faithful God.

July 18ᵗʰ

Proverbs 4:18

But the path of the just is like a shining sun
That shines ever brighter unto the perfect day

Comment

It is nice and joyful to let Jesus guide you every day. Let Him be central in your life and as you step out today and every day your path will be illuminated with His eternal light. God wants the best for you. Let Him guide you every moment of your day and you will be blessed.

July 19ᵗʰ

Proverbs 4:26
Ponder the path of your feet
And let all your ways be established
Do not turn to the right or the left
Remove your foot from evil

Comment

Before you make any small or big decision ask Jesus to guide you in all your decisions. Walking alone without God's guidance is a sure recipe for failure and destruction. Only Jesus can guarantee you success if only you let Him.

July 20th

Proverbs 5:21

For the ways of man are before the eyes of the Lord
And He ponders all his paths

Comment

Whatever you do today or whatever decisions you make in your life, God knows everything and He knows what is best for you. Take advantage of His grace by asking Him to lead you so that you don't make any unnecessary mistakes. No one knows you the best as Jesus does so why don't you allow Him to be your Lord?

July 21st

Psalm 124:2

If it had not been the Lord on our side
When men rose up against us

Comment

Jesus will fight all your battles, and this can start today. With Him on your side victory is certain. There has never been a battle which He has failed. All your enemies will be defeated when Jesus is your commander. Allow Him to fight for you and victory is yours.

July 22nd

Psalm 124:3

Then they would have swallowed us alive
When their wrath was kindled against us
Then the waters would have overwhelmed us

Comment

Without Jesus, your enemies will defeat you. You will not do anything on your own and you will not defeat anything that maybe troubling you. Only God can provide you with assurances of victory if you make Him your Lord. Do that today and feed on His promises.

July 23rd

Psalm 124:8

Our help is in the name of the Lord
Who made heaven and earth?

Comment

There is no name under heaven that can save you but the name of Jesus. Make Him your Savior and let Him run your life. God is the only secure and true source of victory. Your life and success depend on Him. Pray today that He protects, defends, and supports you all the way.

July 24th

Psalm 125:1

Those who trust in the Lord are like mount Zion
Which cannot be moved but abides forever

Comment

Nothing is as important as trusting in the Lord. He is unmovable; He is a formidable force that is eternal. Trust Him and see what kind of blessings will be poured on your life.

July 25th

Psalm 126:5

Those who sow in tears
Shall reap in joy

Comment

Sometimes you may not understand the paths Jesus crafts for you. Things may seem too dark, insurmountable, or difficult. But know this. Even though your path may be clouded with uncertainties the end result will always be victory for you. With Jesus on your side victory is always guaranteed.

July 26th

Psalm 127:1

Unless the Lord builds the house
They labor in vain who build it
The watchman stays awake in vain

Comment

Let Jesus be a part of whatever project you undertake. Let Him be a part of your studies, of your work, of your family life and of everything that involves you. Involving God in all your activities will assure you of true success. Let Him build you.

July 27th

Psalm 127:2

It is vain for you to rise up early
To sit up late
To eat the bread of sorrows
For so He gives his beloved sleep

Comment

Do you want real rest? Do want to enjoy a good night's sleep? Do you want to make good plans for your morrow? Let Jesus handle this for you. Today try to have quite time with Him and set all your plans for the day before Him and see how these unfold. I can assure you that you will be blessed.

July 28th

Psalm 130:3

If you Lord shall mark iniquities
O Lord who would stand?

Comment

No one living is perfect. We all have imperfections, but the good news is that Jesus covers these in His precious blood. When God looks at us He does not see our imperfections but instead sees the perfection of Jesus. God is faithful and He will demonstrate His faithfulness in your life if you allow Him to.

July 29th

Psalm 130:5

I wait for the Lord my soul waits
And in his Word I do hope

Comment

You will do well if you make Jesus number one in your life even today. No one and nothing can compare with Him. Read His Word every day and claim the promises He has in store for you.

July 30ᵗʰ

Psalm 121:1

I will lift up my eyes to the hills
From whence comes my help

Comment

Take time to pray and let your burdens be lifted to Jesus. Everything you need will come from Him. He is the source of good things you may need in life and let Him do that for you. Pray every day and put on a mindset of praise, worship, and prayer.

July 31ˢᵗ

Psalm 121:2

My help comes from the Lord who made heaven and earth

Comment

Everything you need comes from God. Whatever troubling situation you may find yourself in ask Jesus to deliver you and He will honor you. Make Him the source of all your help and let Him provide all your needs. Feed on His faithfulness and your life will be a blessing to yourself and others.

August 1st

Psalm 121:5

The Lord is your keeper
The Lord is your shade at your right hand
The sun shall not strike you by day
Nor the moon by night

Comment

Only God can keep you and protect you from all trials. He is your shield and your fortress. Ask Him to walk with you every moment of your life. His presence will ensure your safety and security. Be aware of this and let Him guide you all the way.

August 2nd

Psalm 123:1

Unto you, I lift up my eyes
O, You who dwell in the heavens

Comment

Worship Jesus every day and every moment. Let Him show you the path you are supposed to walk in. When in difficult circumstances send a prayer to Him and He will be right there to meet you. He is God and He has never failed in anything. All His promises are sure and true and they will always come to pass as long as you claim them. Do that today.

August 3rd

Psalm 123:2

Behold, as the eyes of servants look to the hand of their masters
As the eyes of a maid look to the hand of her mistress
So our eyes look to the Lord our God
Until He has mercy on us

Comment

Let your desires and needs be known to Jesus. Only He has the power to address them. Look up to Him and lift all your problems to Him and you will never be disappointed.

August 4th

Psalm 119:89

Forever, O Lord
Your word is settled in heaven

Comment

No one can counter God's Word. Read and chew on it every day and if possible, start your today by praying to God and then reading and digesting His Word. Read the Word and listen to Him in moment of silence. When this becomes your habit, you will change. You will have a new mindset set on God. This is what matters in life.

August 5th

Psalm 119:90

Your faithfulness endures to all generations
You established the earth and it
abides forever

Comment

God is faithful and will always be faithful. He is just and He wants the best for your life. Trust Him today and see how He proves His faithfulness and guides you through the day.

August 6th

Psalm 119:105

Your Word is a lamp to my feet
And a light to my path

Comment

The Word of God is food for your soul. Read it every day and digest it. Let it become part and parcel of your being and you will never be the same. The Word of God is the best blueprint for your life. Let it speak to you and obey its instructions.

August 7th

Psalm 119:147

I rise before the dawning of the morning
And cry for help
I hope in your Word

Comment

Read the Word of God every day. Try to make it a habit to rise up early and read and meditate on the Word. The blessings you will reap from this practice will be immense and your life will be purposeful and full of meaningful.

August 8th

Psalm 119:164

Seven times a day I praise you
Because of your righteous judgments

Comment

God is worthy to be praised. Let your lips praise Him every moment of your life even now. Let praise constantly come from your mouth. Sing, meditate, and contemplate His greatness all the time.

August 9th

Psalm 142:5

I cried out to you, O Lord
I said you are my refuge
My portion in the land of the living

Comment

God is your refugee and a fortress in time of trouble. He is your deliverer and high tower. He is your shield and strength. Today as you go about your business, trust Him with all your heart and soul.

August 10th

Psalm 143:8

> Cause me to hear your loving kindness in the morning
> For in you do I trust?
> Cause me to know the way in which I should walk
> For I lift up my soul to you

Comment

Today ask God to guide you and let Him walk with you. Read His Word and apply it in your life. His Word is powerful. It will change you if you allow it to.

August 11th

Psalm 144:2

> My loving kindness and my fortress
> My high, tower and my deliver
> My shield and the one in which I take refuge
> Who subdues my people under me?

Comment

Jesus is the true refugee who can shield you from every dart the devil throws at you. He is kind and faithful and He will not fail you. He has already won the battle and the devil knows this. All his old tricks are no match for Jesus. Commit all your worries, fears and plans to God and you will experience success in your life.

August 12th

Psalm 139:23
Search me, O God and know my heart
Try me and know my anxieties
And see if there is any wicked way in me
And lead me in the way everlasting

Comment

It is only God who knows the condition of your heart. Ask Him to purify you from all kinds of impurities that you may be harboring. Let Jesus take stock of your heart and allow Him to remove all those issues preventing you from making progress. He will give you a new heart and He will guide you all the way.

August 13th

Psalm 141:3

Set a guard over my mouth
Keep watch over the door of my lips

Comment

Keeping quiet is an important virtue. Don't just make speak because you want to be heard. Learn to control your tongue and speak only when it is appropriate for you. When you speak let your words be encouraging words to those who hear them. Let your speech be illuminated with heavenly glory so that those who hear you will be blessed and praise God.

August 14th

Psalm 141:5

> Let the righteous strike me
> It shall be a kindness
> And let him reprove me
> It shall be as excellent oil
> Let my head not refuse it

Comment

When you walk with Jesus and allow Him to take control of your life people will notice it. They will notice something different about you and consequently will want to get close to you. This difference about you is only made possible when you make Jesus your Lord and Savior. Do that today and you will reap untold blessings?

August 15th

Psalm 142:2

> I pour out my complaint before Him
> I declare before him my trouble

Comment

Are you in trouble today? Is something troubling your mind? Is fear and worry stalking you? Whatever it is that you are facing take it to Jesus in prayer. Only He has the power to bring under control every negative circumstance or situation you may be facing. When Jesus is in control all will work to your advantage. This is a promise, claim it.

August 16th

Psalm 138:3

In the day when I cried out you
answered me
And made me bold with strength in
my soul

Comment

When you make a genuine plea to Jesus to address any excruciating
or troubling circumstance/s in your life, He will answer you. God
does not fail his own people. If you honor Him, He will honor
you in return. Do that today.

August 17th

Psalm 138:7

Though I walk in the midst of trouble
You will revive me
You will stretch out your hand
Against the wrath of my enemies
And your right hand will save me

Comment

It does not matter to God what you are facing. Just trust Him
and He will make everything easy for you. When you are feeling
down pray that He revives you and He will do that. When you
are pressed down to the limit cry out and stretch out your hand to
Him. Pay attention on Him and see how your situation unfolds.
If you let Him control your circumstances victory is guaranteed.

August 18th

Psalm 139:7

Where can I go from your spirit?
Or where can I flee from your presence?

Comment

God is everywhere. You cannot run away from Him. Let your mindset dwell on His presence and contemplate the great things He can do for you. Take Jesus at His words and He will never fail you.

August 19th

Psalm 139:14

I will praise you for I am fearfully and wonderfully made
Marvelous are your works
And that my soul knows very well

Comment

Your body is the temple of the living God. Take care of it and guard it jealously and in so doing you will be honoring God.

August 20th

Psalm 139:17

How precious are your thoughts to me
O God?
How great is the sum of them

Comment

God wants the best for your life. He has given you His son Jesus Christ through whom is the promise of eternal life. Accept Jesus in your life and claim all the promises He has in store for you.

God is just waiting to lavish you with His blessings, and it is up to you to claim them.

August 21st

Psalm 131:2

Surely I have calmed and quieted my soul
Like a weaned child with his mother
Like a weaned child is my soul within me

Comment

Let your mind be calmed and rest in Jesus. He will not let you down but will give you true peace and joy.

August 22nd

Psalm 133:1

Behold, how good and how pleasant it is
For brethren to dwell together in unity

Comment

Unity and love for each other is one of the testimonies of being a child of God. Pray that you will enjoy unity in your family and with other fellow believers. If you let unity take its course in your circumstance this might be a testimony of the goodness of God in your life.

August 23rd

Psalm 135:5

For I know that the Lord is great
And our Lord is above all gods

Comment

No one is above God. He is the creator of the universe and of everything in the universe. Worshiping Him is your privilege. Walk with Him because He wants to be your friend.

August 24th

Psalm 137:1

Oh give thanks to the Lord for He is good
For His mercy endures forever

Comment

Giving thanks is a type of worship. Give thanks in everything. When you wake up in the morning, when you are bathing, when you are eating breakfast or lunch, when you are driving to work, when you are working, when you knock off from work, when you retire for bed always remember to give thanks to God for His goodness.

August 25th

Psalm 137:2

Who gives food to all flesh?
For his mercy endures forever

Comment

It is God who provides all your needs. Your food, clothes, shelter, energy to work and everything else comes from Him. Praise Him.

August 26th

Psalm 148:13

Let them praise the name of the Lord
For his name alone is exalted
His glory is above the earth and heaven

Comment

Praise God every second, every minute, every hour, and every day of your life. Praise is good because it will not only lift you to the glory of God, but it will position you to a different level of spiritual existence.

August 27th

Psalm 149:4

For the Lord takes pleasure in his people
He will beautify the humble with salvation

Comment

God wants the best for you. He has in store the best blessings you can ever imagine. Be humble and let Him offer you His salvation which is free of charge and the blessings will flow.

Psalm 150:6

Let everything that has breath praise
the Lord
Praise the Lord

Comment

Praise, praise, praise Jesus today. He is worthy of being praised and of being glorified. You will be blessed if you allow praise to constantly come out of your mouth.

August 28th

Proverbs 2:33

But whoever listens to me will dwell safely
And will be secure without fear of evil

Comment

Your true safety and security are only found in Jesus. Listen to His voice through quite times and through reading His words every day. Do that today.

August 29th

Proverbs 2:6

> For the Lord gives wisdom
> From his mouth come knowledge
> and understanding

Comment

Do you want wisdom for your life? Do you want true knowledge? Ask Jesus in sincerity and He will give it to you. Wisdom is crucial to your life because without it your life may be devoid of meaning. Only Jesus can provide the true wisdom so necessary in your life. Ask Him today.

August 30th

Proverbs 3:5

> Trust in the Lord with all your heart
> And lean not on your own understanding
> In all your ways acknowledge him
> And he shall direct your paths

Comment

Trust is an important theme that reoccurs so many times in the Bible. God wants His children to trust Him completely. Why does He ask you to trust Him? Because He wants to demonstrate His power in your life, He wants to give you the best if you let Him. Begin to trust Him today.

August 31st

Proverbs 3:25

Do not be afraid of sudden terror
Nor of trouble from the wicked when
it comes

Comment

God will protect you from all evil and from all harm the devil intends for you. Do not forget to ask Him to protect you every day. When you ask God to protect you believe that He will protect you. Stay calm and let not fear overwhelm or overtake you. God is faithful and He will not let you down.

September 1st

Proverbs 326

For the Lord will be your confidence
And will keep your foot from being caught

Comment

When you put God first in your life, He will take care of your needs. Only God can direct your steps and only He can show you the right places you should walk in. If your foot slips, He will hold you up. In order to experience God's care, you need to learn to trust Him and this is only possible if you communicate with God on an everyday basis. Start today.

September 2nd

Psalm 146:2

While I live I will praise the Lord
I will sing praises to my God while I have
my being

Comment

Praise is crucial for your spiritual growth. Jesus deserves your praise and worship because He is God and He only is the creator. Pray that you learn to praise Him as you navigate through the day. Bring all your concerns and worries to Jesus and He will take care of them.

September 3rd

Psalm 146:3

Do not put your trust in princes
Nor in a son of man in whom there is
no help

Comment

Only God is to be trusted. Do not put your trust in man because man will fail you. But God never fails His children who trust Him. He has not lost any battle. It is important to recall your past victories Jesus has won for you and put these into perspective. These victories will anchor you and enhance your trust in God.

September 4th

Proverbs 146:4

His spirit departs he returns to his earth
In that very day his plans perish

Comment

Do not forget that one day you will die. On that day everything will cease, all your plans will evaporate. But when you have Jesus as your personal Savior you have the promise of eternal life. Death will not have power over you. Genuinely accept Jesus into your life and begin to walk with Him and you will have the assurance of eternal life.

September 5th

Psalm 147:11

The Lord takes pleasure in those who fear Him
In those who hope in His mercy

Comment

Fear God and give Him glory. The most crucial duty in this world is to praise and fear God. God holds in high esteem those who fear Him truthfully. Show Him your honor and gratitude through daily prayer, consistent meditation, and ardent reading of His word. Your life will be rich, rewarding and will be a blessing to others.

September 6th

Psalm 147:15

He sends his command to the earth
His Word runs very swiftly

Comment

God controls everything in the universe and on planet earth. He does whatever He pleases on earth and in the universe. He is God and no one can challenge His authority. If you let Him become your personal Savior, He will speak Words of favor in your life.

September 7th

Psalm 147:16

He gives snow like wool
He scatters the frost like ashes

Comment

God controls nature and everything in it and all things obey Him. He controls the weather including all the seasons. When you take a stroll in nature pay attention to the marvelous things God has made and give Him glory for those things.

September 8th

Psalm 145:14

The Lord upholds all who fall
And raises up all those who are
bowed down

Comment

If you fall trust God, He will raise up when you fall. You are not perfect and sometimes you will hit bumps and fall. This is okay because you are human and all of us do fall sometimes. The most significant step you can take when caught in this situation is to praise God, repent if there are any unrepented sins in your life and allow Jesus to wash you with His blood. For example, King David always repented after sinning and God always accepted Him back. God will also accept you back if you ask Him to.

September 9th

Psalm 145:15

The eyes of all look expectantly to you
And you give them their food in
due season

Comment

All your needs in terms of food, clothes, shelter, job…come from God. He is the creator and He owns everything. He will address your needs if you ask Him to. Bring all your requests and concerns to Him and you will be blessed today.

September 10th

Psalm 145:16

You open your hand
And satisfy the desires of every living

Comment

It is Jesus who satisfies all your desires and needs. Praise Him, bless Him, worship Him, adore Him, and shout to Him the only one and eternal God. Every living thing depends on Him for survival. The key is to trust Him. But in order for you to trust Him you need to know Him and you can only do this through daily prayer and through the reading of His Word. Start today.

September 11th

Psalm 145:19

He will fulfill the desire of those who
fear him
He also will hear their cry and save them

Comment

God is the only one that can satisfy all your needs. If anything, important is lacking in your life ask Jesus and He will provide what you need for your well-being. Even when you fall into all kinds of danger or pitfalls Jesus will be there to pick you up. Allow Him to act in your life and you will be amazed at the way things unfold in your life. Don't lock yourself up when the situation appears gloomy and dark or when it seems that your life is hanging on the edge of a cliff. There is hope for you and Jesus is the answer.

September 12ᵗʰ

Proverbs 15:8

The sacrifice of the wicked is an
abomination to the Lord
But the prayer of the upright is his delight

Comment

God is interested in hearing your prayers and in meeting all your needs. He is always interested in showering you with blessings He has in store for you. Trust Him and claim these blessings because they are yours just for the asking. He is waiting on you.

September 13ᵗʰ

Proverbs 15:29

The Lord is far from the wicked
But He hears the prayers of the righteous

Comment

God is just a second away from you. His presence is always with you. When you cry out to Him with genuine prayers, He will answer you. Make it a habit to have conversations with Him every day. Establish quite times where God will speak to you. It is good to know that you are talking to the creator of the universe.

September 14ᵗʰ

Proverbs 16:1

The preparation of the heart belong to man
But the answer of the tongue is from
the Lord

Comment

You can do whatever your heart tells you. You can follow your thoughts and feelings. But remember that only God knows what is best for you. He knows you more than you know yourself. So, when you direct your thoughts to Him He will answer you. Gods answer to your prayer is the best answer you can ever dream of. Pray to Him and watch how He will answer your prayers. You will not be disappointed.

September 15ᵗʰ

Proverbs 16:16

How much better it is to get wisdom than gold
And to get understanding is to be chosen rather than silver

Comment

True wisdom and understanding can only come from God. Do not trust worldly wisdom because it misleads and does not last. If you ask for Godly wisdom it will be given to you and your life will find true meaning. Godly wisdom will turn you into a useful individual and you will positively impact those people around you.

September 16ᵗʰ

Proverbs 17:22

A merry heart does well like medicine
But a broken spirit dries the bones

Comment

Be cheerful and do not allow sadness, fear and worry to get hold of you. These are areas that can cause risk to your health. When saddened by pressures of this world lift your heart and spirit to

God. God will grant you His joy and happiness. The outcome will be good health and an improved persona.

September 17ᵗʰ

Proverbs 13:19

A desire accomplished is sweet to the soul
But it is an abomination to fools to depart from evil

Comment

Do those things that are in your power to do. Every goal that you fulfill will bring unimaginable blessings. Remember people that are not right with God will do wicked acts because their nature is predisposed to negative behaviors. But you are a child of God and let Jesus run your life through His Holy spirit. Jesus will pour joy into your heart every time you do something good to your fellow human being. Enjoy life by letting God make you a blessing to others.

September 18ᵗʰ

Proverbs 13:11

Wealth gained by dishonesty will
be diminished
But he who gathers by labor will increase

Comment

Work is important to you. God has ordained work and through it come numerous blessings. Get God's blessings by becoming a productive heavenly citizen. Jesus will give you the strength you need for work if you ask Him and He will make you a blessing to your family, community, and nation.

September 19th

Proverbs 14:32

The wicked is banished in his wickedness
But the righteous has a refugee in his death

Comment

When you die, death will have no strength over you. However, if you desire this to be possible in your life there is a caveat. You need to trust in Jesus because it is only, He who guarantees eternal life. When you have Him, you have eternal life at your fingertips. Be excited because death no longer has a hold on you.

September 20th

Proverbs 14:23

In all labor there is profit
But idle chatter leads only to poverty

Comment

Hard work has its rewards. This is God's law and if you work hard, you will reap the benefits of hard work. Do not allow yourself to become a devil's den. Laziness, cheap chatter, gossip, and complacency among other things can be dangerous tools the devil uses to turn you into a liability. Use your gifts and talents to enjoy a meaningful and rewarding life.

September 21st

Proverbs 22:4

By humility and fear of the Lord
Are riches and honor and life

Comment

God loves the humble but hates the proud. Many times, in the Word of God pride is mentioned as something that God seriously condones and, He warns his children not to fall prey to this cancer. If you want your life to be in sync with God's word, ask Him to teach you humility. God's lessons in humility might not be something you will enjoy. If it takes crucibles to clean you up let God do His work in you. The result is always marvelous. Today, you will become a new shining jewel.

September 22ⁿᵈ

Proverbs 23:17

Do not let your heart envy sinners
But in the fear of the Lord continue all
day long

Comment

There is nothing about wicked people that should move you to envy. Let your focus be on Jesus. Think about Him every day, meditate on His word, talk to Him as you work or walk, think about what he has done for you. When you do this your whole character will be transformed and your perception of life will change for the better.

September 23ʳᵈ

Proverbs 23:18

For surely there is a hereafter and your
hope will not be cut off

Comment

Let your mind always contemplate heavenly glories prepared for you. Remind yourself that heaven is real and that one day you will be there. Let this promise not slip through your hands. But keep it real by constantly dwelling on Jesus. Let Him be your ever-present companion to guide you until you cross the bridge.

September 24th

Proverbs 24:10

If you faint in the day of adversity your strength is small

Comment

God will permit trials to come into your life. Don't despair because trials are meant to make you grow stronger in faith. Trials including suffering are Gods tools for chiseling and making you into what He wants you to be. When trials are tougher than you may handle God will provide a way of escape. He has promised that in His Word and you just need to claim that promise today.

September 25th

Proverbs 24:16

For a righteous man may fall seven times and rise again
But the wicked shall fall by calamity

Comment

Being a child of God does not mean that you are exempt from troubles. God will use trials to test your faith. Sometimes He will permit unexpected challenges to hit you. But remember that even if you succumb to these problems God will pick you up repeatedly. Only the person who does not trust in Jesus has no hope of rising again when he or she falls prey to trials. But you friend are a child of God and Jesus will always be there for you. Let this hope be yours today.

September 26ᵗʰ

Proverbs 25:19

Confidence in an unfaithful man in time
of trouble
Is like a bad tooth and a foot out of joint

Comment

Do not put your confidence in man when faced with crucibles.
Trust in Jesus and He will never fail you. Let Him know all your
troubles and confide in Him to resolve all your challenges.

September 27ᵗʰ

Proverbs 25:14

Whoever boasts of giving is like a cloud
and wind without rain

Comment

Do not be proud of any good thing you do, or you might have
done. Let your boasting be only in Jesus and what He has done
for you. Talk about Gods wonderful grace and His precious gift
of eternal life through His son Jesus Christ.

September 28ᵗʰ

Proverbs 26:27

Whoever digs a pit will fall into it
And he who rolls a stone will have it roll
back on him

Comment

Be careful not to fall into the trap of setting up people and taking
advantage of them. The same gimmicks or tricks you use on
people will come back to haunt you. If you want a good reputation

and to be held in high esteem let people, see your wonderful works today and all glory will be given to the Lord.

September 29ᵗʰ

Proverbs 26:12

Do you see a man wise in his own eyes?
There is more hope for a fool than for him

Comment

Do not pretend to know everything when you do not. True wisdom comes by allowing God lead you every day of your life. Place your trust in Jesus and let Him guide you in all things and your life will be rich. Treat other others as better then yourself and God will lift you up.

September 30ᵗʰ

Proverbs 20:24

A man's steps are of the Lord
How then can a man understand his own way?

Comment

God will guide your steps if you let Him. He is the only one who knows what is best for you. When things get rough today it is very easy for you to lose track of your life. If you need direction in your life ask God to lead you. He knows and understands where you need to go and how you can get there. Why don't you let Him lead you today?

October 1ˢᵗ

Proverbs 20:3

It is honorable for a man to stop striving
Since any fool can start a quarrel

Comment

It does not pay to quarrel or to engage in unnecessary striving or quarrelling. Starting strife leads to troubling situations that may not be resolved easily. Whenever somebody steps on your toes, pray for him or her. Sometimes this might not be easy but pray for the Holy Spirit to give you courage. It is important to strive to live at peace with all men and, if need be to make every effort to do so.

October 2ⁿᵈ

Proverbs 20:29

The glory of young men is their strength
And the splendor of old men is their
gray head

Comment

Young men look up to adults for direction and guidance. They also look up to them for wisdom. Older men with wisdom should feel obliged to mentor young people because they have accumulated longer years on earth. If you have young people that you know share your wisdom with them so that their life can be more focused, meaningful, and directed.

October 3ʳᵈ

Proverbs 21:30

There is no wisdom or understanding or
counsel against the Lord
But deliverance is of the Lord

Comment

No one can come against Gods wisdom. If He (God) wants to do something, He will do it without anyone's permission. Whatever He desires or plans will happen because nothing can stand in Gods way. Just believing this will help you trust God including following His directions and plans for your life. His plans are the best for your life and whatever problem you may be facing right now God has innumerable ways of solving it. He is God and there is nothing impossible with Him, just trust Him and obey His word.

October 4th

Proverbs 18:10

> The name of the Lord is a strong tower
> The righteous run to it and are safe

Comment

Are you weary of this life's challenges? Run to Jesus the author and finisher of your faith. Jesus never fails and He wants the best for your life. He is the best safety you can ever have in times of persecution or when tormented. He is the best friend that stands by you always. He never disappoints those who trust Him. He will shield you with His presence.

October 5th

Proverbs 18:24

> The man who has friends must himself
> be friendly
> But there is a friend who sticks closer than
> a brother

Comment

It is good to have good, dependable, and trustworthy friends because they can be a good resource in times of trouble. Although this is good, never put your complete trust in friends because they are just as humans as you are. They are fallible, make mistakes and there is no guarantee that their trustworthiness is without fault. Jesus is the best guarantee for success and victory. He can never fail you if only you honor Him by trusting Him completely. Don't trust your friends but trust Jesus.

October 6ᵗʰ

Proverbs 19:23

The fear of the Lords leads to life
And he who has it will abide in satisfaction
He will not be visited by evil

Comment

Fearing God and giving Him glory always brings blessings. God will reward you if you show Him reverence. Fear of the Lord acknowledges that Jesus is God and, that if you take hold of His promises, your life will never be the same beginning today. Fearing God will prompt Jesus to guide and protect you from the attacks of the enemy. The enemy may intimidate you with fear, worries and discouragement but when you fear God, He will protect you from these. If you want to enjoy true peace and happiness fear God and make Him first in all you do.

October 7ᵗʰ

Proverbs 19:21

There are many plans in a man's heart
Nevertheless the Lords counsel will stand

Comment

Every person has or makes plans which he or she wants to actualize. In this technological age some people are lured by the media, which often influences their plans. Many plans people make do not come to pass because they are not anchored in Jesus. If you want your plans to come to fruition, make them and then let Jesus have the final say. You cannot read into your future, but Jesus can and therefore in all your plans, let Jesus have the upper hand and they will succeed.

October 8ᵗʰ

Psalm 1:6

For the Lord knows the way of
the righteous
But the way of the ungodly shall perish

Comment

Putting your trust in Jesus will assure you of His guidance every step of your day. It is very rewarding to trust Jesus because only He knows what is best for your life. Those who don't believe in God have no part in His plans. But if you love Jesus and make Him Lord of every detail of your life He will make your plans succeed.

October 9ᵗʰ

Psalm 3:8

Salvation belongs to the Lord
Your blessing is upon your people

Comment

Only Jesus can give you eternal life. Believing in Him and living with the promise of eternal life assured is the most crucial thing in your life. Nothing in this world can compare with the gift of eternal life that only Jesus can provide. Trust Him and claim and keep this promise today.

October 10th

Psalm 4:3

> But know that the Lord has set apart for Himself him who is godly
> The Lord will hear when I call to him

Comment

If you are a true and genuine child of God, know that you are special in the eyes of Jesus. Walk with Jesus today and if you have made Him Lord and Savior of your life you, will be blessed. He will hear your prayers when you call upon Him.

October 11th

Psalm 5:11

> But let all those rejoice who put their trust in you
> Let them ever shout for joy, because you defend them

Comment

Trusting God is important because it results in full joy and protection. Jesus has not failed any one of His children who trust in Him. Take Him by His word today and put your complete trust in Him. Knowing Him closely means you have to read the Word everyday so you can hear his voice speaking to you. You will be blessed.

October 12ᵗʰ

Psalm 6:9

The Lord has heard my supplications
The Lord will receive my prayer

Comment

Let all your prayers ascend to Jesus because it is only Him that can answer all your prayers and supplications. Take all your burdens and concerns to Him (Jesus) and He will hear you and grant your desires as He sees fit. God is interested in doing the best for His children who trust Him. Do that today and you will not be disappointed?

October 13ᵗʰ

Psalm 7:10

My defense is of God
Who saves the upright in heart?

Comment

Only God can be your best defender. Trust and make Him your defense to shield you from all evil and attacks from the enemy. Imagine being protected by the most powerful being in creation, God. This is the most wonderful privilege and blessing you will not want to miss today. God is God and if He is on your side nobody can overcome you.

October 14ᵗʰ

Psalm 9:10

And those who know your name will put their trust in You
For You, Lord have not forsaken those who seek You

Comment

Trusting God means that you are honoring Him. It also demonstrates your confidence in Him as creator of the universe. God will honor those who put their complete trust in Him. He will not forsake you if you make Him Lord of your life.

October 15th

Psalm 11:7

For the Lord is righteous
He loves righteousness
His countenance beholds the upright

Comment

Doing right is what we have all been called to do. By all means possible to do right today and ask that the Holy Spirit helps you in this task. Jesus will reward you if you show that you want to live a righteous life that honors Him. He will give you His Holy Spirit who will help you to become what Jesus wants you to become. Allow Jesus to be Lord of your life and His face will shine on your face for others to see and wonder.

October 16th

Proverbs 29:23

A man's pride will bring him low
But the humble in spirit will retain honor

Comment

God hates pride. Don't let this cancer ruin you. However, God loves the humble in spirit. With humility come many blessings including honor. Pray that God will give you the strength to overcome pride. Further, pray that God will allow His Holy Spirit to give you the gift of humility. Once humility becomes part and parcel of your character you will begin to appreciate life including many of its blessings.

October 17th

Psalm 29:25

The fear of man brings a snare
But whoever trusts in the Lord shall be safe

Comment

Trusting in Jesus is one way of your affirmation that nothing is impossible with God. God honors those who trust in Him. He will protect you if you trust Him completely. He will meet all your needs if you trust Him completely. Take advantage of Jesus' promises and claim them today.

October 18th

Proverbs 29:26

Many seek a Kings favor
But justice for man comes from the Lord

Comment

Only God can vindicate you when you are in trouble. People may mistreat you at work, at school, or at home. You may suffer wrong punishments or endure unfair treatment. Remember God is watching, and He is the best judge. He will ensure that justice prevails and this without fail. If you are experiencing any social injustice in your life today just commit your situation to the Lord and He will vindicate you. God does not fail. Although the situation may seem impossible to you God is crafting and arranging everything in place on your behalf and when all pieces begin to fall in place you will be surprised at how everything fits together.

October 19ᵗʰ

Proverbs 30:5

Every Word of God is pure
He is a shield to those who put their trust
in Him

Comment

Read the word of God every day. The Word of God is food for your soul. Without it you are spiritually dead. There is power in God's word and if you read it every day and digest it fully your life will change. If you let Gods Word fashion your life, you will begin to experience His presence as never before. He will be your shield from all assaults of the enemy.

October 20ᵗʰ

Proverbs 27:1

Do not boast about tomorrow
For you do not know what a day may
bring forth

Comment

God knows your future. You do not have the ability to read into the future. Only He can do this for you. If you want to have a safe and secure future commit it to Jesus. Jesus knows what is best for you, He also knows what is best for your family and He knows every different circumstance of your life. So, if you are talking or planning for tomorrow let your plans or talk demonstrate dependence on God's will and He will honor you.

October 21st

Proverbs 27:2

> The refining pot is for silver and the
> furnace for gold
> And a man is valued by what others say
> of him

Comment

Don't talk about or make selfish statements about yourself that border on pride. God does not like this way of thinking because it is a precursor to pride. He hates pride. Whatever accomplishments or achievements may accompany your efforts in any area don't brag. Put God first in your life and He will let others see your good works and they will speak well of you. In the end glory and honor will be ascribed to God the originator of every blessing.

October 22nd

Proverbs 28:20

> A faithful man will abound with blessings
> But he who hastens to be rich will not
> go unpunished

Comment

Riches are a gift from God. Don't rush to get rich when it's not your time to get rich. If its Gods will, you will be blessed with riches at the time He has determined for you. Don't let your heart be solely focused on earthly and materialistic treasures. You can get filthy rich today and become a pauper the following day. In His own time and method Jesus will bless you and, if it's in His wisdom that you be blessed with wealth, He will do this. Just wait for Him to come through.

October 23rd

Proverbs 28:26

He who trusts in his own heart is a fool
But whoever walks wisely will be delivered

Comment

Don't follow what your heart says or leads you to do. The heart if not controlled by the Holy Spirit can mislead you. Instead, let the wisdom of Jesus guide you every day and you will find meaning for your life. Only Gods wisdom can deliver you from all your troubles and from the chaos of this world. In order to attain God's wisdom, you need to begin trusting Jesus completely.

October 24th

Psalm 13:6

I will sing to the Lord
Because he has dealt bountifully with me

Comment

Praise is crucial to God. He is God and He deserves your praise and worship. If you are in tune with His will for your life, He will bless you and, in turn, you will become a blessing to your family and society at large. Let Jesus work through you so that you can bless every person God allows to cross your path. Ask Jesus for spiritual discernment when opportunities for blessing other people arise.

October 25th

Psalm 13:13

Consider and hear me O Lord my God
Enlighten my eyes
Lest I sleep the sleep of death

Comment

Whenever you are in doubt, whenever something serious is troubling you ask Jesus for enlightenment. Jesus will give you peace and joy during whatever situation you are going through. Even if you died today God will be on your side. You will be protected until your glorious entry into heaven.

October 26th

Psalm 16:7

I will bless the Lord who has given me counsel
My heart also instructs me in the night seasons

Comment

Bless Jesus today because He is Lord over your life. Read His word every day beginning this morning and at the end of the day take stock of the daily events you went through. Pay attention to peculiar incidents that may have been orchestrated by providence. If you notice anything amiss don't let fear or worry overwhelm you. In a spirit of humility let Jesus instruct your thoughts and allow Him into your heart to be your master guide.

October 27th

Psalm 17:5

Uphold my steps in your paths
That my footsteps may not slip

Comment

Walk in the paths of righteousness today. Ask Jesus to walk with you and by your side. If by chance your steps slip don't let this trouble you or ruin your day. Whisper a prayer to Jesus and trust and wait on Him. He will be there for you just at the right time.

October 28th

Psalm 18:29

For by you I can run against a troop
And by my God I can leap over a wall

Comment

With God on your side all things are possible. Let your life demonstrate a living faith in Jesus. He (Jesus) has conquered all foes, and He is eagerly waiting to supply all your needs including victory when in trouble. Don't be overcome by fear or worry when the situation seems impossible. Trust in God and He will fight the battles for you.

October 29th

Psalm 18:31

For who is God except the Lord?
And who is a rock except our God?

Comment

God is your rock that cannot be moved. He is the ancient of days and a sure beacon of hope if you trust Him. He is God and there is no other. Let this truth sink into your mind today. If any trial or obstacle comes your way, you must recall that there is a God who is too big for any temptation or problem you may face. Trust and obey Him.

October 30th

Psalm 19:14

Let the words of mouth and the meditation
of my heart
Be acceptable in your sight
O Lord my strength and my redeemer

Comment

Set aside time each day for meditation. Meditation is meaningful if you base it on the Word of God. Read the Word everyday including today and claim its promises. As the day unfolds wait and see how the Word shapes your day. At the end of the day as you retire for bed focus on the Word and discover some of the ways the Word has been a blessing to you. Let your thoughts stay focused on the goodness of God and His power to bless you in innumerable ways.

October 31st

Psalm 19:1

> The heavens declare the glory of God
> And the firmament shows His handiwork

Comment

If possible, try to look at the night skies and gaze at the stars, the moon and all the starry hosts of the heavens. All these heavenly bodies are sure evidence of God's creative power and of His sovereignty. He is God of the heaves and of your life. What a privilege. Praise Him today and claim His promises and your life will never be the same.

November 1st

Psalm 20:9

> Save, Lord
> May the King answer us when we call?

Comment

Only God can deliver you out of all your challenges. Sometimes you may face difficulties you don't understand. Some challenges can be perplexing but just trust Jesus today and He will deliver you out of all your obstacles. Remember nothing is impossible with Jesus.

November 2ⁿᵈ

Psalm 21:2

> You have given him his heart's desire
> And have not withheld the request of
> his lips

Comment

Take all your requests and desires to God. Only He can fulfill them. But to have your desires met by God you need to walk with Him every day. This means that Jesus needs to occupy first place of in your life. Let Him lead you and see how rich your life will become.

November 3ʳᵈ

Psalm 22:24

> For He has not despised nor abhorred the
> affliction of the afflicted
> Nor has He hidden his face from Him
> But when He cried to Him He heard

Comment

If it appears that God is not answering your prayers wait on Him. In His own time and way God will show up and shower you with His loving kindness. Don't give up, stay connected with Jesus and feed on His promises.

November 4th

Psalm 22:11

> Be not far from me
> For trouble is near
> For there is none to help

Comment

In this world the Devil will always cause havoc to children of God. You may be going through trying times today but remember Jesus is with you. If He is besides you have nothing to worry about or fear. Don't let fear or worry get in your way. Run to Jesus our refugee and fortress who never losses.

November 5th

Psalm 23:6

> Surely goodness and mercy shall follow me
> All the days of my life
> And I will dwell in the house of the
> Lord Forever

Comment

Jesus wants the best for you. The condition is that you remain faithful to Him and He will never disappoint you. All the days of your life will be a blessing even though sometimes you may face circumstances beyond your comprehension. Trust Him.

November 6th

Psalm 25:18

> Look on my affliction and my pain
> And forgive all my sin

Comment

If there is anything in your life that is holding you back from receiving God's blessings, confess your sins to Jesus and He will forgive you. Forgiveness of your sins releases you from the pressures and burdens you may be carrying on your own.

November 7th

Psalm 25:20

Oh keep my soul and deliver me
Let me not be ashamed for I put my trust in you

Comment

Placing your trust in Jesus is crucial. God will not disappoint His children who put their trust in Him. You will not be ashamed or disappointed. God will honor your faith.

November 8th

Psalm 27:5

For in time of trouble
He shall hide me in His pavilion
In the secret place of His tabernacle
He shall hide me
He shall hide me; He shall set me high on a rock

Comment

In times when you don't understand what is going on in and around your life pray and take refuge in Jesus. He is the best anchor and support you can ever have. He will hide you under His feathers and wings and He will not allow your feet to slip.

November 9th

Psalm 28:1

To you I will cry O Lord my Rock
Do not be silent to me
Lest if you are silent to me
I become like those who go down to the pit

Comment

Bring all your perplexities to Jesus. Let Him address them by His mercy and grace. Don't withhold anything from Him because you cannot solve anything in your own effort. Be persistent in your prayer and continually read the Word. He will answer you.

November 10th

Psalm 28:7

The Lord is my strength and shield
My heart trusted in Him, and I am helped
Therefore my heart greatly rejoices
And with my song I will praise Him

Comment

Only Jesus can give you the strength in times of trouble. Trust Him and He will see you through. Remember God never fails those who place their trust in Him.

November 11th

Psalm 30:11

You have turned my mourning
into dancing
You have put off my sackcloth and clothed
me with gladness

Comment

There are rewarding results from trusting Jesus. If you are faithful and consistent in your walk with God He will bless and give you victories in your life.

November 12ᵗʰ

Psalm 31:1

In you O Lord I put my trust
Let me never be ashamed
Deliver me in your righteousness

Comment

Trust Jesus and He will bless you. He will honor your faith and guide you in your path. Let Him start leading your life beginning today. You will be blessed.

November 13ᵗʰ

Psalm 31:3

For you are my rock and my fortress
Therefore for your name's sake
Lead me and guide me

Comment

Let Jesus lead and guide you today. He is the best compass and safety you can ever have when confronted with difficulties. Run to Him and you will be safe.

November 14th

Psalm 32:6

> For this cause everyone who is godly shall
> pray to you
> In a time when you may be found
> Surely in a flood of great waters
> They shall not come near him

Comment

If you trust in Jesus, no trouble shall defeat or overtake you. You will be able to overcome any challenge in Jesus' name. Pray every day and let your mindset be controlled by the Holy Spirit and focused on Jesus.

November 15th

Psalm 33:18

> Behold the eye of the Lord is on those who
> fear Him
> On those who hope in His mercy

Comment

If you trust in Jesus and if you hope in His glory, He will protect you, He will provide all your needs and He will fill your heart with peace and joy today.

November 16th

Psalm 33:19

> To deliver their soul from death
> And to keep them alive in famine

Comment

God wants the best for you. He wants to give you eternal life even as you live this day. Let your mind be focused on him today. As you do so He will keep you strong when you face difficulties. During days when you cannot make ends meet Jesus will provide for you. He will meet all your needs. Just trust Him.

November 17ᵗʰ

Psalm 34:8

Oh taste and see that the Lord is good
Blessed is the man who trusts in Him

Comment

Trusting the Lord is the best thing you can do. He will never disappoint those who trust in Him. Let Jesus lead and guide you all the way and pour all your problems on Him. He will handle them on your behalf as you need not carry all your burdens by yourself. He wants to take you to higher heights in your life and this can only happen if you allow Him to.

November 18ᵗʰ

Psalm 34:4

I sought the Lord and He heard me
And delivered me from all my fears

Comment

Nothing is impossible or too hard for the Lord. Whenever you find yourself in trouble or hot waters cry out to Jesus and He will save you. Even when fear strikes you take it to the Lord in prayer. Remember as long if you want to know Jesus more the devil will never leave you alone. But do not be scared because the devil has already lost the battle. Lean on Jesus today and He will give you the victories you need.

November 19th

Psalm 34:4

I sought the Lord and He heard me
And delivered me from all my fears

Comment

When in trouble seek Jesus and He will not disappoint you. Bring all your issues, personal or public, to Him and lay them at His feet. He will take care of every problem you are battling with. Remember, in order to gain victory, you need to have faith in Jesus, you need to place your compete trust in Him and He will deliver you. Jesus has not failed any battle. He is the creator God and He can do anything. Believe that.

November 20th

Psalm 35:22

This you have seen O Lord
Do not keep silence
O Lord do not be far from me

Comment

When things do not seem to be working out for you God is with you. He knows what you are going through and He will be there for you. Talk to Him and walk with Him every day and every moment of your life. If you allow Him to walk with you He will give you peace and joy beyond measure.

November 21st

Psalm 36:7

How precious is your Loving Kindness
O God
Therefore the children of men put their
trust under the shadows of your wings

Comment

God is full of mercy and grace. All He wants for you is to place your trust in Him and He will save you from all your troubles. Try Him and your life will not be the same. He is going to hide you in His presence and believe me this is the best place you can ever be.

November 22nd

Psalm 36:8

They are abundantly satisfied
With the fullness of your house
And you give them drink from the river of your pleasures

Comment

God owns everything and He wants to give you the best you can ever imagine. His presence always comes with joy and peace. Let Him give you a portion of His joy and peace. His pleasures never cease. If you let Him take lead of your life you will become a fountain of living water for your friends and family.

November 23rd

Psalm 36:9

For with you is the foundation of life
In your light we see light

Comment

This world is full of darkness but in Jesus is the light that can dispel this darkness. If you have some darkness in your life Jesus Christ will drive it out if you allow Him to. He is the light of the world. Your life will be full of meaning and purpose if you let Him come into your life. Your life will become light and all those who see you and the changes you exhibit may be attracted to this light. Today let your light shine before this dark world.

November 24ᵗʰ

Psalm 37:4

> Delight yourself also in the Lord
> And He shall give you the desires of
> your heart

Comment

As you begin this day focus your mind on Jesus. Think about Him and about what He has done for you. He came into this world and died for you. He was resurrected and ascended into heaven. He is there right now. He also wants you to join Him in heaven soon. Until then He wants you to have a test of heaven by meeting your desires daily. Let all your desires be known to Jesus and depend on Him. Claim His promises and watch how He meets your desires. He is faithful.

November 25ᵗʰ

Psalm 37:19

> They shall not be ashamed in the evil time
> And in the days of famine they shall be
> satisfied

Comment

During tough times Jesus will defend you. During loneliness He will be a friend by your side. During sickness He will be a surprise visitor by your side. During worry and doubt He will help you think straight. During fear He will give you assurance of His presence. During depression, frustrations, and disappointments He will calm your thoughts and feelings. Jesus is everything you need.

November 26th

Psalm 37:3

Trust in the Lord and do well
Dwell in the Land and feed on
his faithfulness

Comment

Trust, trust, trust in Jesus. Let Him work in you through His holy spirit and you will never be disappointed. Surrender your life to Him completely and claim promises from His Word. He is ready to shower you with blessings He has in store for you. Just trust Him and live a faithful life.

November 27th

Psalm 37:40

And the Lord shall help them and
deliver them
He shall deliver them from the wicked and
save them
Because they trust in Him

Comment

If you trust in Jesus today and rest of your life, He will prove His faithfulness to you. As long as you show your true and complete reliance on Him you will not be disappointed. Jesus will protect you from your enemies and from any troubling situation you may be facing. Trust Him.

November 28th

Psalm 38:22

Make haste to help me
O Lord, my salvation

Comment

Run to Jesus whenever you face insurmountable problems. Let your prayers be known to Him and He will deliver you from all troubles. Make it your special privilege to take all problems you may be facing to the creator of the universe. He knows every detail of your life and He knows what is best for you. Just trust Him.

November 29th

Psalm 38:15

> For in you O Lord I hope
> You will hear O Lord my God

Comment

Let all your hopes, desires, dreams, and ambitions be anchored in Jesus. He has the power to solve every challenge you are facing right now. Don't delay in taking all your requests and concerns to Him. Do that and watch how God proves His faithfulness.

November 30th

Psalm 44:5

> Through You we will push down
> our enemies
> Through Your name we will trample those
> who rise up against us

Comment

The name of Jesus is powerful. It is above every name. It is a protective shield. It's a blessing to those who lean on it. Lean on Him and claim victory over every obstacle.

December 1st

Psalm 46:1

God is our refugee and strength
A very present help in trouble

Comment

When you let Jesus hide you when faced with troubles rest assured that all will be well with you. His presence is the best place you can ever find refuge. Come to Him now in prayer and allow Him to keep and hide you in His glorious presence. There you will find peace, joy, and real happiness for your soul.

December 2nd

Psalm 46:2

Therefore we will not fear
Though the earth be removed
And though the mountains be carried into
the midst of the sea

Comment

Fear has to do with lack of faith. The devil will do everything to cause fear in your mind. He will throw all kinds of assaults at you to cause great fear and anxiety in your heart. But do not let him or his tricks intimidate you. Believe and trust in Jesus' power and all will be well.

December 3rd

Psalm 41:13

Blessed be the Lord God of Israel
From everlasting to everlasting

Comment

God is God and there is none like Him. He is everlasting and all life, including yours, exists in Him. We live, move, and have our being in Him. He holds your and my breath in His hands. Praise Him in songs, in your thoughts, and in all you do today. God deserves worship and praise.

December 4th

Psalm 41:2

The Lord will preserve him and keep him alive
And he will be blessed on the earth
You will not deliver him to the will of his enemies

Comment

If you trust the Lord with all your heart, mind, and soul He will deliver you from all your troubles including from your enemies. When you walk with Jesus it means enjoying and living a blessed life and, even if trouble may come your way, joy will overflow your heart. Walking with Jesus will allow you to enjoy heavenly protection from all your enemies. Jesus never fails just trust today.

December 5th

Psalm 42:11

Why are you cast down O my soul?
And why are you disquieted within me?
Hope in God
For I shall yet praise Him
The help of my countenance and my God

Comment

In this life God will allow temptations and adversity to challenge and test your faith. Sometimes you will be overwhelmed when trials come your way. Your faith will be tested to the limits, but don't worry because Jesus is right there for you and with you standing right beside you. He will carry you in His arms and He will give you victory over all your problems and obstacles.

December 6th

Psalm 39:12

Hear my prayer O Lord
Give ear to my cry
For I am stranger with you
A sojourner as all my fathers were

Comment

Make prayer your breath every moment of today. Talk to Jesus in all your situations and let Him know everything that is troubling you. Focus on heaven and the promises He has promised you. You are not a citizen of this world; you are just a stranger passing through it like Jesus was when He was on earth. It is your right to worship Jesus, to walk with Him and to claim His promises. Do this and you will be blessed.

December 7th

Psalm 39:11

When with rebukes you correct man for his iniquity
You make his beauty melt away like moth
Surely everyman is vapor

Comment

Your life does not belong to you. It belongs to God. Any time He can take it away from you. If God punishes you no one can save you from His chastisement. If He blesses you no one will block your blessings, so trust God today.

December 8th

Psalm 40:17

But I am poor and needy
Yet the Lord thinks upon me
You are my help and my deliverer
Do not delay O my God

Comment

God thinks the best of you. Although you might be going tough times now, Jesus loves you. He wants to shower you with blessings He has in store for you. He looks at you with a compassionate gaze eagerly waiting to bless you. You need to place all your burdens on Jesus, and you need to allow Him lead you all the way. Let Him guide you in all troubling situations and you will be blessed.

December 9th

Psalm 66:5

Come and see the works of God
He is awesome in His doing toward the
sons of men

Comment

Tell others what God has done for you. Let men see the powerful revelations of God in your life. Testify and let God receive the praise and the glory. God is powerful and nothing can stand in His way if wants to exalt you, nothing can and will pull you down.

December 10th

Psalm 66:9

Who keeps our soul among the living?
And does not allow our feet to be moved

Comment

Only Jesus will keep you safe from the devil. He will keep and preserve your soul today. Rest in His presence and you will be saved from all attacks the enemy may place in your way. If you make God, your confidant your path will be safe and you will rest in perfect peace.

December 11th

Psalm 66:10

For you God, have proved us
You have refined us as silver is refined

Comment

God is constantly working in you and through you. He knows what you need in your life and He will give you the best as long as you trust Him. Sometimes He will allow you to be confronted, disturbed and shaken with difficulties so that He can fashion and shape your character. In the end you will rejoice as your character conforms to Christ's Character. You will become a precious jewel in His sight.

December 12th

Psalm 66:12

You have caused men to ride over our
backs
We went through fire and through water
But you brought us out to rich fulfillment

Comment

Don't worry whenever you go through trials and difficulties. God will be with you and He will not allow you to be drowned by your problems. Just trust Him and allow Him to take control of your life today. Jesus cannot fail to deliver you from any problems that seem like mountains to you. He is God and nothing is impossible with Him, believe that.

December 13th

Psalm 61:3

For you have been a shelter for me
And a strong tower from the enemy

Comment

Run to Jesus and you will be safe in His presence. He is a strong tower and fortress. He is our shield from all attacks of the enemy. Jesus is the greatest name on earth and in all creation. Strive to develop an intimate relationship with Him. Talk with Him and walk with Him every moment of the day and let Him handle all your challenges.

December 14th

Psalm 61:6

He only is my rock and my salvation
He is my defense
I shall not be moved

Comment

Make Jesus your rock and foundation today. When you anchor yourself in Him your life will be more meaningful, and nothing shall stand in your way. You will not be the same. Jesus is the master who can give your life's true purpose. Allow Him to be the foundation of your life and you will not be moved.

December 15th

Psalm 63:7

Because You have been my help
Therefore in the shadow of your wings I
will rejoice

Comment

Praise God when you experience victory. Worship Him because He
is worthy to be praised. Learn to take all your personal problems
to Him. He will take you under His wings and there is no better
place to be than in His presence. In his presence is the fullness
of joy.

December 16th

Psalm 63:6

When I remember You on my bed
I meditate on You in the night watches

Comment

Read the Word daily and as you go about your daily business the
Holy Spirit will bring into your remembrance the Word at the
right and appropriate time. Even before you retire for bed make
it a habit to read the Word and the Holy Spirit will seal the Word
in your mind. The more you read the Word the more you will be
drawn to Jesus.

December 17th

Psalm 54:6

I will truly sacrifice to God
I will praise your name; O Lord for it
is good

Comment

Praise God every day and let your life be a daily testimony and sacrifice to Him. God is good and He will do the best for your life if you let Him. As you experience His goodness share your testimonies with others so that God can receive the glory and honor.

December 18th

Psalm 54:7

For He has delivered me out of all trouble
And my eye has seen its desire upon
my enemies

Comment

No trouble is too big for God. He is God, the creator of the universe. Claim His faithfulness by faith and permit Him to fight all the battles for you today. You will rejoice as you see and experience victory after victory in your life. Stay close to Him and don't fear anything or worry about anything. God is in control.

December 19th

Psalm 56:3

Whenever I am afraid
I will trust in You

Comment

Trust Jesus and He will protect you. He is above everything, and His power cannot be compared to anything. You can only trust Jesus if you develop an intimate relationship with Him. This comes by reading His Word every day, praying, and walking with Him daily. God will not disappoint you if you trust Him.

December 20ᵗʰ

Psalm 56:9

> When I cry to you
> Then my enemies will turn back
> This I know because God is for me

Comment

Do you want to experience God's presence in your life? Pray in earnest to Jesus and trust Him for answers. You will be amazed as you begin to see answers to your prayers. As long as you make Jesus the center piece of your life, He will give you victory over all your troubles and problems you may be facing today. He is God and He knows every detail of your life. He knows the best that you need.

December 21ˢᵗ

Psalm 59:16

> But I will sing of Your Power
> Yes, I will sing aloud of Your mercy in
> the morning
> For You have been my defense
> And refugee in the day of my trouble

Comment

It is a blessing to have devotion first thing in the morning. If you start the day with God, He will guide you through and through. All your concerns and circumstances for that day will pass through His eyes. He will address them as He sees fit. He is the creator, and He knows what is best for you. So, if something seems perplexing to you do not worry about it because God is in control. Surrender to Him.

December 22nd

Psalm 68:35

> O God, You are more awesome than Your holy places
> The God of Israel is He who gives strength and power to His people
> Blessed by God

Comment

Every perfect and good gift comes from God. He will encourage and strengthen you to face problems that may seem insurmountable. He will give you peace when nothing seems to be working for you. He will stand by your side to guide you in the steps you are supposed to walk in. He will fill your heart with peace and unspeakable joy when you are overwhelmed with fear or worry. He is God and there is no one who can compare with Him.

December 23rd

Psalm 68:28

> Your God has commanded Your strength
> Strengthen O God what You have done for us

Comment

Do you want to navigate life with a relaxed mind? Do you want the assurance of victory in all your battles? Do you need strength for today and tomorrow and to face whatever the day may bring? Trust in Jesus today and He will not let you face all your mountains alone.

December 24th

Psalm 69:14

> Deliver me out of the mire
> And let me not sink
> Let me be delivered from those who
> hate me
> And out of the deep waters

Comment

Only Jesus can deliver you from all troubles. When you are losing hope and nothing seems to be falling in place cry out to God and He will save you. God will honor your trust because He is a faithful God. Allow Him to go before you in all situations. Let Him hold your hand as a child walking beside its father or mother. Your true safety can only be found in Jesus.

December 25th

Psalm 49:15

> But God will redeem my soul from the
> power of the grave
> For He shall receive me

Comment

All your days on earth are determined by God. If it is not your time to go you will not go no matter what happens or what the enemies plot against you. You can be involved in a car accident but survive. You can be shot but live. You can have a deadly disease but survive and continue to live. Your life is in the hands of God and as long as you are faithful to Him, He will not allow your life to be taken before your time. Enjoy today knowing that your days are only determined in heaven. Your life is safe in Him.

December 26ᵗʰ

Psalm 49:6

Sing praises to God, sing praises
Sing praises to our King, sing praises

Comment

God lives in an atmosphere of worship. Praise Him in song, praise Him in music, and praise Him in all kinds of biblical ways that you may think of. If you make praise an important piece of your life, you will begin to live your life in a new spiritual and heavenly dimension. Start praising Him today and experience His glory.

December 27ᵗʰ

Psalm 50:10

For every beast of the forest is mine
And the cattle on a thousand hills

Comment

Everything belongs to God. Your life, your family, your job, your dreams, your ambitions, your car, your bank account, your plans, and any other thing you may think of. If you let this philosophy sink into your mind, you will be acknowledging that God is God of your life, and He will bless you with unimaginable and unexpected blessings.

December 28ᵗʰ

Psalm 50:23

Whoever offers praise glorifies me
And to him who orders his conduct aright
I will show him the salvation of God

Comment

Make praise and worship the most important item in your life. Let Jesus guide you in everything you do. Ask Him to give you the Holy Spirit. The Holy Spirit will change your life and your behavior will reflect the character of Jesus. The character of Jesus is the best you can ever reflect. It will shine as a light in dark places and consequently you will attract people to Jesus who is living in you.

December 29th

Psalm 51:1

Have mercy upon me God
According to Your loving kindness
According to the multitude of your mercies
Blow out my transgressions

Comment

God is faithful. He is full of grace and mercy, and He wants to give you His grace so that your life can shine. Feast on His mercies and faithfulness today. Let His grace protects you and let His loving-kindness help you grow in faith.

December 30th

Psalm 51:7

Purge me with hyssop and I shall be clean
Wash me and I shall be whiter than snow

Comment

Is your life riddled with sin? Are you tired of perpetual habits that are eating you up? Is any past sin stalking you? Are you scared of relapsing into some hidden sin? Ask Jesus to wash you with His blood and you will be cleaner than anything you can imagine.

Don't take your sins to none other than Jesus. Only He has the power to restore you to your rightful place. Let Him do that for you today.

December 31ˢᵗ

Psalm 52:8

> But I am like a green olive tree in the house of God
> I trust in the mercy of God forever and ever

Comment

If you make Jesus the master of your life, your life will continuously produce new fruit. You will keep on growing in faith. There will always be something about you that people will notice and may desire. Your character will shine, and people will see the heavenly light through your behavior and actions. Trust in God and let Him control your life. You will be amazed at how your life will be transformed into the likeness of heavenly glory. You will become an agent of light wherever you are.

All things are possible to him or her who believes, and they are less difficult to him or her who hopes. They are easier to him or her who loves. And they are easiest to those who persevere in the practice of all three virtues mentioned above. The goal of knowing God and growing spiritually is to become the most perfect worshippers of God that we can possibly be, in this life and throughout all eternity.

When we begin a spiritual journey, it is important to thoroughly examine what we are. We find our ourselves to be miserable or we do not deserve the name of Christians. We are subject to all kinds of suffering. Our circumstances trouble us and cause continuous changes in our health, our emotions, and our mental and physical dispositions. However, God humbles us through this same suffering and pain, inside and outside. Therefore, it should not surprise us that people cause us troubles, temptations, oppositions, and difficulties. We should accept these and bear them for as long as God wishes and view them as highly beneficial to our faith and spiritual development.

Our God is always willing and ready to bless those who love Him. There is no sweeter and delightful life than that of continual communion with God. Only those who experience this communion with God will enjoy a growth in their faith and bliss and perfect peace that comes from Him. In this life we will encounter difficulties, sometimes intense and painful trials that seem too much for us. Yes, we can rely on God our heavenly father to deliver and guide us in ways we could never imagine. God does not expect that we endure on our own, but He does want us to respond with unwavering faith.

God understands our trials and pain and longs to be the One we cling to through good times and bad. You can choose to look elsewhere for comfort, or you can use your hardship as an opportunity to connect with God. God looks past our flaws and instead sees the precious child He created. As a result of His great love, He sent Jesus Christ to save our lives so we could be with Him in this life and the next in heaven. No matter how difficult our circumstances are, the Lord opens the way to faith and abundant life.

Our God goes ahead of us to prepare the way, and He walks with us through every situation. Let us pray for acute awareness of His presence each day. The following psalms provide words of wisdom and encouragement to those who want to live faithfully today and every day. These psalms expressed through inspirational insights will uplift and strengthen those who may be in their valley and want to feel God's presence close to them in a special way. For those on the mountain top He will keep them in perfect peace for as long their eyes are focused on Him.